Studien zu Staat, Recht und Verwaltung
Studies on State, Law and Administration

edited by

Prof. Dr. Gabriele Britz
Prof. Dr. Wolfgang Hoffmann-Riem
Prof. Dr. Laura Münkler
Prof. Dr. Jens-Peter Schneider

Volume 41

Nicole Koblenz | Nicholas Otto | Gernot Sydow [eds.]

Future-Proofing in Public Law

European, International, and Comparative Perspectives

Nomos

Onlineversion
Inlibra

The Deutsche Nationalbibliothek lists this publication in the Deutsche Nationalbibliografie; detailed bibliographic data are available on the Internet at http://dnb.d-nb.de

ISBN 978-3-7560-3541-0 (Print)
978-3-7489-6605-0 (ePDF)

1st Edition 2026

Table of Contents

Introduction: Future-Proofing in Public Law

Nicole Koblenz/Nicholas Otto/Gernot Sydow[*]

How can intergenerational problems, such as global warming or biodiversity loss, be solved in a way that is fair to all generations? Can intergenerational representation contribute to sufficient climate protection? To what extent does representative democracy need to be updated to ensure its resilience in increasingly complex and crisis-ridden times? What is, and can be, the contribution of human rights protection to addressing these challenges? In short: Is public law fit to address the (un)foreseeable challenges brought by the future? Is it, thus, 'future-proof'?

These were some of the central questions addressed by early career scholars from different countries at the Second Münster Conference on Public International and Comparative Law in September 2024. The conference was particularly inspired by the growing prevalence of innovative institutions – such as the *Assemblée Citoyenne du Futur* in France, the *Rat für Generationengerechtigkeit* in Germany and the *Future Generations Commission* in the UK – which ultimately aim to ensure future-proof decision-making. The popularity of such formats might suggest that democratic institutions and decision-making procedures might require structural reforms to adequately take into account the interests of future generations and/or to initiate reforms deemed necessary, for example, in the area of climate protection. However, the fading of the initial euphoria surrounding these instruments suggests a more nuanced perspective: Major institutional and procedural reforms may sometimes be necessary, but in other instances, democratically produced law, guided by the rule of law and human rights, may already be well suited to tackle future challenges – and always has been. Therefore, the notion of 'future-proofing', which we aim to coin

* Dr. Nicole Koblenz, LL.M., and Dr. Nicholas Otto are postdoctoral researchers at the Institute for International and Comparative Public Law at the University of Münster. Prof. Dr. Gernot Sydow, M.A., is Full Jean-Monnet-Professor at the University of Münster and co-directs the Institute for International and Comparative Public Law.

further[1] with this volume, not only assesses possible means of making public law fit for the future. It also leaves room for debate as to whether future-proofing in and of public law is necessary at all, and to what extent current legal mechanisms have already been designed with the future in mind.

The volume collects the results of the conference and is divided into three sections: The first section presents different perspectives on the role of individual rights as a means of making public law future-proof, whether in relation to well-established human rights or the rights of future generations, which have not yet been fully incorporated, with contributions by *Marco Antonio Simonelli, Barbara Jakkel, Juan Alonso Tello Mendoza* and with a co-authored piece by *Derya Nur Kayacan Fidan* and *Maria Liana Vodiță*. The second section contains two articles by *Tavini Nanayakkara* and *Giulia Taraborrelli*, which assess how legal regulation of the online sphere can be made future-proof. Finally, the papers by *Andrea Fiorentino, Giulia Mannarini* and *Jan Philipp Huth* in the third section evaluate different strategies of creating future-proof democratic decision-making, considering both the benefits and drawbacks of potential institutional and procedural reforms. Here, the authors focus particularly on means of participatory and deliberative democracy. Reflecting the variety of solutions to the above-mentioned challenges, which are being discussed worldwide, all of this volume's contributions include an international, supranational and/or comparative legal perspective.

Münster, October 2025

Nicole Koblenz
Nicholas Otto
Gernot Sydow

---

1 In legal contexts, the term is only being used occasionally so far – see, e.g., Katalin Sulyok, 'Future proofing EU law – Does the European Union have a legal obligation to protect future generations?' (2025) 34 Review of European, Comparative & International Environmental Law 420, Brian Opeskin, *Future-Proofing the Judiciary – Preparing for Demographic Change* (Palgrave 2021), Sofia Ranchordás and Mattis van't Schip, 'Future-Proofing Legislation for the Digital Age' in Sofia Ranchordás and Yaniv Roznai (eds), *Time, Law, and Change – An Interdisciplinary Study* (Bloomsbury 2020), and the papers resulting from the symposium on 'Future-Proofing Law: From rDNA to Robots', which have been published in (2017) 51 UC Davis Law Review.

Whatever works? Instruments for Protecting Future Generations within Contemporary Constitutional Democracy

*Marco Antonio Simonelli**

The present contribution examines how contemporary constitutional democracies are attempting to address the structural short-termism that marginalises the interests of future generations. In particular, the paper explores four main avenues through which democracies have sought to integrate the long-term dimension into governance: the constitutional entrenchment of 'future clauses', the establishment of ombudspersons for future generations, the creation of future committees in legislatures, and the judicial enforcement of intergenerational obligations. Through a comparative analysis of national experiences across Europe, Latin America, and beyond, it assesses the design, effectiveness, and limitations of these institutional arrangements, showing how they seek to reconcile the need for democratic legitimacy of public policy and the necessity of orienting them towards the long-term. The article concludes by suggesting that while no single mechanism can guarantee adequate protection for future generations, a combination of constitutional, parliamentary, and judicial tools offers the most promising path.

I. Introduction

In his book *What We Owe the Future*, Oxford philosopher *William MacAskill* makes a compelling case for future generations, emphasising that the vast majority of human lives, estimated at 99.5 %, are yet to be lived, urging present generations to act as stewards of the future rather than mere custodians of the present.[1] Unfortunately, as humanity faces a series of unprecedented existential challenges, ranging from the fight against climate change and the governance of Artificial Intelligence to the demographic transformation of societies, the inability of contemporary democracies to address issues requiring long-term policies is becoming all

* Assistant Professor of Constitutional Law, University of Barcelona.
1 William MacAskill, *What We Owe the Future* (Basic Books 2022) 15.

the more manifest. Indeed, whilst contemporary constitutional democracy claims to uphold values like equality, social justice, and the fundamental rights of its citizens, these principles essentially apply only to living citizens. Future generations – the unborn –, who will inherit the consequences of current policy decisions, still remain largely excluded from democratic decision-making. Not only, despite bearing the consequences of today's policy choices – many of which, according to scientific consensus, are projected to be catastrophic – future generations' interests are essentially ignored by today's rulers, who seem to operate under a logic of temporal irresponsibility well encapsulated by the cynical maxim '*après moi, le déluge*'.[2]

This flaw appears to be inherent in the very design of contemporary liberal and representative democracy. The functioning of contemporary democracies is indeed based on the representation mechanism, through which elected officials, acting on behalf of their electors, translate and reflect their will within legislative processes. Ultimately, the legitimacy of representative constitutional democracy as a whole is derived from the idea that elected representatives are accountable, through periodic elections, to the electorate. Yet, future generations obviously cannot participate in elections. In theory, it should not be an issue, as this trustee model of representation implies, that representatives are supposed to adopt policies that should benefit society as a whole and ensure its prosperity in the long term, even if the adoption of such policies conflicts with short-term popular demands, with the 'whims of the masses'. However, it is almost a commonplace that representative democracy is biased against the future. The capacity of elected representatives to ponder adequately the long-term consequences of public decisions is indeed practically nullified by the dependency of government and parliament on the electoral cycle, as the necessity to secure re-election inevitably leads the incumbent ruling majority to implement policies that prioritise the short over the long term.[3] This structural inability to pursue long-term objectives and the sheer scale and complexity of future generations' interests, thus, make it unwise to rely exclusively on the good judgment of present-day representatives for ensuring intergenerational justice. As such, complementary institutional solutions must be developed to ensure that future generations are not

2 The maxim is famously attributed to the King of France Louis XIV, and it was then reprised by Carl Marx in *The Capital* to describe capitalists' attitude towards the future.

3 Jörg C. Tremmel 'Establishing Intergenerational Justice in National Constitutions', in Edward Elgar (ed), *Handbook of Intergenerational Justice* (Edward Elgar Publishing 2006) 187–188.

merely an afterthought in democratic governance but are actively and meaningfully included in policy decisions. Even though presentism is still firmly entrenched within contemporary constitutional democracy, with most democratic systems lacking formal mechanisms for addressing the interests of those yet to be born, in the last decades things started to change, as several states around the world have been putting into place innovative arrangements to promote intergenerational justice and introduce the long-term dimension in public policy.

The aim of this contribution is precisely to explore those institutional solutions for the protection of future generations, to identify which are the most promising ones. Through a comparative review of the existing mechanisms, as well as of the most significant normative proposals, this contribution will evaluate their design, effectiveness, and limitations in responding to the temporal challenges that contemporary democracies are facing. To reach this stated aim, the paper will proceed along the following lines. Section II. reviews the different types of constitutional 'future clauses' and illustrates how national courts have interpreted them. Section III. analyses the different institutional solutions devised to include future generations' interests in the elaboration of public policy by parliament and government. Section IV. briefly illustrates the roles of courts as enforcers and guarantors of the rights of future generations. Section V. identifies the shortcomings common to all these solutions and concludes.

Before embarking on this task, it must be clarified that this work proceeds from the assumption that future generations can no longer be considered just as passive recipients of decisions made by today's governments and that their interests need to be adequately taken into account in the present political discourse. Drawing from *Robert A. Dahl's* theory of democracy, which considers inclusiveness, intended as the breadth of interests taken into account in policy-making, one of the decisive indicators for measuring democratic quality,[4] the contribution assumes that the consideration and protection of future generations is not just an ethical imperative but also a structural requirement for enhancing the democratic

4 Famously *Dahl* identified five criteria for evaluating democratic quality: equality in voting, effective participation, enlightened understanding, final control over the agenda, and inclusion. See: Robert A. Dahl, *Democracy and Its Critics* (Yale University Press 1989).

character of contemporary constitutional democracies.[5] In this sense, the question this contribution will try to answer is not *whether* democracies should protect the interests of future generations, but *how* they can do so without eroding their legitimacy.

Also, the present work will not discuss the theoretical question of whether future generations are capable of being rights-holders,[6] but it will simply assume that intergenerational justice,[7] intended as the idea that future humans shall enjoy the core of basic human rights essential for their well-being,[8] should become a fundamental constitutional principle of contemporary democracy. It is worth underscoring that this definition of intergenerational justice resembles that of sustainable development contained in the famous 1987 *Brundtland Report* as a form of development 'that seeks to meet the needs and aspirations of the present without compromising the ability of future generations to meet their own needs'.[9] However, also considering that the very notion of sustainable development has received serious criticism from academics of different disciplines,[10] in the following pages, our main focus will be on those institutional and

5 Some scholars have instead argued that any solution for the protection of future generations would inevitably result in a lowering of the democratic level of a polity as it implies a reduction of the 'ability of "the people" to rule itself democratically by introducing an asymmetry between rulers (the living and the unborn) and the ruled (the living)'. See, Ludvig Beckman, 'Democracy and Future Generations. Should the Unborn Have a Voice?', in Jean-Cristophe Merle (ed), *Spheres of Global Justice* (Springer 2013).

6 For an insight on the problems and opportunities posed by the recognition of rights to future generations see: Axel Gosseries, 'On Future Generations' Future Rights' (2008) 16 Journal of Political Philosophy 4, 446–474.

7 For a more thorough discussion on the definition of intergenerational justice see: Richard P. Hiskes, *The Human Right to a Green Future. Environmental Rights and Intergenerational Justice* (Cambridge University Press 2008), in particular 5–25.

8 Since a habitable environment is the necessary precondition for the enjoyment of all fundamental rights, the contribution will mainly deal with environmental change related solutions.

9 *Report of the World Commission on Environment and Development: Our Common Future*, para 49. Available at: https://sustainabledevelopment.un.org/content/documents/5987our-common-future.pdf (all links were last accessed on 10 July 2025).

10 From the very moment of its appearance the notion of sustainable development has been criticised for its vagueness, allowing for an easy 'greenwashing' of public policies, for assuming that human development invariably coincides with economic growth, and for ignoring that the planet has already reached its 'carrying capacity'. For a more detailed analysis of the flaws of the notion see Jem Bendell, 'Replacing Sustainable Development: Potential Frameworks for International Cooperation in an Era of Increasing Crises and Disasters' (2022) 14 Sustainability, in particular 6-10.

normative solutions that have their explicit rationale in the protection of future generations and the promotion of intergenerational justice.

As a final point, it must be underlined that representative constitutional democracy will constitute the theoretical framework of the discussion. Rather than proposing a wholesale redesign of democratic institutions, this contribution proceeds from the assumption that meaningful improvements in the protection of future generations can emerge through gradual, incremental reforms embedded within existing constitutional frameworks.[11]

II. The Constitutional Entrenchment of Intergenerational Justice

Thomas Jefferson was probably the first voice to claim that constitutional law should worry about intergenerational fairness, famously affirming that 'the earth belongs in usufruct to the living'.[12] In particular, *Jefferson* identified as an obstacle to intergenerational justice the rigidity of the constitution, as he considered that earlier generations should not have the power to impose their will on future ones ('the dead have no rights'), and suggested that each generation, identified with a timespan of nineteen years, should have the right to draft a new constitution 'to choose for itself the form of government it believes most promotive for its own happiness'.[13] In similar terms, the *Jacobin* Declaration of Rights of Man and Citizen of 1793, in its Article 28, affirmed that '[a] people has always the right to review, to reform, and to alter its constitution. One generation cannot subject to its law the future generations'. As it is well known, this declaration never entered into force, and it remains the only historical constitution which manifested such concern for the right of future generations to choose their own form of government. This radical conception of popular sovereignty is, in fact, incompatible with the contemporary understanding of the constitution as a normative text characterised above all by its rigidity and longevity. More-

11 The question of whether those reforms may be sufficient to prevent the most ominous consequences of climate change far exceeds the scope of this work. It must be, however, underscored that many scholars from different disciplines are arguing that only a radical change will suffice. See for instance Kohei Saito, *Capital in the Anthropocene* (Cambridge University Press 2024).

12 *Letter from Thomas Jefferson to James Madison*, 6 September 1789. The letter can be read at: https://founders.archives.gov/documents/Madison/01-12-02-0248.

13 *Letter from Thomas Jefferson to Samuel Kercheval*, 12 July 1816. The letter can be read at: https://founders.archives.gov/documents/Jefferson/03-10-02-0255.

over, despite its declared intent, it does not appear suitable to guarantee intergenerational justice, as there is no assurance that the interests of those yet to be born will be taken into account in each revision process.[14]

The first contemporary constitution to explicitly consider future generations is the Japanese Constitution of 1946. In particular, Article 11 declares that all fundamental rights guaranteed in the Constitution 'shall be conferred upon the people of this and future generations as eternal and inviolate rights'.[15] The Japanese Constitution is, still nowadays, the only constitution worldwide to explicitly recognise future generations as rights-holders.[16] Yet, from this affirmation, no practical consequences flow, as, according to Japanese courts, fundamental rights are only acquired at birth.[17] In this sense, Article 11 is better understood as imposing a moral obligation on the State with an eminently symbolic value.

Another path followed by constitutional legislators around the globe for protecting future generations has been to entrench environmental clauses within constitutional texts.[18] Those provisions began to appear in constitutional texts during the 1970s, two prominent examples being Article 45 of the 1978 Spanish Constitution and Article 66 of the Portuguese Constitution of 1976, enshrining the right to a healthy environment. It is significant to note that both these provisions affirm the fundamental right to a healthy environment,[19] and a corresponding duty not only of the State,

---

14 For other arguments in defence of constitutional rigidity for the protection of future generations see Axel Gosseries, 'Constitutions and Future Generations' (2008) 17 The Good Society, 32-34.

15 This provision is complemented by Article 97, which essentially reinforces the eternity clause of Article 11 concerning fundamental rights. All the texts of the Constitutions have been consulted in their English version on the database *Constitute* (constituteproject.org).

16 Yoshinobu Nakanishi, 'The Rights of and Obligations towards Future Generations' in Hélène Ruiz Fabri, Valerie Rosoux and Allessandra Donati (eds), *Representing the Absent* (Nomos Verlag 2023) 241.

17 Takayuki Shinohara, 'Interpretation of Articles 11 and 97 of the Japanese Constitution – do they guarantee effective rights to "future generations"?' [2019] *SAFNA Blog* https://safna.org/2019/10/12/interpretation-of-articles-11-and-97-of-the-japanese-constitution-do-they-guarantee-effective-rights-to-future-generations/.

18 Tania Groppi, 'Sustainability and Constitutions. The Constitutional State and the Dilemma of the Future Generations' (2016) 1 Diritto pubblico comparato ed europeo, 43–78.

19 According to a consolidated constitutional interpretation, Article 45 of the Spanish Constitution constitutes first and foremost an obligation imposed upon the State to provide adequate protection of the environment.

but also of every citizen to protect it, thus emphasising the solidarity on which the recognition of the right to a healthy environment is grounded. In a recent judgment interpreting Article 45, the Spanish Constitutional Tribunal affirmed that this solidarity also embraces future generations as Article 45 contains 'an obligation of intergenerational solidarity to conserve and improve the natural environment so that future generations have the opportunity to enjoy their own right to life, physical and moral integrity and the development of their life projects in conditions equivalent to those available to us today'.[20]

Starting from the early 1990s, we have witnessed the rise of future generations in constitutions around the world. In Europe, in particular, most of the constitutions approved in the aftermath of the dissolution of the USSR affirmed the responsibility of the living towards future generations, recognising the latter as rights-holders. Admittedly, most of these affirmations are contained in the preambles to the constitutional text,[21] therefore, their capacity to orient the action of state authorities is limited.

A more cogent form of recognition of intergenerational responsibility is represented by Article 20a of the German Basic Law ('GG'), introduced in 1994. The provision reads: '[M]indful also of its responsibility toward future generations, the state shall protect the natural foundations of life and animals within the framework of the constitutional order by legislation and, in accordance with law and justice, by executive and judicial action.' Until recently, Article 20a was regarded primarily as a state objective clause – a normative mandate for public authorities rather than a directly justiciable right. As such, it was often invoked rhetorically in political discourse and environmental policymaking but was deemed unsuitable to be enforced in court. This interpretation aligned with the traditional German distinction between State duties (*Staatszielbestimmungen*) and subjective rights of individuals (*Abwehrrechte*). With its historic 2021 ruling in *Neubauer*,[22] the German Federal Constitutional Court completely shifted this paradigm. In this decision, the Court found that the Federal Climate Change Act of 2019 was incompatible with the Basic Law insofar as it failed to regulate emissions reductions beyond 2030 sufficiently. The Court held that insuffi-

20 STC 142/2024, of 20 November 2024, FJ 3.

21 That is the case of the following constitutions: Azerbaijan (1995); Czechia (1993); Estonia (1992); Latvia (1991); Moldova (1994); Poland (1997); Ukraine (1996); Uzbekistan (1992).

22 BVerfG, 24 March 2021 (*Neubauer et al*), 1 BvR 2656/18.

cient planning placed an unjustified burden on younger and future generations, effectively limiting their fundamental freedoms, such as the general right of personality (Art. 2(1) GG) in conjunction with Art. 20a. The most innovative element of the judgment is the Court's interpretation of Article 20a as creating a duty of the State to protect intertemporal freedom (*intertemporale Freiheitssicherung*),[23] whose respect requires the legislature to distribute the costs of climate protection fairly across generations. In a nutshell, this ruling elevated Article 20a from a mere state objective to a normatively operative principle capable of being applied in fundamental rights adjudication.[24]

More recently, countries like Norway, in 2014, and Italy, in 2022, have amended their constitutions to include an explicit responsibility towards future generations. In the case of Italy, a third paragraph was added to Article 9 of the Constitution to include as duties of the Republic the protection of the environment, biodiversity, and ecosystems, for safeguarding the interests of future generations. In its first interpretation of this new provision, in the 2024 *Priolo* case,[25] the Italian Constitutional Court affirmed 'that current generations have a clear duty to preserve the conditions for [future generations] to enjoy an environmental heritage that is as intact as possible' and struck down a provision allowing the government to keep an industrial plant operating indefinitely under a strategic-interest exception.[26] In this sense, the Italian Court made clear that with the constitutional reform, Article 9 was transformed into a directly enforceable provision, capable of being used as a yardstick in judicial review of legislation. Similarly, Article 112 of the Constitution of Norway states that '[n]atural resources should be made use of on the basis of comprehensive long-term considerations whereby this right [to a healthy environment] will be safeguarded for future generations as well'. According to a consistent interpretation of Norwegian courts, decisively confirmed in 2020 by the Norwegian Supreme Court,

23 Not to be mistaken with protection duties of the state stemming directly from the fundamental freedoms, which the German Constitutional Court ruled were not violated in this case.

24 On this point and for further details on the interpretation of Article 20a GG as a norm conferring fundamental rights upon individuals and future generations see Louis J. Kotzé, 'Neubauer et al. versus Germany: Planetary Climate Litigation for the Anthropocene?' (2021) 22 German Law Journal, in particular 1436–1437.

25 Italian Constitutional Court 13 June 2024 (*Priolo*), n 105.

26 An English summary of the judgment can be found at https://www.cortecostituzionale.it/documenti/english/legal_summary_105_of_2024.pdf.

Article 112 of the Constitution is not merely a declaration of principle, but a substantive rights provision that can be invoked before tribunals.[27]

More innovatively, Ecuador's 2008 Constitution departs from the anthropocentric model altogether, recognising the rights of nature (*derechos de la naturaleza*) and thereby implicitly affirming the rights of future generations by protecting ecosystems regardless of their instrumental value to current human needs (Articles 71-74).[28] Indeed, despite being clearly distinguishable categories, in Latin America, the rights of nature and the rights of future generations are often considered to be part of the same phenomenon.[29] This approach is manifest in the landmark decision of the Colombian Supreme Court STC 4360-2018, which recognised the Colombian Amazon as a subject of rights and at the same time framed environmental protection as a duty owed to future generations.[30] In Europe, such an approach based on the constitutional recognition of the rights of nature seems instead to be encountering more resistance, as for the moment only Spain, in 2022, has passed a law recognising legal personality to an element of nature, the Mar Menor lagoon in the Murcia Autonomous Community.[31] Such an approach is closely reminiscent of the constitutionalism of

---

27 Petra Minnerop and Ida Røstgaard, 'In Search of a Fair Share. Article 112 Norwegian Constitution, International Law, and an Emerging Inter-Jurisdictional Judicial Discourse in Climate Litigation' (2021) 44 Fordham International Law Journal 4, 857.

28 The debate around the possibility of recognising rights is generally considered to have begun in the first years of the 1970s with the publication of the study by Christopher D. Stone, 'Should Trees Have Standing? – Toward Legal Rights for Natural Objects' (1972) 45 Southern California Law Review, 450–501.

29 Luis Angel López Zamora, 'The Recognition of the Rights of Nature in Latin America. The Lost Linkage with the Rights of Future Generations' in Hélène Ruiz Fabri, Valerie Rosoux and Allessandra Donati (eds), *Representing the Absent* (Nomos 2023) 494.

30 Colombian Supreme Court, 5 April 2018, 4360.

31 Law 19 of 30 September 2022, *para el reconocimiento de personalidad jurídica a la laguna del Mar Menor y su cuenca*. For a comprehensive critical reading of the law focused on the problems connect with the representation of rights of nature see Blanca Soro Mateo and Santiago M. Álvarez Carreño, 'Derechos de la naturaleza y Constitución, a propósito del caso de la laguna del Mar Menor' [2024] Revista d'estudis autonòmics i federals 34, 61-122. The same authors also published a shorter commentary of the law in English language. See 'The Mar Menor Lagoon Enjoys Legal Standing: and now, what?' [2022] *Verfassungsblog* https://verfassungsblog.de/the-mar-menor-lagoon-in-spain-enjoys-legal-standing-and-now-what/.

common goods of *Ferrajoli*,[32] who advocated a change of paradigm in the very notion of constitutionalism, as it should shift from the protection of fundamental rights to that of fundamental common goods, such as clean air, water, forests, and biodiversity.[33] Since the depletion of those common goods threatens not only the well-being of current populations but also the rights of those yet to be born, granting constitutional protection to those fundamental goods also protects the interests of future generations. Yet, recognising nature's legal personality constitutes an even more radical departure from the paradigm of liberal constitutionalism than that proposed by *Ferrajoli*, as it implies establishing nature not just as an object of constitutional protection but as a subject capable of exercising rights. Further, if we consider that in European constitutional law, only in exceptional circumstances are environmental associations granted standing before courts to defend collective environmental rights,[34] a generalised recognition of rights to nature would appear somewhat inconsistent. Rather than recognising rights of nature, which often end up being litigated in courts with questionable outcomes,[35] a more convincing solution within existing constitutional frameworks may lie in recognising the principle of solidarity, on which the effectiveness of the right to a healthy environment depends, through emphasising the individual duties attached to this right.

All in all, nowadays around 80 constitutions worldwide contain some reference to future generations' interests and rights. In general, the introduction of these future clauses has been especially frequent in the field of environmental protection, as the degradation of the environment and the depletion of natural resources are amongst the most pressing issues

32 Not to be confounded with the more conservative common good constitutionalism of *Adrian Vermeule*. See Adrian Vermeule, *Common Good Constitutionalism* (Polity 2022).

33 Luigi Ferrajoli, *Per una Costituzione della Terra. L'umanità al Bivio* (Feltrinelli 2022). There, the author also argues that the most efficient way for guaranteeing the future of the planet is enlarging the paradigm of rigid constitutionalism to a global scale. Obviously, the implementation of such a proposal would require a major shift in the current world political scenario that is characterised more by its fragmentation rather than its unity. In this sense, apart from its theoretical appeal the concrete chances of the realisation of such a theory are rather thin.

34 The issue will be discussed in more detail in Section IV.

35 For a more thorough critic of the idea of nature rights, see Mauricio Guim and Michael A. Livermore, 'Where Nature's Rights Go Wrong', (2021) 107 Virginia Law Review 7, 1347–1419.

looming over future generations.[36] Also, it must be emphasised that when future clauses are included in the substantive part of constitutions, they are generally framed as constitutional mandates to state authorities, i.e. they are state duties and not enforceable individual rights. Another common element to future clauses is that they are based on the underlying ambition to compel governments to take the interests of future generations into account in their decision-making processes. The assumption is that by elevating intergenerational concerns to constitutional status – alongside equality, liberty, or democracy – governments will be normatively bound to weigh the long-term environmental, fiscal, or social consequences of their actions.

However, the open-ended nature of many of these provisions often results in vaguely defined legal obligations, leaving courts and administrative actors largely responsible for determining their scope and application. Emblematic in this respect is the case of Hungary, where, in 2011, one of the broadest and most relevant constitutional reforms protecting future generations was implemented. Both in the preamble and the substantive provisions, there is a strong emphasis on the responsibility towards future generations. Article P of the new Fundamental Law, for instance, declares that 'natural resources, in particular arable land, forests and drinking water, biodiversity, in particular native plant and animal species, as well as cultural assets shall form the common heritage of the nation, [and] it shall be the obligation of the State and everyone to protect and maintain them, and to preserve them for future generations.'[37] Also, Article 30 attributes to the Commissioner for Fundamental Rights the task to 'protect the interests of future generations'. Despite this strong constitutional commitment, Hungary's subsequent institutional developments resulted in an overall weaker protection of future generations,[38] demonstrating how constitutional provisions can be rendered largely symbolic in the absence of robust institutional safeguards; first and foremost an independent constitutional court and judiciary.

36 Renan Araujo and Leonie Koessler, 'The Rise of the Constitutional Protection of Future Generations' (2021) 7 LPP Working Paper https://ssrn.com/abstract=3933683 or http://dx.doi.org/10.2139/ssrn.3933683.

37 To mark a difference with the 1949 Constitution adopted under the Communist regime, the 2011 Fundamental Law followed a *three-layered system of references* – letters, Roman numerals, Arabic numbers – where the main articles ('Fundamentals') were Articles A to I.

38 ibid.

Ultimately, while constitutional entrenchment of intergenerational principles represents an important step, expressing a normative commitment to the future, it shall not lead to an overestimation of the power of constitutions to transform political practices. Its practical effectiveness indeed remains, as the Hungarian and Japanese cases demonstrate, largely dependent on the capacity and willingness of state authorities, in the first place, constitutional and supreme courts, to translate constitutional provisions into enforceable standards of intergenerational justice. Also, the transformative potential of such provisions ultimately depends on whether they are integrated into actual practices of governance, first of all through legislation. In the following section, we shall thus review the institutional solutions that have been implemented or proposed in order to include future generations' interests in the formulation of public policy.

III. Including Future Generations' Interests in the Public Decision-making Processes

While constitutional entrenchment represents a fundamental step towards reorienting constitutional democracies to the future, it is within legislative bodies that most binding policy decisions are adopted. Consequently, ensuring that long-term interests are reflected in law-making has become a critical concern in the design of intergenerational safeguards. This section explores the principal mechanisms through which contemporary democracies have attempted to integrate future-oriented reasoning into legislative deliberation. These include essentially the establishment of ombudspersons tasked with providing expertise-based and moral advocacy and the creation of specialised parliamentary committees with a long-term mandate. Each of these institutional arrangements reflects a different balance between democratic legitimacy and normative ambition, allowing to identify the main challenges connected with the consolidation of intergenerational justice into democratic governance.

1. Ombudspersons for Future Generations

One of the most widely discussed institutional mechanisms for representing the interests of future generations is the establishment of an ombudsperson for future generations,[39] whose explicit mandate is to advocate for the rights of future generations in contemporary politics. One of the reasons advanced by its proponents is that, given its 'innocuous character' – ombudspersons typically lack binding powers – the introduction in the legal system of an ombudsman for future generations should be relatively easy.[40] Yet, despite strong academic advocacy, only two countries, Hungary and Wales,[41] have introduced such an institution. Hungary introduced the Ombudsman for Future Generations in 2007, granting the office-holder investigative powers in environmental matters and a formal role in legislative review. The Commissioner could initiate proceedings before administrative and constitutional courts as well as submit *amici curiae*, which have played a significant role in the Hungarian context.[42] Yet, the independence and autonomy of the Hungarian Ombudsman have also been affected by the rule of law backsliding in Hungary; as of 2011, the Ombudsman was absorbed into the more general Office of the Commissioner for Fundamental Rights, significantly weakening its visibility and autonomy. While the initial design reflected a serious commitment to institutionalising intergenerational advocacy, the subsequent rollback underscores the fragility of non-binding structures in politically adverse environments.

Wales introduced an ombudsman for future generations in 2015 with the Well-being of Future Generations Act, heralded 'as a landmark piece of sustainable development legislation'.[43] This piece of legislation established the Future Generations Commissioner as an institution tasked with advocating long-term thinking in decision-making processes, having the duty to 'act as a guardian of the ability of future generations to meet their needs'.

---

39 See amongst many Ludvig Beckman and Frederik Uggla, 'An Ombudsman for Future Generations: Legitimate and Effective?' in Iñigo González Ricoy and Axel Gosseries (eds), *Institutions for Future Generations* (Oxford University Press 2016), in particular fn 1.

40 ibid 125.

41 According to the Welsh devolution settlement, the Senedd (the Welsh Parliament) has powers to legislate on matters that are not reserved to the United Kingdom Parliament, thereby including the protection of future generations.

42 Marcel Szabó, 'Representing the Interests of Present and Future Generations at the Same Time – A Case Study of the Hungarian Ombudsman for Future Generations' in Hélène Ruiz Fabri, Valerie Rosoux and Allessandra Donati, *Representing the Absent* (Nomos 2023) 421.

43 Elen Stokes and Caer Smyth, 'Hope-Bearing Legislation? The Well-being of Future Generations (Wales) Act 2015' (2024) 13(3) Transnational Environmental Law, 569–587.

The Commissioner is appointed by the Government following a public selection process for a seven-year non-renewable mandate. The Commissioner is notable for the broad scope of its competences, as it may provide advice and assistance to public bodies and to 'any other person' wishing to contribute to the achievement of the seven well-being goals, defined in the Act, encompassing environmental protection but also health, equality, and social cohesion. Public bodies are under a legal duty to act 'in accordance with the sustainable development principle', and the Commissioner advises, monitors, and reviews their respect for the principle. However, as in the Hungarian case, the Commissioner's powers are purely advisory: it cannot veto legislation, block government projects, or impose sanctions for non-compliance. More generally, according to Welsh courts, a lack of compliance by public authorities with the provisions of the Well-being of Future Generations Act is not amenable to judicial review.[44]

In this regard, as with all ombuds institutions, the effectiveness of an ombudsperson for future generations relies less on legal coercion than on normative persuasion and soft accountability mechanisms. This is why authors insist on the importance of office holders being persons with strong communicative skills;[45] otherwise, their lack of binding powers makes them easy to marginalise and ignore. Also, to strengthen the position of the ombudsperson vis-à-vis the government and the parliament, it should be provided with sufficient independence guarantees, first and foremost immovability and a long non-renewable mandate, and with budgetary autonomy, without which it risks becoming little more than a symbolic institution incapable of structurally embedding future generations' interests within the decision-making architecture of constitutional democracy. Ultimately, provided that the institutional design is adequate, the establishment of an ombudsperson for the future may represent a useful institutional innovation, which can act as an advocate for future generations, contributing to introducing a future-oriented language into policy-making. However, the effectiveness of its actions faces the same challenges and shortcomings as general ombudspersons, the most significant being that ombudspersons are most effective when they operate in a receptive environment.

44 ibid 573–576.

45 Beckman and Uggla (n 39) 130.

2. Parliamentary Committees for Future Generations

Another institutional mechanism devised to include future generations' interests in the decision-making processes is the establishment of dedicated parliamentary committees tasked with scrutinising legislation and policies from a long-term perspective.

Among the earliest and most notable examples is the *Knesset's* Commission for Future Generations, created in Israel in 2001 through the enactment of the *Commission for Future Generations Act*. Though not formally a parliamentary committee, the office functioned in close conjunction with legislative committees and participated in the drafting of legislation. Its mandate was to examine proposed laws and assess their impact on future generations. To fulfil this mandate, the Commission was granted the power to scrutinise each legislative act and to appear before the relevant *Knesset* committee whenever it considered that the bill would have a significant impact on future generations.[46] The assessment of the Commission was contained in a report, and until its submission, legislation could not be passed. The Commission was presided over by a Commissioner elected by an *ad hoc* committee composed of an equal number of experts, appointed by the Speaker of the *Knesset*, and of MPs.[47] The establishment of the Commission had a significant impact as its activities affected a broad spectrum of legislative proposals: those related to natural resources, but also those concerning technology and education.[48] Upon expiry of the legislative term in 2006, the Commissioner was not reappointed and finally, in 2011, the *Knesset* passed a law dissolving the Commission for Future Generations. The Israeli Commission for Future Generations was the first wholesome attempt to represent future generations within the legislative procedure, and its dissolution, which was allegedly due to the cost of its operation as well

---

46 On this point, and for further details on the functioning of the Commission, see the chapter written by the person who presided the Commissioner during its five years of existence, *Shlomo Shoham*. See Shlomo Shoham and Friederike Kurre, 'Institutions for a Sustainable Future: The Former Israeli Commission for Future Generations' in Marie-Claire Cordonier Segger, Marcel Szabó and Alexandra R. Harrington (eds), *Intergenerational Justice in Sustainable Development Treaty Implementation* (Cambridge University Press 2021) 334.

47 ibid 335.

48 Edith Brown Weiss 'Implementing intergenerational equity' in Fitzmaurice M. (ed), *Research Handbook on International Environmental Law* (Edward Elgar Publishing 2010) 110–111.

as its growing interference with parliamentary activity,[49] only confirms the importance of constitutional entrenchment to consolidate advancements in the protection of future generations.

A more lasting example is provided by Finland, which, already in 1993, embedded long-term policy evaluation into the parliament through the Committee for the Future (*Tulevaisuusvaliokunta*). The Finnish Committee was the first permanent committee in the world with a specific mandate for the future. Despite being a permanent committee, it does not have law-making powers, i.e. it does not participate in the legislative process, nor does it routinely scrutinise or review legislative bills.[50] This exclusion has proven decisive in allowing the body to overcome partisan lines in carrying out its mission, which is to foster 'a dialogue with the government on future problems and opportunities'.[51] In this regard, the primary task of the Committee for the Future is to prepare the response of the Finnish parliament to the Government's Report on the Future, which is presented once per electoral term. Since the answer of the Committee is usually published at the end of the electoral term, its content is primarily directed to the future government, something that constitutes a further incentive for the Committee to overcome partisan logic. The Committee's second task is to issue, upon request of the parliament, a statement regarding a government bill on which another committee is preparing a report. However, such statements are seldomly issued by the Committee,[52] which actively avoids being involved in the legislative procedure. Finnish scholars are instead unanimous in considering that the main strength of the Committee for the Future is its power to set its own agenda, allowing it to act as a 'parliamentary think-tank' for the future.[53] In conclusion, while it does not formally speak on behalf of future generations, as the Welsh ombudsman does,

49 Shoham and Kurre (n 46) 336.

50 Vesa Koskimaa and Tapio Raunio, 'Encouraging a longer time horizon: the Committee for the Future in the Finnish Eduskunta' (2020) 26(2) The Journal of Legislative Studies, 160.

51 This is how the Committee describes its mission on its official website. See, https://www.eduskunta.fi/EN/valiokunnat/tulevaisuusvaliokunta/Pages/default.aspx.

52 According to *Koskimaa* and *Raunio*, in the period 2000–2018 the Committee only issued one such a statement, see Koskimaa and Raunio (n 50) 163–164.

53 Paula Tihonen, 'Power over Coming Generations: Committee for the Future in the Eduskunta, the Parliament of Finland' in Marie-Claire Cordonier Segger, Marcel Szabó and Alexandra R. Harrington (eds), *Intergenerational Justice in Sustainable Development Treaty Implementation* (Cambridge University Press 2021) 402.

the Finnish Committee represents a blueprint for integrating long-term thinking into parliamentary deliberation in a systematic, non-partisan way.

Following Finland's lead, a growing number of legislatures have experimented with parliamentary committees that aim to embed long-term thinking into policy-making.[54] Currently, seven national parliaments across the world have established a standing committee for the future. In Europe, Austria established the Senate Committee for Technology, Innovation, and the Future in 2015, and was followed by Lithuania (2020) and Iceland (2021), which established committees for the future within their unicameral parliaments. In Latin America, Brazil (2013) and Chile (2012) created a Senate Committee for the Future, whereas Uruguay (2020) decided to create a Bicameral Special Committee for the Future, and more recently Paraguay (2022) established a Committee for the Future within the Chamber of Deputies.[55] All these committees are established as permanent and their institution reflects an increased attention by national legislators towards long-term thinking.[56] What is also remarkable about these committees is the breadth of their remit: they are called upon to formulate recommendations and elaborate policies on a wide array of issues – from demographic change and technological disruption to climate change, AI, public health, and social equity – often spanning the entire scope of government agendas. In this sense, their institution can be considered a signal that the consideration of the interests of future generations is going beyond the issue of climate change, as those committees may function as fora in which parliaments can engage in forward-looking analysis and policy foresight.[57] In

54 In addition to the creation of future-oriented parliamentary committees, some legislatures have opted for a more technocratic approach by institutionalising foresight research units that support long-term thinking. Examples include South Korea's National Assembly Futures Institute, Estonia's Foresight Centre, and the Scottish Parliament's Futures Forum.

55 A more complete list of parliamentary committees tasked with long-term thinking, containing also non active bodies, can be found in Paola Aceituno, *Parliamentary Committees for the Future: A Legislative Movement to Overcome Political Myopia* [2025] United Nations University Centre for Policy Research https://unu.edu/cpr/blog-post/parliamentary-committees-future-legislative-movement-overcome-political-myopia.

56 For a discussion of the common features to these committees and the significance of this trend see Vesa Koskimaa and Tapio Raunio, 'Expanding anticipatory governance to legislatures: The emergence and global diffusion of legislature-based future institutions' (2022) 45(2) International Political Science Review, 261–277.

57 ibid.

general, albeit their functions and competences vary significantly,[58] the fact that a body within the parliament is tasked with a mandate to consider the long-term consequences of public policies represents a partial solution to the democratic conundrum we discussed in the introduction, namely that MPs are periodically accountable to the electorate, but the general interest of the society needs to be projected beyond the electoral cycle. Creating a parliamentary committee with a mandate for the future indeed helps to realign the functioning of parliaments with the idea that representation entails an obligation to legislate for the *common good,* rather than for the aggregation of immediate preferences.

In a nutshell, parliamentary committees for the future may serve as a useful democratic corrective to the structural short-termism embedded in majoritarian institutions. However, it should not be overlooked that, as long as the composition of those committees reflects that of the chamber within which they are created, their capacity to orient the legislative agenda towards the future may be blurred by the lack of incentives to compel the majority to think in the long-term, especially when the same party or coalition controls both the legislative and the executive. In this sense, the solution adopted in Brazil and Chile, where a future committee has been established within the Senate – which in the two countries has a mandate twice as long as that of the Chamber of Deputies (8 years in both cases) and functions as a powerful check on the executive powers – seems capable of reducing that risk, whilst at the same ensuring that long-term planning extends beyond the electoral cycle of both the Deputies and the President. If we add that also in Austria, a committee for the future has been established within the *Bundesrat,* it may be possible to infer from such a trend that the establishment of those committees represents a welcome revitalisation of the function of senates as reflection chambers. On another note, as the example of the Israeli Commission well illustrates, it is fundamental for the full consolidation of those committees that they are grounded on a solid legal basis, whose modification should ideally require at least an absolute majority of parliament, so as to reduce the risk of regression in the path towards a more future-proof legal system.

58 For an overview of the different competences of those committees see: UNDP (2024). *The use of futures in parliaments. A guide for Transformative Actions* Policy Documents Series, in particular the comparative table at 25–26 https://www.undp.org/latin-america/publications/use-futures-parliaments.

Finally, it shall be noted that there have been more ambitious proposals for embedding the protection of future generations within the legislative power. In particular, it must be discussed the proposal for the creation of a *Chambre du Futur*, widely discussed in France in recent years. The proposal envisages the creation of a third, future-focused parliamentary chamber, with 90 members (60 drawn by lot from a list prepared by environmental NGOs, 30 by lot from citizens), equipped with the power to initiate legislation and a suspensive veto on laws conflicting with long-term interests.[59] The adoption of this proposal seems to imply a radical departure from the model of representative democracy, as it breaks with the idea that representatives sitting in parliament are accountable to their electors. However, as long as such a chamber would not be composed of elected representatives, and it does not have binding law-making powers, it seems more convincing to consider such a body, as *Tremmel* does, as a power distinct from the legislature, the 'Future Branch'.[60] Put in this perspective, the proposal for a Chamber of the Future can be considered to be a more ambitious way, compared to ombudspersons, to establish an advocate of future generations within the so-called fourth branch. Be that as it may, as seen for ombudspersons, or the Israeli Commissioner for Future Generations, national parliaments tend to resist the introduction of external bodies tasked with monitoring their activities, evidently preferring to internalise long-term thinking by entrusting it to dedicated committees.

All in all, it can be concluded that parliamentary committees focused on the long term represent a pragmatic method for strengthening the protection of future generations without altering the institutional framework of representative democracy or undermining its legitimacy.

59 A more detailed description, in French language, can be found on the website of the *Fondation pour la Nature et l'Homme*, which originally launched the proposal. Available at: https://www.fnh.org/la-proposition-de-la-fnh-pour-une-democratie-du-long-terme-la-chambre-du-futur/.

60 Jörg C. Tremmel, 'The Four-Branches Model of Government: Representing Future Generations' in Marie-Claire Cordonier Segger, Marcel Szabó and Alexandra R. Harrington (eds), *Intergenerational Justice in Sustainable Development Treaty Implementation* (Cambridge University Press 2021) 754–780.

IV. The Judicial Protection of Future Generations

An alternative route to securing the rights of future generations lies in the judicial enforcement of long-term principles by constitutional courts or other judicial bodies. Constitutional judges, being already tasked with upholding constitutional rights, may be seen as appropriate arbiters for ensuring that government policies do not infringe upon the rights of future generations. In the same vein, the Venice Commission in its 2020 Opinion on Iceland's constitutional reform explicitly endorsed the entrustment of the protection of future generations to the judicial branch, stating that '[a]s the future generations do not take part in present day democracy and do not vote in present day elections, the judicial branch appears to be best placed to protect the future generations against the decisions of present-day politicians'.[61] As we have seen, several courts around the world have already begun to engage with this issue, particularly in the context of environmental law.

At least in the European context,[62] the case that paved the way for climate change litigation is the 2019 judgment of the Dutch Supreme Court in *Urgenda*.[63] The judgment upheld the judgments of the lower courts ordering the government to reduce greenhouse gas emissions by at least 25 % by 2020 compared to 1990 levels. One of the most salient passages of the judgment is when the Supreme Court addresses the argument of the Government that it was not for the courts to undertake the political assessment necessary for a decision on the appropriate reduction of greenhouse gas emissions. In its reply, the judgment emphasises that a 'fundamental rule of constitutional democracy' is that 'if the government is obliged to do something, it may be ordered to do so by the courts, as anyone may be, at

61 See CDL-AD(2020)020-e. *Opinion on four draft constitutional bills on the protection of the environment, on natural resources, on referendums and on the president of Iceland, the government, the functions of the executive and other institutional matters*, adopted by the Venice Commission at its 124th online Plenary Session (8–9 October 2020), para 114.

62 As we have already discussed, Latin American Constitutionalism has been pioneer in elaborating solution for the future-proofing of constitutional democracy, yet the actual implementation of those solutions has mostly remained confined to that continent. See above, Sec. II.

63 Dutch Supreme Court, *Urgenda Foundation v. State of the Netherlands*, 20 December 2019, [2015] HAZA C/09/00456689.

the request of the entitled party'.[64] Despite recognising a wide margin of discretion to the government and the parliament concerning the reduction of greenhouse gases, the Supreme Court reaffirmed the competence of 'courts to decide whether, in availing themselves of this discretion, the government and parliament have remained within the limits of the law by which they are bound'.[65] What must be noted is that, according to the Supreme Court, the law binding the Dutch authorities is the European Convention on Human Rights, and in particular its Articles 2 and 8. Despite the lack of any ECtHR case law concerning the applicability of those two provisions to climate change at that time,[66] the judgment concluded that the Dutch State breached its positive obligation flowing from Articles 2 and 8 ECHR to protect its citizens against foreseeable and serious harm to their rights to life and to a healthy environment. All in all, the *Urgenda* judgment marked a landmark moment in climate litigation, establishing that states can be held legally accountable for insufficient climate action based on human rights obligations.

As we have already discussed, a similar path was followed by the constitutional courts of Germany and Italy, albeit both those courts could rely on a constitutional provision recognising intergenerational solidarity. In the *Neubauer* case, for instance, the German court relied on the country's obligations under the Paris Agreement as an interpretive lens for Article 20a of the Basic Law, thus linking global climate governance to domestic constitutional duties.[67] The 2024 judgment of the Italian Constitutional Court in *Priolo* follows the same logic as *Urgenda*, as it reaffirms that judges can scrutinise administrative and political decisions concerning the balancing of environmental protection with other public interests.[68]

64 ibid para. 8.3.1. The text of the judgment in English language is available at: https://climatecasechart.com/wp-content/uploads/non-us-case-documents/2020/20200113_2015-HAZA-C0900456689_judgment.pdf.

65 ibid para 8.3.2.

66 A circumstance that is recognised by the same Supreme Court. See ibid para 5.6.3.

67 BVerfG, 15 December 2022, 1 BvR 2146/22.

68 Some commentators have argued that the core of the Italian Constitutional Court decision is actually reaffirming its competence to reviewing the balancing of political actors on a case-by-case basis and criticised the judgment for failing to elaborate a systemic approach to deal with environmental protection and the protection of future generations. See Marta Pecchioli , 'The Priolo Case in Light of the 2022 Constitutional Reform: Historic Judgment or Deadlock for the Protection of Environmental Protection' (2025) 17(1) Italian Journal of Public Law, in particular 387–424.

In what may be considered the transnational echo of the *Urgenda* judgment, the European Court of Human Rights has entered the terrain of climate litigation with its groundbreaking decision in *Verein KlimaSeniorinnen Schweiz and Others v. Switzerland.*[69] The ECtHR for the first time found that a state's failure to adopt adequate mitigation measures against climate change can amount to a violation of the ECHR. Drawing on developments in comparative and international climate jurisprudence, the Strasbourg Court held that Switzerland had breached its positive obligations under Article 8 ECHR to protect its citizens against the adverse consequences of climate change. Significantly, the ruling attaches considerable weight to the protection of future generations. First, emphasising that future generations suffer 'a distinct representational disadvantage',[70] and 'that collective action through associations or other interest groups may be one of the only means' through which their voice can be heard, the Strasbourg Court granted standing to the *Klimaseniorinnen* association.[71] Second, the judgment seems to attach a decisive weight to the protection of future generations also in the finding of a violation, as it affirms that 'to avoid a disproportionate burden on future generations, immediate action needs to be taken and adequate intermediate reduction goals must be set for the period leading to net neutrality'.[72]

A common element in all these judicial decisions is their heavy reliance on international and supranational climate commitments, particularly those established in the Paris Agreement and EU secondary legislation. Courts have drawn normative strength in particular from Article 2.1(a) of the Paris Agreement, which commits states to hold the increase in the global average temperature to 'well below' 2 °C above pre-industrial levels, and to pursue efforts to limit the increase to 1.5 °C. With those judgments, national courts thus transformed essentially political targets, deprived of judicial enforcement mechanisms, into legal norms capable of integrating the parameters for judicial review of legislation. More generally, this strategy reflects a broader judicial trend toward integrating international norms into

69 *Verein KlimaSeniorinnen Schweiz and Others v. Switzerland* (GC), 09 April 2024, 53600/20.

70 ibid para 420.

71 ibid paras 489, 526.

72 ibid para 549. The ruling has been hardly criticised for its creative interpretation of Article 8 ECHR. See, for instance, George Letsas, 'The European Court's Legitimacy After KlimaSeniorinnen' (2024) 5(4) European Convention on Human Rights Law Review, 444–453.

binding domestic adjudication, which is especially visible in the domain of environmental and intergenerational justice.

Whilst climate change litigation contributes to strengthening the normative force of global climate objectives, it also has its vulnerabilities. First, courts are often forced to rely on non-self-executing or politically ambiguous instruments to impose binding obligations on states. Moreover, the judiciary's role is reactive, meaning that it can only address issues after they arise, being structurally incapable of proactively shaping policy. In this sense, while international and EU climate agreements have become crucial tools in the hands of judges, their effectiveness depends on the political system's readiness to comply with judicially imposed mandates.

From a systemic point of view, the judicialisation of climate policy raises democratic concerns about courts stepping into policy domains traditionally reserved for elected branches. Such an approach indeed contributes to an ongoing trend of contemporary constitutional democracies consisting of a shift of decision-making powers away from democratic institutions towards unelected bodies, such as constitutional courts and the judiciary. In a nutshell, while judges may be better positioned to enforce long-term principles, since they are not accountable to present electors and thus should be able to quash decisions that do not pursue long-term benefits for the society as a whole, increasing their role in policymaking inevitably comes at the expense of democratic accountability. Such a risk was explicitly recognised by the Strasbourg Court, which adverted that 'opening broad access to the judicial branch as a means of prompting changes in general policies regarding climate change' may disrupt 'national constitutional principles and the separation of powers'.[73] National constitutional courts seem to have also pondered such a risk. In *Neubauer*, the German Constitutional Court denied standing to environmental associations – despite admitting that this would considerably strengthen the enforcement of Article 20a –[74] and in a subsequent decision it affirmed that an action based on Article 20a must in principle be directed against the totality of permitted emissions,[75] thus limiting the potential of Article 20a as an instrument of climate change litigation. In *Priolo*, the Italian Constitutional Court demonstrated an awareness

73 *Verein KlimaSeniorinnen Schweiz and Others v. Switzerland*, para 484.

74 BVerfG, 24 March 2021 (*Neubauer et al*), 1 BvR 2656/18, para 136. The text of the judgment, in its English translation, is available at https://climatecasechart.com/wp-content/uploads/non-us-casedocuments/2021/20210324_11817_order-1.pdf.

75 BVerfG, 15 December 2022, 1 BvR 2146/22.

of the risk of an excessive involvement of the judiciary in climate policy, affirming that when the Government declares that an industrial plant is of strategic national interest and, after balancing the interests involved, authorises its continuation despite its negative environmental impact, ordinary judges are bound by that declaration.[76] At the same time, it must be noted that, unlike in Germany, in Italy individuals do not have access to the constitutional court, therefore, the fulfilment of the mandate contained in Article 9(3) of the Italian Constitution by public authorities can be enforced by judges only through the submission of an incidental question of constitutionality.

All in all, whilst judicial enforcement of future clauses is an indispensable tool for compelling political actors to long-term thinking, excessive reliance on judges to safeguard future interests may trigger a backlash against democratic powers, which can further alienate the electorate from the decision-making process and thereby threaten the legitimacy of constitutional democracy, fuelling illiberal and populist movements.

V. Conclusion

After this brief review of the main solutions devised by constitutional democracies around the world for protecting the interests of future generations – constitutional embedment, ombudspersons, parliamentary committees, and judicial enforcement – it is evident that each approach has its strengths and limitations. Aside from the weaknesses already signalled, there is an inherent limitation to all those solutions: the most pressing challenges that future generations face – such as climate change, nuclear proliferation, and global inequality – transcend national borders. In this sense, any institutional solution adopted at the national level would inevitably suffer from the impossibility of providing local solutions to global problems. As a result, many scholars are advancing proposals addressed at the international level, such as the creation of an international authority tasked with safeguarding the interests of future generations.[77] However, in light of the *de facto* collapse of the post-war liberal world order, any

76 Italian Constitutional Court, Judgment of 13 June 2024 (*Priolo*), n. 105, *Considerato in diritto* 4.3.

77 More specifically, *Ferrajoli* calls for an extension of the paradigm of rigid constitutional to the global scale. See Ferrajoli (n 33) in particular 90–113.

proposal aimed at its reform currently amounts to little more than wishful thinking.

This of course shall not lead to overlooking the fundamental role of international and regional organisations in the protection of the rights of future generations, especially in the fight against climate change. The United Nations' Sustainable Development Goals (SDGs), adopted in 2015, despite all the criticisms, have been pivotal in calling on States to pursue more forward-looking policies. Similarly, the Paris Agreement on climate change underscores the responsibility of current generations to mitigate global warming for the benefit of future generations.[78] The UN Secretary-General's report, 'Our Common Agenda' (2021), also highlights the need to enhance intergenerational solidarity by considering the establishment of a UN Special Envoy for Future Generations, which would act as a global representative for long-term humanity interests.[79] Although these frameworks signal a commitment on the part of a vast number of UN Member States to think in the long-term, they remain largely aspirational and rely on the voluntary cooperation of states. Within the EU, with the installation of the second *von der Leyen* Commission in the summer of 2024, future generations are starting to appear, albeit not in a central position, in the European political discourse. In the July 2024 Political Guidelines presented by *von der Leyen*, there is only one reference to future generations, generically affirming the moral duty to 'ensure that decisions taken today do not harm future generations'.[80] At the same time, it must be noted that the second *von der Leyen* Commission is the first to have a commissioner for intergenerational fairness.[81]

Yet, regardless of these apparent advancements, the broader framework of international cooperation unquestionably finds itself in a deep crisis. Multilateralism is under strain, as growing geopolitical competition, nationalist retrenchment, and the erosion of shared normative commitments have weakened the ability of international institutions to respond effectively to

---

78 The Paris Agreement actually refers to 'intergenerational equity'.

79 Our Common Agenda. Report of the Secretary General. Available at: https://www.un.org/en/content/common-agenda-report/assets/pdf/Common_Agenda_Report_English.pdf.

80 See *Europe's Choice. Political Guidelines for the Next European Commission*, 19 https://commission.europa.eu/document/download/e6cd4328-673c-4e7a-8683-f63ffb2cf648_en?filename=Political%20Guidelines%202024-2029_EN.pdf.

81 The Commissioner for Future Generations, however, does not have any Directorate General in his portfolio.

long-term global challenges.[82] In this context, it is no longer sufficient to call for reforms at the level of international organisations alone. What is needed is a rethinking of the very foundations upon which international cooperation rests – namely, the constitutional commitments and institutional architectures of nation-states themselves.

This contribution has sought to contribute to such a rethinking by shifting the focus from the often aspirational discourse of global governance to the concrete, if not uneven, ways in which constitutional democracies are beginning to integrate the protection of future generations into their legal and institutional frameworks. By documenting national-level innovations, this work has shown that rather than reconfiguring the architecture of representative democracy, national legislatures tend to proceed with a piecemeal approach, without radically altering the basic structures of contemporary constitutional democracy.

Going back to the question we asked in the introduction, namely, what are the institutional arrangements which best protect future generations, the answer is that a combination of different institutional arrangements appears the most promising alternative. In particular, the constitutional entrenchment may serve to introduce 'future clauses' modelled on those already present in the constitutions of Germany, Italy, and Norway, amongst others. Future clauses, phrased in open-ended terms, leave the legislator with a certain margin of discretion as to the best way to fulfil its mandate of protecting future generations. At the same time, they provide a constitutional basis for *ad hoc* independent autonomous bodies, such as ombudspersons and parliamentary committees, which may help to orient the actions of the ruling majority to a more long-term approach.[83] Finally, judges are also called to play a role in reviewing public policies for their compliance with the principles of intergenerational justice that are being introduced in constitutions around the world.

In conclusion, adopting a long-term approach is not only a normative imperative but a litmus test for the capacity of constitutional democracies

---

82 For a deeper analysis of the crisis of the international order as a consequence of the crisis of democracy see Peter Trubowitz and Brian Burgoon, *Geopolitics and Democracy: The Western Liberal Order from Foundation to Fracture* (Oxford University Press 2023).

83 The United Nations' Sustainable Development Goals (SDGs), adopted in 2015, explicitly recognise the need for long-term thinking by calling on member states to pursue policies that balance the needs of the present without compromising the ability of future generations to meet their own needs (n 9).

to meet the existential challenges of our time. The protection of future generations demands a set of institutional reforms that integrate long-term thinking into the very structure of democratic governance. In the past, national democracies have demonstrated the capacity to evolve to meet the demands of present citizens; the challenge contemporary democracies are now facing is not to reconcile with the electorate's preferences. Rather, parliaments and governments shall prove capable of understanding the dimension of the challenges threatening the very survival of civilisation and move towards a national and international order that is, indeed, fit for the future.

The Human Rights Approach to Climate Change and Anthropocentrism of Human Rights

*Barbara Jakkel**

We live in the 'Anthropocene', in which human destructive activity is having such a major impact on Planet Earth that it has become the main culprit in the global ecological crisis involving climate change, biodiversity loss, and overall pollution. The scientific conception of the Anthropocene makes it inevitable for societies to reconsider the myriad economic and legal institutions used to regulate the relationship between humans and the environment. Indeed, a critique from the environmental ethics perspective states that the ecological crisis has been brought about by an anthropocentric view that emphasises the exclusivity of human interests, subordinating non-human beings to these human interests.[1] *These eco- or biocentric approaches, giving rights to nature or constitutionalising biodiversity, seem rather exotic to a European lawyer, as in climate policy discussions in this region we make efforts to increase the role of human rights. In this paper, I will point out that legal solutions that go beyond an anthropocentric perspective should not be understood as a kind of exoticism, but as a fundamental challenge to human rights-based climate protection that seeks to extend the language of rights beyond humans and calls for a non-human-centred protection of the environment. I will argue that, while this challenge must be taken seriously, there are good reasons to continue to use the language of human rights to express our climate change-related demands.*

---

* Dr Barbara Jakkel, PhD student, Faculty of Law and Political Sciences, University of Debrecen.

1 Environmental ethics: It is a systematic philosophical and ethical examination of human values and attitudes towards nature and the biosphere, emerged as an important subfield of philosophy during the 1970s. It is now a flourishing area of research. See more about it: John Baird Callicott, 'Environmental Ethics' in Stephan G. Post (ed), *Encyclopedia of Bioethics* (3rd ed 2004); Clare Palmer, Katie McShane and Ronald Sandler, 'Environmental ethics' (2014) 39 Annual Review of Environment and Resources 419.

I. Introduction

In 2011, *Nori Huddle* and *Richard Frederick Wheeler* filed a lawsuit against the government of Ecuador's Loja province claiming that they both owned land along the Vilcabamba River in the Loja province. During the widening of a nearby road, the provincial government released excavated material and construction debris into the river. The blockages altered the course of the river, causing massive flooding. The floods increased the risk of landslides, damaged local ecosystems, and reduced local landowners' access to land and water. *Huddle* and *Wheeler* were desperate to save their land and sued the provincial government on behalf of the Vilcabamba River. As this was a constitutional lawsuit brought on behalf of nature, the lawsuit was not to compensate *Huddle* and *Wheeler*, but solely to restore the river's natural ecosystem.[2] As *Huddle* and *Wheeler* were defeated in the municipal court, they appealed to the Loja Provincial Court, which ruled in favour of the Vilcabamba River in March 2011.

The case has been described in the literature as the world's first successful Rights of Nature (RoN) lawsuit.[3] It illustrates the possibility of how a prima facie tort against the interests of landowners can be transformed into a tort against nature itself. And the merit of the provincial judge is no less than that he was able to decouple the RoN and the harm to nature from human interests.

Is this the right legal response to the global ecological crisis? There is a broad scientific consensus that the ecological crisis is anthropogenic, whether we are talking about biodiversity loss, climate change, or overall pollution.[4] The scientific concept of the Anthropocene epoch captures well the way we think about the state of nature and the role of humanity. Taking this line of thought further, environmental ethics criticise 'anthropocentrism', the traditional Western ideology, which emphasises the exclusivity

2 Richard Frederick Wheeler y Eleanor Geer Huddle c/ Gobierno Provincial de Loja, juicio 11121-2011-0010 (30 March 2011); Papers analysing the decision: Natalia Greene, 'The first successful case of the Rights of Nature implementation in Ecuador' https://www.earthlaws.org.au/wp-content/uploads/2016/07/RON_Vilcabamba-Ecuador-Case-complete.pdf, accessed 10 October 2024); Craig Kauffman and Pamela Martin, 'Can rights of nature make development more sustainable? Why some Ecuadorian lawsuits succeed and others fail' (2017) 92 World Development 130.

3 See n 2.

4 Markku Oksanen, 'On tackling the environmental crisis through human rights' (2020) 75 Rivista di Estetica 104.

of human interests at the expense of the interests of other non-human beings (animals and nature).[5] The critique says that this human-centred ideology is responsible for the global environmental crisis. For this reason, environmental ethics advocate legal solutions that are not anthropocentric; the lawsuits based on the RoN mentioned above have emerged precisely as a response to the critique of anthropocentric law. At the same time, the role of human rights based environmental litigation is increasingly coming to the fore in the service of more effective solutions to global environmental problems, with global warming-related climate challenges being a striking example.

Thus, although human rights and the environmental crisis were originally understood as separate issues, they have been regularly discussed together in legal and policy documents and relevant research since the 1970s.[6] From a philosophical point of view, the ultimate question is whether we humans are responsible for the environmental crisis because of the rights we have secured for ourselves.[7] Human rights 'not only regulate our relations with our fellow humans but also provide us with a superior status with respect to the natural world. When understood in this way, are human rights drivers of the environmental crisis as they encourage and justify unsustainable use of the land, the waters and the air; or are they an essential element in the search for a way out of the crisis?'[8]

In this paper, I will show that there is an ideological conflict between the human rights approach and certain statements of environmental ethics. First, the paper provides an insight into the development since the 1970s during which the human rights approach to climate change has gradually gained ground in global climate policy, in the courts and also among researchers working on legal solutions to climate change. Afterwards, the paper introduces the concept of the Anthropocene and the critique of environmental ethics (which is directed against ideologies that support the exclusivity of human interests), showing biocentric and ecocentric legal solutions. By this, it does not, of course, dispute the significant progress that has been reached against the effects of climate change thanks to the human rights-based climate cases, of which an important recent example is

---

5 Laÿna Droz, 'Anthropocentrism as the scapegoat of the environmental crisis: a review' (2022) 22 Ethics in Science and Environmental Politics 25.

6 Oksanen (n 4).

7 Oksanen (n 4).

8 Oksanen (n 4).

the *KlimaSeniorinnen v. Switzerland* case at the European Court of Human Rights.[9] At the same time, this paper also does not intend to explicitly address the many difficulties that human rights-based environmental litigation faces. Instead, the paper will present arguments for a human rights approach that can be considered acceptable in the light of the challenges coming from environmental ethics.

The paper inevitably touches upon the extent to which public law can be made future-proof. One of the most pressing problems causing uncertainty for future generations is climate change, which is only one symptom of the global ecological crisis that defines our age. One of the public law solutions to the problem of climate change is the initiation of national and international climate litigation. A promising litigation strategy in these climate lawsuits is to treat climate change as a human rights violation, which could, thus, also drive forward the future-proofing of public law.

II. The Relevance of a Human Rights Approach to Climate Change

1. Human Rights in Global Climate Policy

For a long time, the human rights narrative was not present at all in the basic principles of global climate policy. Until recently, two approaches have dominated policy thinking on climate change:[10] on the one hand, an approach of economists using a loan-benefit analysis and seeking to maximise net benefits, which seeks to design the optimal climate policy along these lines; on the other hand, the approach of political leaders sharing burdens between states and distributing the economic costs of climate change along these lines.

However, a series of weather-related disasters (from Superstorm *Sandy*, Typhoon *Haiyan* and Cyclone *Pam* to massive floods in Pakistan, a crippling drought in Ethiopia and heat waves in central Europe) has highlighted the human victims of climate change worldwide.[11] In developed countries, such events cause significant material and infrastructural damage,

9 *Verein KlimaSeniorinnen Schweiz and Others v. Switzerland*, 09. April 2024 App no 53600/20.
10 Derek Bell, 'Climate change and human rights' (2013) 4 WIREs climate change 159.
11 Jacqueline Peel and Hari Osofsky, 'A Rights Turn in Climate Change Litigation?' (2018) 7 Transnational Environmental Law 37.

injuries and, in many cases, the loss of lives. In developing countries, where events such as severe storms, floods, or droughts can destroy homes, shorten food supplies and the access to clean water, and deprive people of their livelihoods, the number of fatalities from extreme weather disasters is often even higher. These weather-related disasters – which are predicted to become more severe and frequent due to climate change – have obvious implications for the enjoyment of human rights.[12] As the UN Human Rights Council recognised in its Resolution 7/23: 'Climate change poses an immediate and far-reaching threat to people and communities around the world and has implications for the full enjoyment of human rights.'[13]

The human rights perspective rejects an economic approach based on a cost-benefit analysis because it would allow for some to suffer very great harms so that others benefit more overall.[14] On the other hand, it also challenges the focus on 'who pays', which dominates international climate negotiations, and calls us instead on 'who suffers' from climate change and how their suffering can be prevented.[15] While the representatives of the human rights approach do not deny the need to talk about sharing the costs of mitigation and adaptation, they believe that the focus should be on achieving the following two objectives: firstly, humanity must take stock of what is needed prevent climate change from undermining human rights; secondly, there should be convincing reasons for why all humans should bear their fair share of the costs of mitigation and adaptation in order to avoid a contribution in the violation of someone's human rights.[16]

The UN Office of the High Commissioner for Human Rights' (OHCHR) study on climate change and human rights explains that there is broad international consensus that climate change has a negative impact on the realisation of human rights in general.[17] Although the universal human rights treaties do not include a specific right to a safe and healthy environment that may be threatened by climate change, the study emphasised

---

12 See e.g.: https://science.nasa.gov/climate-change/extreme-weather/, accessed 9 September 2025.

13 UN Human Rights Council Resolution 7/23 available at https://www.uncclearn.org/wp-content/uploads/library/a_hrc_res_7_23.pdf, accessed 11 October 2024.

14 Bell (n 10) 159.

15 Bell (n 10) 159.

16 Bell (n 10) 160.

17 UN High Commissioner for Human Rights (OHCHR) study on climate change and human rights available at https://www.refworld.org/reference/themreport/unhrc/2009/en/65384, accessed 11 October 2024.

that all UN human rights treaty bodies recognise the link between the environment and the realisation of a range of human rights. The collective right to life, health, food, water, adequate housing, and self-determination, as well as the procedural rights to access information and to participate in decision-making about environmental risks, are all prerequisites for the realisation of the right to a healthy environment. In addition, environmental disasters exacerbated by climate change can affect human rights in a wide range of ways, for example due to death, disease, malnutrition (right to life, right to health), food security (right to food), impacts on water resources and threats to access to safe drinking water (right to water), and the loss of habitable land (right to adequate housing). In addition to the overall impacts of climate change on human rights, the OHCHR study also found that the impacts will be unevenly distributed: the effects of climate change will be felt most by persons who are already vulnerable due to factors such as gender, age, minority status, or disability.[18]

At the global level, there is also serious inequality:[19] low-income countries, which produce the least greenhouse gases (GHGs), are affected more by climate change than high-income countries, which produce significantly more GHGs. In addition, low-income countries are much less able to adapt to climate change than high-income countries.[20] As a consequence, the most severe impacts of climate change will be felt by those whose rights are already insecure, as climate change will be felt most in the world's poorest countries, where basic rights protections are already weak.[21]

As a result of the above mentioned, it is now well established in global climate policy that climate change has an impact on human rights. Both the jurisprudence[22] and the literature[23] on climate claims use human rights language and strongly point to the fact that climate change raises a number of human rights concerns.

---

18 ibid 5.

19 Barry Levy and Jonathan Patz, 'Climate Change, Human Rights and Social Justice' (2015) 81 Annals of Global Health 310.

20 Stephen Humphreys, *Human Rights and Climate Change* (Cambridge University Press 2009) 1.

21 ibid 10.

22 See under 2.

23 See under 3.

2. Human Rights in Courts

The claim of a human rights violations in the context of climate change first appeared in courts in 2005 in a petition to the Inter-American Court of Human Rights on behalf of Canada's *Inuit* Indigenous peoples. This was the first attempt to articulate the claim for redress of climate change harms from a human rights perspective. The *Inuit* petition pointed at how climate change is already affecting, and will in the future threaten, the human rights of *Inuit* people due to rising temperatures and further melting of the ice sheets on which their culture, identity and economy depend.[24]

In 2015, a judge of the Lahore High Court in Pakistan 'made history' by ruling that the Pakistani government's delay in implementing the country's climate policy framework violated the fundamental rights of its citizens.[25]

A few months before the Pakistan ruling, amid much greater media attention, a district court in The Hague ordered the Dutch government to adopt stricter measures to reduce GHGs,[26] except that in this case the court did not find a violation of the applicants' human rights, although it did give serious consideration to the human rights-based arguments and used them as an interpretative tool in considering whether the Dutch government had breached its duty of care to the *Urgenda* Foundation and the Dutch population.

In its ruling of March 24, 2021, in the *Neubauer* case, the German Federal Constitutional Court published its decision striking down parts of the Federal Climate Change Act as incompatible with fundamental rights

24 The Inuit communities' 2005 petition to the Inter-American Court of Human Rights and the decision are available at https://climatecasechart.com/non-us-case/petition-to-the-inter-american-commission-on-human-rights-seeking-relief-from-violations-resulting-from-global-warming-caused-by-acts-and-omissions-of-the-united-states/, accessed 11 October 2024.

25 The Ashar Leghari v. Pakistan decision is available at Case No 25501/2015 https://climatecasechart.com/wp-content/uploads/non-us-case-documents/2015/20150404_2015-W.P.-No.-25501201_decision.pdf, accessed 11 October 2024.

26 The decision Urgenda Foundation v. The Netherlands is available at C/09/456689/HA ZA 13-1396 https://www.globalhealthrights.org/wp-content/uploads/2016/03/Urgenda-Foundation-v-State-of-Netherlands.pdf accessed 11 October 2024. For a summary of the decision in Hungarian, see Katalin Sulyok, 'Challenges and successes of the Climate Paper – lessons from the Urgenda judgment' 13(1) Public Law Review 1–7.

(Article 2.2 and Article 20a of the German Basic Law[27]) for failing to set sufficient provisions for emission cuts beyond 2030.[28]

And the recent case of the European Court of Human Rights called *KlimaSeniorinnen v. Switzerland*,[29] mentioned in the introduction, also shows that more and more courts consider the applicability of fundamental rights arguments in climate cases. Since the European Convention on Human Rights (ECHR) does not explicitly provide for the right to a healthy environment, plaintiffs in climate change cases before the ECHR typically rely on Articles 2 (right to life) and Article 8 (right to respect for family and private life) of ECHR. This practice is colloquially referred to as 'greening' of fundamental rights as in such cases courts examine violations of existing fundamental rights in environmental cases.[30]

Besides court decisions, it is fruitful to examine the human rights approach to climate change through a theoretical lens of the relevant literature.

3. What Makes the Human Rights Approach Attractive?

In order to understand what proponents of a human rights approach to climate change consider to be the appeal of this perspective, it is necessary to consider the implications of different philosophical approaches to human rights.

Two of the greatest challenges in contemporary human rights philosophy are the clarification and justification of human rights, which are the subject of an endless debate between moral and political philosophers.[31]

Political conceptions of human rights attribute one or more constitutive political functions to human rights, and thus human rights in this approach

27 Basic Law for the Federal Republic of Germany in english version: https://www.gesetze-im-internet.de/englisch_gg/englisch_gg.html, accessed 9 September 2025.

28 Order of the First Senate of 24 March 2021 – 1 BvR 2656/18 et al.; available at https://www.bundesverfassungsgericht.de/SharedDocs/Entscheidungen/EN/2021/03/rs20210324_1bvr265618en.html; brief summary of the case: https://climatecasechart.com/non-us-case/neubauer-et-al-v-germany/, accessed 09 September 2025.

29 Association of ClimateSenior Women of Switzerland and Others v. Switzerland App no 53600/20, https://hudoc.echr.coe.int/eng-press?i=003-7919428-11026177, accessed 11 October 2024.

30 Anne van Boven, 'The Greening of Human Rights' (MS thesis, Utrecht University 2021).

31 Gerhard Ernst and Jan-Cristoph Heilinger (eds), *Philosophy of Human Rights – Contemporary Controversies* (Walter de Gruyter 2012).

are used to assess political institutions rather than individual behaviour – an interpretation that is reflected in the prevailing interpretation of international law, which sees states as the duty-bearers of the obligation to respect human rights. According to the political conception, understanding human rights must be based on the practice of human rights.[32]

The political approach of human rights is also reflected in the human rights arguments used in climate cases: when plaintiffs use human rights arguments to hold the state accountable for the insufficiently ambitious emission reduction measures it has undertaken, they do not rely on abstract moral arguments but seek to enforce the achievement of objectives already enshrined in international policy through human rights.

Orthodox conceptions of human rights, known as the moral approach to human rights, are more closely linked to the natural rights tradition. This view holds that the justification of at least some political and legal rights is based on analogous moral rights. Proponents of this view reject the restriction of the role of human rights to the political domain and support philosophical theories of human rights based on different values (such as autonomy or equality).[33] This is why two theorists who are committed to the human rights approach but who have chosen a different focus may make completely contradictory claims about what human rights and their main functions are.[34]

The literature supporting the human rights approach to climate change, as we shall see, mostly provides arguments from a moral conception of human rights to support the applicability of this perspective. *Sinden* for example, starts with the premise that every century has its own defining moral question. In the 20th century, the defining moral evil was the subordination of stigmatised groups and efforts to combat this evil culminated in the mid-century, when the American civil rights movement achieved significant success, inspiring the launch of liberation movements around

---

32 Erasmus Mayr, 'The political and moral conceptions of human rights – a mixed account' in Adam Etinson (ed), *Human Rights: Moral or Political?* (Oxford University Press 2018) 73.

33 John Tasioulas, 'On the nature of human rights' in Adam Etinson (ed), *Human Rights: Moral or Political?* (Oxford University Press 2018) 17–60.

34 James Nickel, 'Assigning Functions to Human Rights: Methodological Issues in Human Rights Theory' in Adam Etinson (ed), *Human Rights: Moral or Political?* (Oxford University Press 2018) 145.

the world.[35] During this period, world leaders were able to work together in political and economic institutions to promote world peace, resulting in the adoption of a second generation of human rights norms, largely fuelled by the horrors of the Holocaust.

Sinden considers the climate crisis to be the most crucial moral issue of the 21st century, as it is the story of the exploitation of the weak by the powerful: despite being a matter for humanity as a whole, it divides us on the other side in terms of culpability and vulnerability; the rich and powerful, who carelessly burn fossil fuels, place heavy moral obligations on the poor and powerless, whose contribution to the planet-warming gases is negligible, yet they are the primary victims of a climate that is spiralling out of control.[36]

Moral issues require a profound response from law, and in the 21st century, human rights are law's best response to moral wrongs of grave, unfathomable scale and scope, because human rights are the strongest condemnation of the exploitation of the weak by the powerful through the law.[37]

This is related to the other important role of human rights, which is that they 'rhetorically carry with them an aura of absolutism' – they often stand above and beyond ordinary law, allowing an independent judiciary to override ordinary legislation by the legislature and the executive. It is for this reason, it is argued, that if climate change is understood as a human rights struggle, it creates an opportunity to take action against the political forces that continue to perpetuate and exacerbate the climate crisis.[38]

Bell sees the attraction of a human rights approach to climate change in that it focuses on the harms suffered by individuals, giving climate change a 'human face' and that characterising something as a human rights issue elevates its status relative to other issues, making the problem more morally urgent. It also draws attention to the victims and demands that their interests will be protected.[39]

---

35 Amy Sinden, 'Climate Change and Human Rights' (2008) 49 Journal of Land, Resources & Environmental Law, Temple University Legal Studies Research Paper, available at https://papers.ssrn.com/sol3/papers.cfm?abstract_id=984266.

36 ibid 6.

37 ibid 20.

38 Amy Sinden, 'A Human Rights Framework for the Anthropocene', in Jordi Jaria-Manzano and Suzana Borras (eds), *Research Handbook on Global Climate Constitutionalism* (Edward Elgar 2019) 132.

39 Bell (n 10) 168.

Kotzé stresses the role of a human rights approach to the charge of anthropocentrism, as he sees the future of humanity in the struggle for survival in the Anthropocene era as depending on how it responds to the myriad challenges it has brought about in this era. And the key to survival may be for humanity to adhere to and stay within certain 'thresholds', which are both moral thresholds and biophysical and geophysical ones. The role of human rights in the Anthropocene is important because, although they are not 'experts' in defining bio- and geophysical thresholds, they can establish obligations, entitlements, moral boundaries, and governance commitments that provide the basis for a legal normative response that is responsive to and able to influence such thresholds in order to increase the chances of survival in the Anthropocene.[40] The attraction of human rights, according to *Kotzé*, lies in their ability to transform society, many socio-political, legal, and economic institutions, and this attraction is heightened in conditions of uncertainty, when people are more inclined to rely on underlying values to determine the rules on which decisions are based.[41]

Now that the main merits of the human approach to climate change were mentioned, the paper shall turn to the understanding of human responsibility for the global ecological crisis.

III. The Concept of the Anthropocene Era and the Critique against Anthropocentrism

The 'Planetary Boundaries Framework' is a natural science concept that defines a safe operating space for humanity based on the inherent biophysical processes that govern the stability of the Earth system.[42] The framework has been revised several times since its inception, and in September 2023, a team of scientists first quantified the nine processes that govern the stability and resilience of the Earth system. The team concluded that six of the nine limits have already been crossed by humanity. Crossing these boundaries increases the risk of large-scale, sudden, or irreversible environmental

40 Louis J. Kotzé, 'Human rights and the environment in the Anthropocene' (2014) 1 The Anthropocene Review 252.

41 ibid 253.

42 Katherine Richardson et al., 'Earth beyond six of nine planetary boundaries' (2023) 9(37) Science Advances. The Planetary Boundaries Framework is available in detail at https://www.stockholmresilience.org/research/planetary-boundaries.html, accessed 11 October 2024.

change.[43] Yet, despite the constant warnings of ecological crisis scientists and more than 30 years of international agreements, global carbon dioxide emissions increased by 70% between 1990 and 2020.[44] Biodiversity is collapsing at an unprecedented rate: within a few decades, a million animal and plant species will be at risk of total extinction, mainly due to human activity.

This is the era of the 'triple planetary crisis', which encompasses the interlinked crises of climate change, biodiversity loss, and widespread pollution[45].[46]

1. The Anthropocene

Paul Crutzen was the first who proposed that we should name our present age 'the Anthropocene era', [47] because human destructive activity on planet Earth has become so significant that it has become the main culprit in the global environmental crisis.[48] The term Anthropocene crisis is used because, although there have always been radical changes in climate history and five previous mass extinction events took place on Earth, atmospheric warming and the current sixth mass extinction event are considered exceptional because of the existence of humans.[49] When a crisis event occurs, non-humans adapt or disappear, but humanity can only adapt to a certain degree and does not want to disappear. The urge to reflect on the state of nature and the role of humanity is reflected in the concept of the Anthropocene.

The era of the Anthropocene has begun between the invention of the steam engine and the first industrial revolution, which precisely captures

43 ibid 1.

44 https://www.unep.org/resources/emissions-gap-report-2022, accessed 05 September 2024.

45 For environmental pollution and its effect on life see e.g.: Mashhood Ahmad Khan and Arsalan Mujahid Ghouri, 'Environmental pollution: Its effects on life and its remedies' (2011) 2(2) Researcher World: Journal of Arts, Science & Commerce 276.

46 https://unfccc.int/news/what-is-the-triple-planetary-crisis, accessed 18 August 2025.

47 The use of the concept of the Anthropocene was first proposed by Nobel Prize-winning chemist *Paul Crutzen*. See Paul Crutzen, 'Geology of mankind' (2022) 415 Nature 23.

48 Alf Hornborg, 'The Anthropocene challenge to our worldview' in Jordi Jaria-Manzano and Suzana Borras (eds), *Research Handbook on Global Climate Constitutionalism* (Edward Elgar 2019) 17.

49 Oksanen (n 4).

the moment when mankind began to act as a geological force on the planet, bringing about destructive changes that will be detectable in the geological rock layers long after mankind has disappeared from the planet's surface. This was the moment when we moved from the geological era of the 'Holocene' to the Anthropocene era of the Earth System.[50]

The true merit of the concept of the Anthropocene is that it goes beyond the possibility of scientific interpretation, as it also raises socio-natural questions that anticipate the questioning of constructs associated with modern Western understanding based on the consciousness of human exceptionalism and the traditional relationship between man and nature.

Although the anthropocentric narrative has been a subject to much criticism since its emergence,[51] *Crutzen's* definition seems to be the most influential conceptual attempt to capture the complex characteristics of our anthropogenically dominated planet.

The reactions to humanity's excessive destruction of the environment are very often moral-based People judge this destructive human activity not only to be unpleasant, unfortunate or irritating, but also immoral, wrong or downright evil.[52] These reactions have led to the application of ethical categories in areas where this was previously uncommon. For a long time, ethical categories were used solely to evaluate human activities. Much of the moral-based response to environmental degradation is also undoubtedly human-centred, since much of the concern about the environment rightly focuses on harm to people or adverse effects on human health and well-be-

50 Eva Horn and Hannes Bergthaller, *The Anthropocene – Key Issues for the Humanities* (Routledge 2019).

51 One of the most prominent criticisms is the 'capitalocene narrative'. The term is a contestation of the Anthropocene, as it substitutes capital, capitalism, for man, the anthropos. This approach attributes the environmental crisis not to humanity in the abstract, but to a historically determinable system of socio-economic relations, capitalism. It is important to see that the capitalocene discourse is not contesting the geological anthropocene theory, but the historical narrative of the anthropocene: its critique is that the current ecological crisis is not caused by humanity, but by Western political and economic systems that entrench unjust systems of distribution of environmental goods and services. It is precisely by attributing the ecological crisis to humanity as a whole that the theory suggests that the vast differences between those responsible and the possibility of individualised accountability are obscured. For further insight into this discussion, see Michelle Scobie, 'Framing Environmental Human Rights in the Anthropocene' in Walter Baber and James May (eds), *Environmental Human Rights in the Anthropocene* (Cambridge University Press 2023) 9.

52 Robert Elliot, 'Normative Ethics' in Dale Jamieson (ed), *A Companion to Environmental Philosophy* (Blackwell Publishers 2001) 177.

ing. Human-centred environmental ethics can, thus, do much to articulate the moral responses that many people give to environmental harm and destruction.

However, many environmental philosophers are unsatisfied with the answers of anthropocentric environmental ethics, as they argue that it is the 'anthropocentric' approach in the first place that is to blame for the current ecological crisis.[53]

2. The Anthropocentrism of (Human) Rights

'Anthropocentrism' is defined by *Hayward* as 'attitudes, values or practices which give exclusive or preferential concern to human interests at the expense of the interests or well-being of other species or the environment'.[54] Thus, anthropocentrism is generally used in environmental ethics as a critical term: to 'overcome' anthropocentrism would be to recognise that man is not the centre of the universe, the purpose of creation, but merely a part of the natural order.

Although the concept of anthropocentrism and its layers of meaning are complex,[55] it can be said that it criticises any social construct that prioritises human interests. The charge against law is that rights and laws, which depend on legal systems created by humans to regulate human behaviour within social and geographical boundaries, are anthropocentric, and therefore, since law is a human instrument, legal protection of the environment always involves anthropocentrism to a certain degree.[56] In the search for legal solutions to the ecological crisis, this is why, according to critics, we must move away from anthropocentrism, because it is unsustainable and has caused the crisis in the first place, by prioritising human interests over environmental values.[57]

53 See the environmental philosophical positions mentioned in the following section (2.).

54 Tim Hayward, 'Anthropocentrism', *International Encyclopedia of Environmental Politics* (2014).

55 Ben Mylius, 'Three types of anthropocentrism' (2018) 15(2) Environmental Philosophy 159.

56 Droz (n 5).

57 Helen Kopnina, Haydn Washington, Bron Taylor and John J Piccolo, 'Anthropocentrism: More than Just a Misunderstood Problem' (2018) 31 Journal of Agricultural and Environmental Ethics 109.

Human rights can be seen as confusing from the point of view of environmental philosophers who reject this anthropocentric approach.[58] Indeed, the human rights approach, in their view, promotes structures, practices, and activities that lead to biodiversity loss, global warming, pollution, and the exceeding of planetary boundaries, as it expresses and justifies what we call human superiority over the rest of nature. Because human rights are the rights of individuals, they belong to them only because they were born as humans and this places human individuals above non-human beings, thus justifying the exploitative human attitude towards the rest of nature.

These accusations by environmental philosophers are not without historical merit either, since, if we look at the social, cultural, and economic dimensions of human rights, there are signs in the most important international declarations and conventions that the natural world is seen as a repository of resources and that the ultimate use of these resources is in the hands of sovereign states.[59]

Existing environmental rights are also mostly anthropocentric in focus, emphasising the benefits of environmental and ecosystem goods and services for human health and well-being.[60] Only a few exceptions to this tendency can be mentioned, such as the constitutional laws of Ecuador[61] and Bolivia,[62] which declare the objective of giving the environment the right to exist, to survive, to preserve, and to renew its life cycles.

The result, according to critics, is that anthropocentric human rights are simply inadequate to confront the economic policies and power struc-

---

58 William Aiken, 'Human Rights in an Ecological Era' (1992) 1(3) Environmental Values 191.

59 As Aiken points out, at the beginning of the UN Universal Declaration of Human Rights in 1948, the human rights debate was not about the relationship between people and the environment, the focus was on the rights to liberty and well-being that were fundamental to human dignity and well-being. Several of the rights declared were rights which, if fully exercised by all peoples, would have adverse environmental consequences (e.g. the right to property, work, rest, leisure, an adequate standard of living, etc.). Article 19 states that the only condition for limiting these rights is 'due recognition and respect for the rights and freedoms of others...' which shows that only the strengthening of human rights can limit human rights, ibid 192–195.

60 Kotzé (n 40).

61 Constitution of Ecuador available at https://www.constituteproject.org/constitution/Ecuador_2021, accessed 11 October 2024, Article 10.

62 Constitution of Bolivia available at https://www.constituteproject.org/constitution/Bolivia_2009, accessed 11 October 2024.

tures of industrial capitalism.[63] Related to this is a further problem with the human rights approach: in the paradigm of sustainable development, human rights are often used to promote socio-economic development at the expense of ecological considerations.[64] In countries where people have a constitutional right to protect the environment for the benefit of present and future generations, these provisions allow for legislative and other measures to be taken to ensure the ecologically sustainable development and use of natural resources, provided that these measures also promote economic and social development. In essence, this creates an opportunity to balance sustainable development with socio-economic interests, the latter taking precedence.[65]

A further difficulty with the human rights paradigm is that the rights-based approach is individualistic, which is contrary to a holistic view of the Earth and its systems, whereas the most popular global governance model for the Anthropocene, Earth System Governance, seeks to provide a holistic and integrated response to the complex problems of the Anthropocene.[66]

Therefore, the conclusion of the critique of the anthropocentric approach is usually that human rights either play no role in addressing the environmental crisis or it blames the human rights approach outright for legally 'entrenching' the superiority of humans and degrading nature to the level of a commodity.

3. Legal Solutions from a Biocentric and an Ecocentric Perspective

As an alternative to anthropocentrism biocentrism and ecocentrism are recommended in the literature. Biocentrism is about giving moral value to all living entities. It is also known as an individualistic approach, which, like anthropocentrism, adheres to the ethical paradigm that only individuals are morally worthy of respect. Ecocentrism, on the other hand, offers a holistic perspective: it considers not only living organisms but the whole ecosystem, including the abiotic parts of nature, to be worthy of moral status.[67]

63 Kotzé (n 40) 259.
64 Robin Craig and Melinda Benson, 'Replacing Sustainability' (2013) 46 Akron Law Review 841.
65 ibid 853.
66 Kotzé (n 40) 255.
67 Hayward (n 53).

A legal solution that rejects an anthropocentric approach and takes an ecological perspective is the RoN movement,[68] which has gained increasing recognition over the last few decades and is seen as having the potential to make a significant contribution to solving the ecological crisis. The RoN movement is based on ecological justice, which is a broader concept according to which not only humans but all biotic and abiotic (sentient and non-sentient) non-human entities are entitled to the moral value of justice.[69] This implies that humans, as moral agents, cannot (at least without a stronger moral justification) deprive these sentient and non-sentient entities of the environmental basis for their continued existence and reproductive capacity.

One practical solution for the recognition of nature's rights was found by the Supreme Court of the Indian state of Uttarakhand: the court transferred the legal guardianship of abiotic systems (glaciers, rivers, streams, lakes, jungles, etc.) to the state authorities and recognised them as legal entities with rights and obligations.[70]

Another solution is to recognise constitutional rights of nature itself. For example, Ecuador amended its constitution in 2008 to recognise that Mother Nature has the right to maintain her existence and respect her regeneration.[71] The text of the constitution states that anyone can enforce these rights by calling on the authorities to respect them.[72] Since then, several successful lawsuits have been brought based on this constitutional amendment, like in 2021, when the Ecuadorian Constitutional Court decided to revoke environmental permits previously granted for two mining concessions in the *Bosque Protector Los Cedros* reserve.[73] The court ruled that the mining concessions in question violated not only several constitutional

---

68 Gilber et al., 'Understanding the Rights of Nature: Working Together Across and Beyond Disciplines' (2023) 51 Human Ecology 363.

69 Himani Bhakuni, 'Perspective Beyond Anthropocentrism – Health Rights and Ecological Justice' (2021) 23(2) Health and Human Rights 7.

70 Lalit Miglani v. State of Uttarakhand & Others, High Court of Uttarakhand Order on Miscellaneous Application CLMA 3003/17, March 30, 2017.

71 Ecuador Constitution (n 61).

72 According to Article 71 of the Equador Constitution: 'Nature, or Pacha Mama, where life is reproduced and occurs, has the right to integral respect for its existence and for the maintenance and regeneration of its life cycles, structure, functions and evolutionary processes. All persons, communities, peoples and nations can call upon public authorities to enforce the rights of nature. To enforce and interpret these rights, the principles set forth in the Constitution shall be observed, as appropriate.'.

73 See the original decision of the Constitutional Court of Ecuador No. 1149-19-JP/21: https://esacc.corteconstitucional.gob.ec/storage/api/v1/10_DWL_FL/e2NhcnBld

rights of the communities living in the area, but also, and most importantly, the rights of Mother Nature (*Pacha Mama*). These rights were specifically granted by the court to the *Los Cedros* reserve.

The ruling is significant because, although the court had already held in a previous case that mangrove ecosystems in general have natural rights, it had not provided a formula that would have specified in detail how these rights should be taken into account in specific cases.[74] The *Los Cedros* case law went further by structuring the legal standard for the application of natural rights in specific cases, recognising *Los Cedros* as a special subject deserving protection.[75]

The theory of RoN and its practical application are still in their infancy, but there are signs that they are gradually being incorporated into the law enforcement practices of some states, with over 150 initiatives currently strengthening RoN worldwide.[76] The supporters of the biocentric perspective also emphasise constitutionalisation, which advocates the inclusion of biodiversity in the constitution. Protecting biodiversity is not only important for maintaining a healthy 'non-human' environment, but also indirectly for humans and for an ecologically sustainable society. Protecting biodiversity ensures that humanity continues to have access to high quality food sources, and it is also essential for medical research and the discovery and development of new medicines.[77] Humans also depend on a biodiverse and ecologically balanced environment for atmospheric regulation of oxygen and greenhouse gases, water purification, soil fertilisation, and groundwater recharge.[78]

GE6J3RyYW1pdGUnLCB1dWlkOic2MmE3MmIxNy1hMzE4LTQyZmMtYjJkOS1mYzYzNWE5ZTAwNGYucGRmJ30= (accessed 18 August 2025); papers analyzing the decision: Mika Peck et al., 'The conflict between Rights of Nature and mining in Ecuador: Implications of the Los Cedros Cloud Forest case for biodiversity conservation' (2024) 6 People and Nature; Tănăsescu Mihnea et al., 'Rights of nature and rivers in Ecuador's Constitutional Court' [2024] The International Journal of Human Rights 1.

74 This previous judgment was made also in 2021 (No. 22-18-IN/21) by the Constitutional Court of Ecuador.

75 Judgment No. 1149-19-JP/21 of the Constitutional Court of Ecuador, for analising the decision, see Gustavo Prieto, 'The Los Cedros Forest has Rights – The Ecuadorian Constitutional Court Affirms the Rights of Nature' [2021] Verfassungsblog https://verfassungsblog.de/the-los-cedros-forest-has-rights/, accessed 10 October 2024.

76 Gilber et al. (n 68) 375.

77 Joshua Bruckerhoff, 'Giving Nature Constitutional Protection: A Less Anthropocentric Interpretation of Environmental Rights' (2008) 86 Texas Law Review 615, 619.

78 ibid 620.

The scientific conception of the Anthropocene era and the critique of environmental ethics against anthropocentrism call for a rethinking of man's responsibility for environmental destruction. The human rights approach partly answers the question of human responsibility, as will be seen below, by drawing attention to the actual human victims of climate change and holding large emitting corporations and insufficiently climate-conscious states accountable. There are, however, some victims that remain invisible through the human rights approach: the non-human beings of the environment. The greater attention to the interests of these non-human beings and the change of attitude that this requires, according to some proponents[79] of environmental ethics, could be a solution to the global ecological crisis.

IV. How can a Human Rights Approach Answer the critique of Environmental Ethics?

As has been shown, the authors who emphasise the importance of a human rights approach in the context of climate change start from a moral conception of human rights. However, it is also clear from the above that the anthropocentric critique coming from environmental ethics targets the moral approach to human rights: it criticises the anthropocentric focus that leaves non-human beings off the moral scales, thus, only focusing on the human victims of the ecological crisis. Advocates of a moral approach to human rights – emphasising the merits of human rights in the context of the ecological crisis –, therefore, cannot afford to ignore this critique. At the same time, it is important to acknowledge that human rights approach currently represents the best moral response of law to the representation of the human victims of climate change

This argument is linked to another argument for a human rights approach to climate change, which *Aiken* calls the 'tourist trail argument'.[80] This is related to the phenomenon that the advance of the human rights narrative in international fora (both in international climate policy and in courts) seems to offer the best chance at present to develop a workable, viable practice in environmentalism. Indeed, by basing environmental responsibility on human rights, we can participate in the debate in the

79 See e.g. Mary Midgley, 'The End of Anthropocentrism?' (1994) Royal Institute of Philosophy Supplements 36, 103; Droz (n 5); Kopnina (n 57).

80 Aiken (n 58) 201.

language used by decision-makers in the international forum and thus have a chance to influence concrete policy. However, an environmentalist position that rejects the human rights approach does not calculate the risk of being easily marginalised, its arguments might not be taken seriously because they are not in the language of the current decision-makers. *Aiken* argues that while it is conceivable that the ecological crisis will usher in a post-industrial, green, decentralised, communitarian era when human rights language will no longer be needed, until then, the human rights approach offers a cautious, effective, and practical approach.[81]

This approach clearly understands the role of human rights in the relevance of policy makers,[82] rather than focusing on individual behaviour. In response to the accusations of environmental philosophy, the policy approach also sometimes goes beyond the tourist trail principle to argue that empirical research shows that in countries where environmental human rights are elevated to constitutional status, the commitment of society to natural values is also strengthened.[83]

V. Conclusion

This paper has not sought to take a position on a particular conception of human rights, nor does it embrace any ideology that rejects the human rights approach to reassessing the role of humans in the ecological crisis. It emphasised the human rights approach to climate change and, at the same time, sought to shed more light on the context, in which the debate on the role of human rights can be understood, and the limits of this approach. Criticism of the anthropocentrism of human rights is a fundamental challenge that cannot be ignored by the literature supporting the human rights approach to climate change, but it would be difficult for critics to deny the current usefulness of human rights in the fight against climate change. Actors of legal practice are therefore right, in my view, to use the existing effective tools to fight the ecological crisis, while remaining open to legal solutions that seem exotic in the current context, but which are likely to become more prevalent in everyday legislative and enforcement debates in the future.

---

81 ibid 201.
82 See at II. 1.
83 Kotzé (n 40) 253.

Finally, we cannot ignore the questions raised in the introduction, which identified the search for a future-proof strategy for dealing with the global ecological crisis. The paper sought to provide a theoretical examination of the human rights approach, contrasting it with the claims of environmental ethics, which criticise anthropocentric ideologies. The text argued that the human rights approach can be considered a promising strategy for the present, but that it is important to bear in mind the consequences of the Anthropocene crisis and that the crisis is likely to generate increasingly creative litigation strategies in the future, which even those, who are currently averse to them and prefer traditional legal solutions, will have to come to terms with.

The Role of Future Generations' Rights in the Interpretation of the Paris Agreement's Temperature Goal

*Derya Nur Kayacan Fidan/Maria Liana Vodiță**

This paper examines the legal enforceability of the 1.5 °C temperature goal set out in the 2015 Paris Agreement in the light of the concept of future generations' rights. While Article 2 of the Paris Agreement references a temperature range between 1.5 °C and 2 °C above pre-industrial levels, this work argues that the 1.5 °C target is, in itself, legally binding, particularly when interpreted in light of the principle of intergenerational equity and human rights. Future generations' rights are understood broadly to include unborn individuals as well as children and others unable to represent their long-term interests. Mainly focusing on a European perspective, this paper draws on relevant frameworks such as the 2023 Maastricht Principles to illustrate the growing relevance of intergenerational equity in the interpretation of legal norms. It also considers the 2025 Advisory Opinion of the International Court of Justice, which confirms the binding nature of the of the 1.5 °C target, as well as relevant jurisprudence that integrates intergenerational concerns into climate litigation. By incorporating human rights considerations, this paper aims to contribute to the broader discourse on the enforceability of climate objectives and the protection of vulnerable populations amidst intensifying climate impacts on current and future generations.

I. Introduction

The Paris Agreement,[1] adopted in 2015, represents a landmark global effort to address climate change by setting out a collective commitment aimed at 'holding the increase in the global average temperature to well below 2 °C above pre-industrial levels and pursuing efforts to limit the temperature increase to 1.5 °C above pre-industrial levels, recognising that this would

* Asst. Prof. Dr. Derya Nur Kayacan Fidan (Turkish-German University Istanbul) and Dr. Maria Liana Vodiță (IU International University of Applied Sciences).

1 Paris Agreement (adopted 12 December 2015, entered into force 4 November 2016) 3156 UNTS 79.

significantly reduce the risks and impacts of climate change' in Article 2. By setting this ambitious goal, the Paris Agreement has since been the basis of the vast majority of international efforts in facing the challenges caused by climate change. The wording of Article 2 of the Paris Agreement thus clearly establishes a legally binding force of the 2 °C temperature goal, with no scope for interpretation beyond that. The question arises, however, whether the stricter 1.5 °C temperature goal, which would overrule the 2 °C goal, is also legally binding for the Contracting Parties to the Paris Agreement given that the wording of Article 2 of the Paris Agreement does not define this without a doubt, but rather indicates a temperature range between 1.5 °C and 2 °C above pre-industrial levels.

The impacts of climate change generally vary across the globe, with some regions already experiencing severe effects from the current 1 °C rise in global temperatures compared to pre-industrial levels.[2] Limiting global warming to 1.5 °C instead of 2 °C would significantly reduce risks such as heatwaves, heavy rainfall, and sea-level rise, but the specific impacts will depend on future greenhouse gas emissions and the pathways taken.[3] Overshooting 1.5 °C even temporarily, however, could lead to greater and more irreversible damage, especially if critical thresholds, or 'tipping points', are crossed, making it essential to stabilise temperatures at or below 1.5 °C.[4] The 1.5 °C goal has therefore notably spurred innovation in renewable energy, encouraged investments in sustainable technologies, and heightened global awareness of the urgency of climate action, promoting a collective commitment to mitigating climate impacts.

Given that recent scientific climate models show significant differences in impacts between a 1.5 °C and a 2 °C rise, including an increased risk of extreme weather events and substantial sea level rise, which would have severe repercussions for future generations,[5] an additional question arises: How can the temperature goal determined by Article 2 of the Paris Agreement be interpreted specifically in the context of future generations' rights?

---

2 Intergovernmental Panel on Climate Change (IPCC), *Global Warming of 1.5 °C: IPCC Special Report on Impacts of Global Warming of 1.5 °C above Pre-Industrial Levels in Context of Strengthening Response to Climate Change, Sustainable Development, and Efforts to Eradicate Poverty* (1st edn, Cambridge University Press 2022) 282 <https://www.cambridge.org/core/product/identifier/9781009157940/type/book> accessed 28 June 2024.

3 ibid.

4 ibid 283.

5 Intergovernmental Panel on Climate Change (IPCC) (n 2).

This work argues that the 1.5 °C temperature goal is, in fact, legally binding for the Contracting Parties to the Paris Agreement. While there is a multitude of arguments supporting this approach, one particularly relevant argument stands out: the concept of future generations' rights as a compelling basis for the interpretation of the Paris Agreement's temperature goal. In this regard, the concept of future generations' rights shall be understood as a broad term that not only includes such persons who have not yet been born, but also those who are currently not able to represent their future interests, even though they will be increasingly and disproportionately affected by today's actions in the future, such as infants and children in general. Herein, this work mainly focuses on the European perspective from a human-rights-focused point of view and aims to explore how the rights of future generations can be integrated into today's interpretation of the relevant legal frameworks, whilst also emphasising the role of human rights within the discussion on the effects of climate change. Additionally, it considers relevant case law and judicial interpretations that strengthen the argument for the 1.5 °C goal as a legally binding commitment, particularly within the context of European jurisdictions. In this sense, the present analysis highlights how the legal interpretation of the Paris Agreement must evolve to reflect the growing relevance of intergenerational justice, and the newest scientific findings related to the effects of climate change in the present and future. By doing so, it emphasises the relevance of the interpretation of existing legislation as a means of future-proofing public law and thus ultimately aims to contribute to the broader discussion on the legal enforceability of climate goals and the protection of vulnerable populations in the face of an escalating climate crisis.

II. The Concept of Future Generations' Rights as Human Rights

The consequences related to climate change pose a threat to human rights, especially those of future generations. The concept of the rights of future generations in the field of environmental law emphasises the importance of considering the well-being and interests of both the current population and those who will inhabit the planet in the future. It entails future generations to have pre-emptively enforceable rights against governments to ensure environmental protection and address climate change, as they will suffer most from the consequences of lack thereof.

The protection of the environment is a matter of public interest recognised in both international and domestic legal frameworks. At the international level, instruments such as the Stockholm Declaration, the Rio Declaration, and the Paris Agreement affirm that states have responsibilities to protect the environment for present and future generations.[6] More recently, the United Nations General Assembly has explicitly recognised the human right to a clean, healthy and sustainable environment, underscoring the global consensus on governments' duties in this field.[7] Similarly, many national constitutions enshrine the right to a healthy environment and impose duties on governments to act in the public interest – for example, Article 56 of the Turkish Constitution, Article 20a of the German Basic Law, the French Charter for the Environment of 2004, Section 24 of the South African Constitution, and Articles 71–74 of the Ecuadorian Constitution.[8] Within this normative context, governments are obliged to prioritise the well-being and concerns of the general public in their actions and decisions. While upholding the public interest, they must ensure that their conduct aligns with democratic principles such as justice, fairness, and equity.[9] This reflects the conception of government as an institution that should 'serve, rather than steer' – that is, to implement policies and processes that genuinely benefit society as a whole rather than merely directing or controlling it.[10] Importantly, the interpretation of what constitutes the public interest is not static; it evolves in light of changing social, economic, and environmental circumstances, which in turn shape the methods by which governments are expected to fulfil these obligations.

Climate change unequivocally represents a matter of public interest given its profound impact on the environment, affecting not only current generations, who are already grappling with extreme weather events linked to cli-

6 Declaration of the United Nations Conference on the Human Environment (Stockholm Declaration) (16 June 1972) UN Doc A/CONF.48/14/Rev.1; Rio Declaration on Environment and Development (14 June 1992) UN Doc A/CONF.151/26 (vol I).

7 UNGA Res 76/300 (28 July 2022) UN Doc A/RES/76/300; UNHRC Res 48/13 (8 October 2021) UN Doc A/HRC/RES/48/13.

8 Constitution of the Republic of Turkey (adopted 7 November 1982, as amended); Basic Law for the Federal Republic of Germany (adopted 23 May 1949, as amended); Charter for the Environment 2004 (France), incorporated into the French Constitution by Constitutional Law No 2005-205 of 1 March 2005; Constitution of the Republic of South Africa, 1996; Constitution of the Republic of Ecuador, 2008.

9 Robert B. Denhardt and Janet V. Denhardt, 'The New Public Service: Serving Rather than Steering' (2000) 6 Public Administration Review 549, 554.

10 ibid 553.

mate change, but also future generations, whose prospects are increasingly at risk in the absence of urgent and proactive measures. What was once regarded as a distant threat is now a pressing reality that demands immediate collective action to mitigate its consequences and safeguard the well-being of both present and future generations. While the present generation is still able to enjoy fundamental human rights, future generations are becoming increasingly more vulnerable and their ability to enjoy their fundamental human rights is steadily diminishing. However, not all States view environmental protection as a public interest that warrants prioritisation, at least not to an extent that could culminate in an effective change. This reluctance may be explained by the perception that climate consequences are not sufficiently immediate to justify far-reaching measures. It can also be linked to structural features of democratic systems, where short legislative terms incentivise politicians to prioritise re-election and present-day challenges over long-term risks such as climate change.[11]

Perhaps the consequences are perceived as insufficiently immediate to justify far-reaching measures. The reluctance of some states to prioritise environmental protection – particularly industrialised states, which are the principal contributors to global emissions – remains a critical barrier to the adoption of effective climate measures.[12]

Against this reluctance, the recognition of the rights of future generations has emerged as a normative framework designed to compel states to adopt a long-term perspective in their decision-making. Scholars and legal experts increasingly advocate for integrating such rights into legal systems as a means to ensure that the needs and interests of those yet to be born are not subordinated to short-term considerations.[13] By putting more emphasis on

11 See Tristan Barczak, 'Demokratische Zukunftsverantwortung Zwischen Verfassungsrecht Und Verfassungspolitik' (2023) 76 Die Öffentliche Verwaltung (DÖV) 925.

12 See Hannah Ritchie, 'Global Inequalities in CO2 Emissions' (*Our World in Data*, 31 August 2023) <https://ourworldindata.org/inequality-co2> accessed 15 August 2025, noting that high- and upper-middle-income States, representing roughly half of the world's population, are responsible for over 80 per cent of global CO2 emissions.

13 Margaretha Wewerinke-Singh, Ayan Garg and Shubhangi Agarwalla, 'In Defence of Future Generations: A Reply to Stephen Humphreys' (2023) 34 The European Journal of International Law 651; Rachel K. Johnston, 'Lacking Rights and Justice in a Burning World: The Case for Granting Standing to Future Generations in Climate Change Litigation' (2016) 21 Tilburg Law Review 31; Bridget Lewis, 'Human Rights Duties towards Future Generations and the Potential for Achieving Climate Justice' (2016) 34 Netherlands Quarterly of Human Rights 206.

the rights of future generations, governance can be reshaped in a manner that is more sustainable and equitable, ensuring that today's actions take full account of their long-term consequences.

This vision has also begun to find expression in international instruments. Already in 1987, the World Commission on Environment and Development, which was established based on a resolution of the United Nations (UN) General Assembly, had pointed out that 'the results of the present profligacy [were] rapidly closing the options for future generations' and urged for the recognition and protection of future generations' rights.[14] The General Conference of the UN Educational, Scientific and Cultural Organization has also acknowledged in its Declaration on the Responsibilities of the Present Generations Towards Future Generations of 1997 the need to safeguard the interests of future generations.[15] More recently, this momentum has deepened. The Maastricht Principles on the Human Rights of Future Generations (the Principles) published in 2023 is among the most recent attempts to articulate a deeper recognition of future generations within human rights law.[16] While non-binding, they carry persuasive authority as an expert restatement of how existing human rights norms should be interpreted in light of intergenerational concerns. Principle 2 in particular underscores that the application of the current human rights framework is not confined to those who are alive today, but extends to all of humanity across time. Accordingly, every generation carries 'the duty to protect and sustain the Earth's natural and cultural heritage for future generations' and, under the current environmental situation, the recognition of the intergenerational dimension of this duty is of particular urgency.[17] The General Conference of the UN Educational, Scientific and Cultural Organization has also acknowledged in its Declaration on the Responsibilities of the Present Generations Towards Future Generations of 1997 the

14 The World Commission on Environment and Development, 'Our Common Future (A/42/427)' paras 26, 97 <https://documents.un.org/doc/undoc/gen/n87/184/67/pdf/n8718467.pdf> accessed 20 August 2024.

15 UNESCO General Conference, 'Declaration on the Responsibilities of the Present Generations Towards Future Generations' <https://www.unesco.org/en/legal-affairs/declaration-responsibilities-present-generations-towards-future-generations> accessed 20 August 2024.

16 'Maastricht Principles on The Human Rights of Future Generations' <https://www.rightsoffuturegenerations.org/the-principles/english> accessed 20 August 2024.

17 ibid 8 and Preamble V.

need to safeguard the interests of future generations.[18] The necessity to consider future generations has also been emphasised by *António Guterres*, the UN Secretary-General, in his report titled 'Our Common Agenda' which represents his vision for future global cooperation and presents a road map to achieve the 2030 Agenda for Sustainable Development.[19] The report includes several suggestions such as the establishment of a 'Futures Laboratory' for impact assessment of major policies, the appointment of a special envoy to represent the interests of future generations and the adaptation of a Declaration on Future Generations to consolidate these efforts.

Building upon these recommendations, the *'Summit of the Future'*, convened in September 2024, constituted a critical juncture for operationalising long-term commitments within the UN framework.[20] Among its principal outcomes was the *Declaration on Future Generations*, formally adopted by consensus on 22 September 2024.[21] While the Declaration stops short of codifying a legally enforceable 'right' of future generations, it unequivocally recognises their 'needs and interests' as considerations that ought to inform the formulation and implementation of present policies, including those with profound environmental and intergenerational consequences.[22] Notably, the Declaration commits Member States to integrate long-term impact assessments,[23] promoting intergenerational equity,[24] and strengthening evidence-based decision-making processes – commitments that are directly pertinent to the interpretation and operationalisation of climate obligations under the Paris Agreement. Moreover, the Declaration supports the appointment of a *UN Special Envoy for Future Generations*, whose mandate is envisaged to include advocacy for the inclusion of future generations' perspectives in international norm-setting and compliance

18 UNESCO General Conference (n 15).

19 UN Secretary-General, 'Our Common Agenda' (2021) <https://www.un.org/en/common-agenda> accessed 21 August 2024; UN General Assembly, 'Transforming Our World: The 2030 Agenda for Sustainable Development (A/RES/70/1)' (2015) <https://sdgs.un.org/2030agenda> accessed 21 August 2024.

20 'Summit of the Future' <https://www.un.org/en/summit-of-the-future> accessed 21 August 2024.

21 UN General Assembly, 'Declaration on Future Generations' [2024] UN Doc A/RES/78/XXX.

22 ibid preamble paras 3–5.

23 ibid para 11.

24 ibid para 4.

monitoring.[25] Although the position has not yet been formally established, preparatory consultations and programmatic groundwork are underway, with the Secretary-General having reiterated his intention to appoint the Envoy by the end of 2025.[26] Taken together, these developments underscore an evolving normative landscape in which the *interests and, arguably, the emerging rights* of future generations are accorded growing weight as interpretative considerations in the legal assessment of states' duties to mitigate climate change.[27]

The same notion of responsibility towards future generations is reflected in the General Comment published by the Committee on the Rights of the Child. In its General Comment, the Committee focused on children's rights in relation to environmental protection and emphasised the obligation of States to take necessary measures to protect children's rights under the Convention on the Rights of the Child from negative implications of climate change.[28] After drawing attention to the principle of intergenerational equity and the interests of future generations, the Committee considered children as a crucial actor in environmental law and underscored their role as the bridge between current and future generations.[29] 'While the rights of children who are present on Earth require immediate urgent attention, the children constantly arriving are also entitled to the realization of their human rights to the maximum extent.'[30] It thus recognised that children's rights and intergenerational equity are inherently linked in the context of environmental sustainability, highlighting the need to safeguard the well-being of both present and future generations.

25 UN Secretary-General (n 19) para 124.

26 UN Secretary-General, 'Remarks at the Informal Interactive Dialogue on the Implementation of the Pact for the Future' (26 March 2025) <https://www.un.org/sg/en/content/sg/statement/2025-03-26/secretary-generals-remarks-the-informal-interactive-dialogue-the-implementation-of-the-pact-for-the-future-bilingual-delivered-scroll-down-for-all-english-version> accessed 27 June 2025.

27 Edith Brown Weiss, *In Fairness to Future Generations: International Law, Common Patrimony, and Intergenerational Equity* (United Nations University/Transnational Publishers 1989); UN Human Rights Council Res 48/13 (8 October 2021) UN Doc A/HRC/RES/48/13.

28 Committee on the Rights of the Child, 'General Comment No. 26 on Children's Rights and the Environment, with a Special Focus on Climate Change (CRC/C/GC/26)' para 20 <https://www.ohchr.org/en/documents/general-comments-and-recommendations/crccgc26-general-comment-no-26-2023-childrens-rights> accessed 20 August 2024.

29 ibid 11.

30 ibid.

Although the phrase 'rights of future generations' is not explicitly used in most of the above-mentioned documents, they all share the common understanding to respect and consider the well-being, needs and interests of future generations. This ideology is referred to as the principle of intergenerational equity. *Weiss* bases the foundation of intergenerational equity on two relationships: the relationship of the current generation with nature and the relationship between different generations. All generations are connected to one another through their relationship with nature, before which all are equal.[31] Intergenerational equity, which is also the foundation of sustainable development, is the concept of fairness in distributing natural resources among generations, meaning that each generation should utilise the resources available to them 'without compromising the ability of future generations to meet their own needs'.[32]

Whether the duty to consider the interests of future generations that the principle of intergenerational equity bestows on the current generation actually correlates with a right for future generations is a controversial topic among legal scholars. Some scholars argue that future generations cannot possess rights since they do not yet exist and, therefore, can neither have nor claim such rights.[33] In order to *have*, one must exist; who does not exist, cannot *have*. But this approach is too mathematical and superficial, neglecting to appreciate the complex nature of this topic. The environment, which belongs to no one yet is entrusted to everyone bestows the responsibility to respect and protect it on all those who enjoy it.[34] Surely, we expect there to be a future generation, although we do not know who exactly they will be. The mere reason that they do not yet exist does not mean that they will not. The fundamental reason behind the foundation of the League of Nations, later the UN, or the European Union, and many other international organisations and international agreements is the will to establish and maintain a world order where there is peace and security in order for humanity to prosper. Simply dismissing the rights of future generations because they do not yet exist falls contrary to the spirit of international law.

31 Weiss (n 27) 20–21.

32 See Edith Brown Weiss, 'Intergenerational Equity' [2021] Max Planck Encyclopedia of Public International Law <https://opil.ouplaw.com/display/10.1093/law:epil/9780199231690/law-9780199231690-e1421> accessed 21 August 2024; The World Commission on Environment and Development (n 14) para 27.

33 Wilfred Beckerman and Joanna Pasek, *Justice, Posterity, and the Environment* (Oxford University Press 2001) 16.

34 Weiss (n 27) 20.

It is further argued that rights are inherently 'claimable', and that since future generations cannot themselves assert claims, they cannot meaningfully be said to hold rights. Yet this view overlooks the fact that rights need not always be exercised directly by the right-holders. Just as children, or persons lacking legal capacity, are represented by guardians who advance claims on their behalf, so too can institutions, states, or designated representatives act as guardians of the interests of those yet to be born. This trusteeship approach regards the present generation as holding the planet on behalf of future generations.[35] Similarly, the Maastricht Principles on the Human Rights of Future Generations affirm that the non-existence of future generations does not prevent the current generation from recognising their rights and acting as duty-bearers in anticipation of their interests.[36] Thus, while future generations cannot themselves appear as claimants, mechanisms of representation can ensure that their rights can still function within the legal system. The recognition of interests in international declarations and instruments reflects this point. If one were to deny that future generations could have rights, one would also need to deny that they have interests – a position flatly contradicted by the growing body of international law recognising precisely such interests.[37] This conceptual understanding of representation also finds reflection in emerging jurisprudence, where courts have increasingly recognised the standing of associations, NGOs, or vulnerable groups to advance claims that indirectly safeguard the rights and interests of future generations, which will be explored in the following section.

Indeed, the Universal Declaration of Human Rights (UDHR) starts with the 'recognition of the inherent dignity and of the equal and inalienable rights of all members of the human family [as] the foundation of freedom, justice and peace in the world'.[38] This recognition of the fundamental equality of all human beings includes also future generations.[39] Equality of all human beings requires protection of everyone's interests, which is achieved through a correlating human right and an obligation to respect

35 ibid 40–44.

36 'Maastricht Principles on The Human Rights of Future Generations' (n 16) Principles 1-2.

37 UNESCO General Conference (n 15); The World Commission on Environment and Development (n 14).

38 Universal Declaration of Human Rights (adopted 10 December 1948 UNGA Res 217 A(III) Preamble.

39 Weiss (n 27) 21.

it. Considering that there will be and that we want there to be a future, this also has to include the interests and correlating rights of future generations.[40] The focus should not be the future generation's ability or inability to *have* something, but rather should be our obligation towards them. Intergenerational equity reflects this perspective and must be understood as an obligation of current generations to responsibly manage resources, mitigate climate change, and promote sustainable development, ensuring that future generations inherit a planet that is habitable, resilient, and conducive to their well-being and prosperity. It represents the current generation's responsibility to include the rights of future generations in today's decision-making process that ultimately and inevitably will affect future generations.

III. The Role of Future Generations' Rights in the Interpretation of the Paris Agreement's Temperature Goal

The issue of future generations' rights is, therefore, becoming increasingly relevant in the context of climate change, including the interpretation of the Paris Agreement's temperature goal. From a legal perspective, the question arises whether human rights can even be pre-emptively claimed regarding the interests of individuals and groups, especially by future generations in accordance with the above-mentioned definition. If this were the case, the subsequent question would then concern the specific interpretation of the Paris Agreement's temperature goal, taking into consideration the principle of intergenerational equity and future generations' rights in this context.

1. The Pre-emptive Enforcement of Future Generations' (Human) Rights

While the concept of future generations' rights has been gaining more and more relevance within the field of human rights law, the question arises whether proactive governmental or state action, *inter alia* aimed at achieving the Paris Agreement's temperature goal, can even be pre-emptively demanded on behalf of certain individuals or groups, including those that would be allocated to future generations. In this regard, one can differenti-

40 Jos Philips, *Actualizing Human Rights Global Inequality, Future People, and Motivation* (Routledge 2020) 63.

ate between human rights as moral rights, which is a concept rooted in various philosophical traditions, on the one hand, and human rights as legal rights in the context of human rights law on the other, although these concepts, despite their conceptual differences, are closely linked due to the existing influence of moral-philosophical understandings in the context of human rights law.[41] From a moral-philosophical point of view, it would be particularly difficult to argue that future people cannot be attributed rights due to their non-existence at present,[42] as has been discussed above.

While the beforementioned theoretical approach to human rights can easily consider obligations to future generations to be at least morally binding on today's society,[43] recognising and enforcing these obligations on the basis of current human rights law is an entirely different matter, especially as it raises a multitude of legal questions. As future generations are not explicitly named as beneficiaries under international or most domestic laws, and government obligations are generally limited to persons under their jurisdiction or effective territorial control, it remains unclear at first glance whether these obligations also extend to future generations and especially to such persons that have not yet been born.[44] In this sense, one can argue that the protection of human rights must also be extended to future generations in the above-mentioned sense, as these rights ought to apply to 'all members of the human family' in accordance with the Preamble to the UDHR, representing an agreeable perspective from a moral-philosophical point of view. Nevertheless, such an interpretation faces certain legal difficulties that must be addressed. Under current legal standards, the main difficulty lies in pre-emptively proving that state actions may eventually result in human rights violations in the future, even though the anticipated harm has not yet occurred. This especially applies to the legal field of climate litigation.

Although human rights laws mandate the prevention of harmful actions in this sense, such violations are typically recognised only when the threat is imminent. However, the relevant jurisprudence differs significantly in regards to recognising such an imminent threat, even concerning the same

41 Bridget Lewis, 'Human Rights as a Basis for Institutions for Future Generations' in Jan Linehan and Peter Lawrence (eds), *Giving Future Generations a Voice* (Edward Elgar Publishing 2021) 63.

42 Robert Elliot, 'The Rights of Future People' (1989) 6 Journal of Applied Philosophy 159, 168.

43 ibid.

44 Lewis (n 41) 66–67.

scope of protection, i.e. the right to life. For instance, in the case of *Teitiota v. New Zealand*, the Human Rights Committee found that although rising sea levels in Kiribati did pose serious risks, they did not amount to actual or imminent harm to the complainant's right to life under Article 6 of the International Covenant on Civil and Political Rights (ICCPR) at the time of the claim.[45] On the other hand, in *Urgenda v. Netherlands*, the Dutch Supreme Court found that climate change did present an imminent threat to both the right to life and the right to respect for private and family life as guaranteed by the Articles 2 and 8 of the European Convention on Human Rights (ECHR), therefore on a regional level, but regarding the same scope of protection regarding the right to life, while determining that the State ought to take the necessary precautionary measures as a result.[46] Despite this broader interpretation of the definition concerning the term 'imminent harm', the challenge of proving violations of future generations' human rights persists under existing legal frameworks, as these continue to emphasise the concept of imminent or immediate harm as the standard despite the inconsistent interpretation by the competent courts.

The requirement for proven imminent harm for the individual in the context of climate litigation cases has, however, recently been redefined in *Strasbourg*, France, with regards to the right to respect for private and family life. In April of 2024, the European Court of Human Rights (ECtHR) delivered a significant ruling in the case of *Verein KlimaSeniorinnen Schweiz and Others v. Switzerland*, stating that the Swiss government failed to adequately address climate change, resulting in violations of Article 8

45 International Covenant on Civil and Political Rights (adopted 16 December 1966, entered into force 23 March 1976) 999 UNTS 171; United Nations International Covenant on Civil and Political Rights, 'Teitiota v. New Zealand, Human Rights Committee, Communication No. 2728/2016, U.N. Doc. CCPR/C/127/D/2728/2016' (United Nations Human Rights Committee 2020) 8, 10 <https://documents.un.org/doc/undoc/gen/g20/237/12/pdf/g2023712.pdf>; Ivanka Bergova, 'Environmental Migration and Asylum: Ioane Teitiota v. New Zealand' (2021) 42 Justice System Journal 222, 223; Duncan Muhumuza Laki, 'The Case of *Ioane Teitiota v. New Zealand* at the Human Rights Committee: A Common Sense Approach' (2021) 115 Proceedings of the ASIL Annual Meeting 161, 161–162.

46 Convention for the Protection of Human Rights and Fundamental Freedoms (European Convention on Human Rights, as amended) (adopted 4 November 1950, entered into force 3 September 1953) ETS No 5; *Urgenda v. Netherlands* [2019] Supreme Court of the Netherlands ECLI:NL:HR:2019:2007; Chris W. Backes and Gerrit A. Van Der Veen, 'Urgenda: The Final Judgment of the Dutch Supreme Court' (2020) 17 Journal for European Environmental & Planning Law 307, 308.

in conjunction with Article 6 ECHR.[47] Here, the ECtHR derived from Article 8 ECHR the positive obligation to establish and enforce a legislative and administrative framework to effectively protect life and health.[48] Unlike other European courts, such as the German Federal Constitutional Court, which in its so-called 'climate ruling' denied a violation of protective duties but acknowledged a violation of intertemporal and intergenerational freedom under the Basic Law,[49] the ECtHR argued based on positive obligations, specifying the state's obligations to set timelines to achieve climate neutrality, and correspondingly, determine a remaining CO_2 budget or other calculation methods to reach the goal of containing climate change, stating that without such measures, adequate regulation would not be possible.[50]

In this case, a group of senior Swiss women, represented by the association *Verein KlimaSeniorinnen Schweiz*, claimed that the Swiss government's insufficient action to mitigate climate change had violated *inter alia* their rights to life and health under the ECHR, arguing that rising temperatures, verifiably and increasingly aggravated by climate change, disproportionately affected their health, particularly during heatwaves, whilst pointing out that 'the global scientific consensus was that many premature deaths and health impairments could be prevented by adhering to the 1.5 °C limit'.[51] The ECtHR held that the Swiss government had failed to fulfil its positive obligations under the ECHR by omitting to take adequate measures to limit greenhouse gas emissions and thus protect the applicants from the effects of climate change.[52] Concerning the necessary evidence in regards to such a violation, the ECtHR argued that while the individual applicants did not meet the criteria for victim status under Article 34 ECHR because they could not demonstrate a direct and imminent threat to their rights, the association itself was found to have the standing to bring the complaint, as it was acting on behalf of a specific and vulnerable group affected by

47 *Verein Klimaseniorinnen Schweiz and Others v. Switzerland* App no 53600/20 (ECtHR, 2024).

48 ibid 538, 545; Michael L. Fremuth, 'Der Klimawandel vor dem EGMR und die Grenzen der Menschenrechtskonvention' (2024) 15 Europäische Zeitschrift für Wirtschaftsrecht (EuZW) 697, 699.

49 *Climate Protection Ruling* [2021] German Federal Constitutional Court (Bundesverfassungsgericht) 1 BvR 2656/18, 1 BvR 78/20, 1 BvR 96/20, 1 BvR 288/20.

50 Fremuth (n 48) 700.

51 *Verein Klimaseniorinnen Schweiz and Others v. Switzerland* (n 38) 64–68.

52 ibid 558–574.

climate change.[53] As a result, the ECtHR allowed for legal protection without requiring individual victim status or direct legal threat, and it elevated Non-Governmental Organisations (NGOs) to a central role in climate protection in the interest of the public and future generations,[54] thus also consequently establishing the possibility of pre-emptively enforcing human rights for vulnerable groups, including those of future generations.

In parallel to these developments within the human rights framework, the International Court of Justice (ICJ) has also supported a long-term, preventive approach to environmental protection that aligns with the rights and interests of future generations. Notably, in its Advisory Opinion on the *Legality of the Threat or Use of Nuclear Weapons*, the Court explicitly recognised the importance of safeguarding the environment for 'generations unborn'[55] and recently reaffirmed this within its 2025 Advisory Opinion on the *Obligations of States in respect of Climate Change*.[56] Moreover, in *Gabčíkovo-Nagymaros*, the ICJ stressed the necessity of reconciling development with environmental protection and acknowledged the irreversible nature of environmental harm.[57] In a similar tone, the Court reaffirmed in *Certain Activities Carried Out by Nicaragua in the Border Area* that states are under a duty to conduct environmental impact assessments where there is a risk of transboundary harm – a procedural obligation that inherently reflects the principle of prevention and supports the long-term protection of environmental interests, including those of future generations.[58] These statements reinforce the idea that the protection of future generations forms part of the evolving landscape of international legal interpretation and must be integrated into the reading of States' climate obligations.

2. The Concretisation of the Temperature Goal on the Basis of the Concept of Future Generations' Rights

It is becoming increasingly clear that States must align their human rights obligations with international environmental law principles, as it is stipulat-

53 ibid 521–526.
54 Fremuth (n 48) 702.
55 *Legality of the Threat or Use of Nuclear Weapons* [1996] ICJ Rep 226 [29].
56 *Obligations of States in respect of Climate Change (Advisory Opinion)* [2025] [155].
57 *Gabčíkovo-Nagymaros Project (Hungary/Slovakia)* [1997] ICJ Rep 7 [140].
58 *Certain Activities Carried Out by Nicaragua in the Border Area (Costa Rica v Nicaragua)* [2015] ICJ Rep 665 [104–105].

ed in paragraph 11 of the Paris Agreement's Preamble, which mandates that 'Parties should, when taking action to address climate change, respect, promote and consider their respective obligations on human rights.' Such an alignment has proven to be particularly relevant in the recent past as the ECtHR, amongst others, has examined potential human rights violations in the context of global temperatures rising above 1.5 °C pre-industrial levels, potentially shaping States' obligations under the UN Framework Convention on Climate Change (UNFCCC) and the Paris Agreement, notwithstanding jurisdictional constraints.[59]

Although Article 2 of the Paris Agreement does not explicitly render the 1.5 °C target legally binding according to its wording, the growing emphasis on the rights of future generations in environmental law substantially enhances its legal force and binding nature.

Together with the scientific data, the temperature goal laid down in the Paris Agreement should be interpreted in light of other relevant legal tools and texts that frame States' obligations in environmental protection. This interpretation should include an assessment based on the principle of intergenerational equity and rights of future generations, together with relevant articles from the UNFCCC, the ECHR and ICCPR, while also taking into consideration the Vienna Convention on the Law of Treaties (VCLT). Article 2 paragraph 1 of the Paris Agreement regulates the temperature goal within the context of the UNFCCC by the setting the aim of 'enhancing the implementation of the Convention' in this regard.[60] The UNFCCC's preamble emphasises the need to protect the climate for 'present and future generations of humankind'. This objective entails the responsibility of present generations to take decisive action to mitigate climate change and ensure the well-being of both current and future generations. With the Paris Agreement further substantiating the principle of 'intergenerational equity' in the sense of the protection of future generations' rights within its preamble, the temperature goal under Article 2 of the Paris Agreement must be interpreted in the light of their protection, as according to Article 31 of the VCLT, the preamble is integral to interpreting a treaty's provisions,

59 Maria L. Voditã, 'The Growing Relevance of the Paris Agreement's 1.5 °C Temperature Goal in the Light of International Human Rights Law and Climate Change Litigation' (*Opinio Juris*, 23 November 2023) <http://opiniojuris.org/2023/11/23/the-growing-relevance-of-the-paris-agreements-1-5-c-temperature-goal-in-the-light-of-international-human-rights-law-and-climate-change-litigation/> accessed 27 June 2024.

60 United Nations Framework Convention on Climate Change (adopted 9 May 1992, entered into force 21 March 1994) 1771 UNTS 107.

as it further determines the treaty's purpose and objectives.[61] This aligns with the ICJ's view within its Advisory Opinion on the *Obligations of States in respect of Climate Change*, according to which 'intergenerational equity is a manifestation of equity in the general sense and thus shares its legal significance as a guide for the interpretation of applicable rules'.[62]

As the principle of intergenerational equity implies a duty to prevent harm to future generations by taking proactive and preventive measures against climate change, the integration of scientific evidence and climate models that forecast the specific consequences of a 1.5 °C versus a 2 °C increase in global temperatures appears crucial when interpreting the Paris Agreement's temperature goal through the lens of future generations' rights. In this sense, it is not sufficient to focus on the Paris Agreement's wording when concretising the relevant temperature goal, especially as scientific findings on the effects of climate change have become more accurate since the Paris Agreement first came into force in 2015.

Additionally, in 2015, the UNFCCC Subsidiary Body for Scientific and Technological Advice (SBSTA) had already declared the 2 °C temperature goal by itself does not align with the UNFCCC's objective. In their 'Report on the Structured Expert Dialogue on the 2013–2015 review', summarising expert deliberation on the adequacy of the long-term global goal under the UNFCCC, the SBSTA emphasised that only limiting warming up to 1.5 °C above pre-industrial levels would be sufficient to uphold the objective of the UNFCCC and meet the Paris Agreement's temperature aim, as 'high risks are projected even for warming above 1.5 °C'.[63] The assessment took place within the framework of Article 2 of the UNFCCC, which defines the central aim of avoiding dangerous human impacts on the climate system. This goal continues to guide how subsequent agreements, including the Paris Agreement, should be understood and applied. It was therefore declared in the report 'that Parties would profit from restating the long-term global goal as a "defence line" or "buffer zone", instead of a "guardrail" up to which all would be safe'.[64] Furthermore, given that scientific models predict

61 Vienna Convention on the Law of Treaties (adopted 23 May 1969, entered into force 27 January 1980) 1155 UNTS 331.

62 *Obligations of States in respect of Climate Change (Advisory Opinion)* (n 56) para 157.

63 United Nations Framework Convention on Climate Change (UNFCCC), 'Report on the Structured Expert Dialogue on the 2013–2015 Review' (Subsidiary Body for Scientific and Technological Advice 2015) FCCC/SB/2015/INF.1 33 <https://unfccc.int/resource/docs/2015/sb/eng/inf01.pdf>.

64 ibid.

significantly more severe impacts at 2 °C of warming compared to 1.5 °C,[65] adhering to the lower threshold becomes not just a target, but an obligation rooted in the duty to protect future generations from foreseeable harm. It can thus be concluded that States must adhere to a temperature goal that not only aligns with the wording of Article 2 paragraph 1(a) of the Paris Agreement, but also take into consideration other relevant aspects such as the UNFCCC's objectives as established by Article 2 paragraph 1 of the Paris Agreement. As a result, exceeding the 1.5 °C goal would likely result in States failing to fulfil their obligations, as the anticipated consequences would contradict the objectives of both the UNFCCC and, consequently, the Paris Agreement.[66]

The question arises, however, whether the principle of 'intergenerational equity' as mentioned in the Paris Agreement's preamble allows for a further concretisation of the temperature goal to an upper limit of 1.5 °C above pre-industrial levels. According to the preamble, which must be taken into consideration when interpreting the temperature goal according to Article 31 VCLT, 'Parties should, when taking action to address climate change, respect, promote and consider their respective obligations on human rights, the right to health, the rights of indigenous peoples, local communities, migrants, children, persons with disabilities and people in vulnerable situations and the right to development, as well as gender equality, empowerment of women and intergenerational equity'. In this sense, the ICJ stated that '[i]ntergenerational equity is an expression of the idea that present generations are trustees of humanity tasked with preserving dignified living conditions and transmitting them to future generations', while also emphasising that 'States must (...) take their obligations under international human rights law into account when implementing their obligations under the climate change treaties and other relevant environmental treaties and under customary international law, just as they must take their obligations under the climate change treaties and other relevant environmental treaties and under customary international law into account when implementing their human rights obligations'.[67] The principle of intergenerational equity thus ought to be placed in the human rights context, thus allowing for an interpretation based on the assumption that the principle of 'intergenerational

65 Intergovernmental Panel on Climate Change (IPCC) (n 2) 282–283.

66 Vodiţă (n 59).

67 *Obligations of States in respect of Climate Change (Advisory Opinion)* (n 56) paras 156, 404.

equity' must be understood as an instrument for human rights protection of future generations. The argument that the principle of intergenerational equity as mentioned in the Paris Agreement's preamble further implies the protection of future generation's rights raises the question of the extent of possible human rights violations based on relevant provisions of international human rights law. Focusing on the European context, this especially entails possible violations under the ECHR on the one hand, and under the ICCPR on the other.

As mentioned above, in the case of *Verein KlimaSeniorinnen Schweiz and Others v. Switzerland*, the ECtHR acknowledged the Respondent State's positive obligations to implement sufficient measures to combat climate change under Article 8 ECHR as well as their failure to comply with these, whilst noting 'that there is a close link between the substantive obligations under the various Convention provisions which come into play in the present context'.[68] In addition to this, the ECtHR determined that 'the Convention should be interpreted so as to achieve internal consistency and harmony between the various provisions and the fact that the State's positive obligations in the environmental context under Articles 2 and 8 largely overlap',[69] whilst hinting that 'the interpretation and application of the rights provided for under the Convention can and must be influenced both by factual issues and developments affecting the enjoyment of the rights in question and also by relevant legal instruments designed to address such issues by the international community', and, more specifically, 'that the Convention should be interpreted, as far as possible, in harmony with other rules of international law'.[70] As a result, an interdependence between the States' obligations under the Paris Agreement as well as the UNFCCC and under international human rights regulations accordingly is observable and must be taken into consideration when interpreting relevant regulations on both ends of this kinship.[71] This assumption is reinforced by the ECtHR, stating that 'the scope of the respondent State's obligation to protect under Articles 2 and 8 needed to be interpreted in the light of the relevant international instruments, which manifested an international trend (and international obligations) on the measures that needed to be taken to address the serious and profound risks of climate change' and specifically

68 *Verein Klimaseniorinnen Schweiz and Others v. Switzerland* (n 47) 292.
69 ibid.
70 ibid 455.
71 Vodiţă (n 59).

referring to 'the commitments undertaken by the State under the UNFCCC and the Paris Agreement, as well as the 2021 Glasgow Climate Pact which had confirmed 1.5 °C as the primary global temperature rise ceiling'.[72]

Based on this interdependence, there is not only the need to interpret the ECHR in the light of the UNFCCC and Paris Agreement as stated by the ECtHR, but also the other way around. In this sense, the right to life as well as the right to respect for private and family life under Articles 2 and 8 ECHR can be attributed a significant influence on the interpretation of Article 2 of the Paris Agreement. As a result, the Paris Agreement's temperature goal must adhere with the State's positive obligations in the environmental context under Articles 2 and 8 ECHR.

Under the ICCPR, the main priority can be attributed to the right to life under Article 6 ICCPR, as considered, for example, in the case of *Teitiota v. New Zealand*. Here, the UN Human Rights Committee recognised that environmental degradation and climate change can pose a real threat to the right to life, thereby expanding the traditional understanding of Article 6 ICCPR to include the protection against life-threatening environmental conditions.[73] This led to a broader interpretation of Article 6 ICCPR, which considers environmental factors as part of the right to life, supporting the argument that the temperature goals outlined in the Paris Agreement must be interpreted with a view towards preventing violations of the right to life due to climate-induced harms.[74] Furthermore, the Human Rights Committee recognised that when States fail to take sufficient action to mitigate climate change, they may be in breach of their obligations under Article 6 ICCPR.[75] This acknowledgment reinforces the notion that international human rights law, including the ICCPR, must be interpreted in light of challenges related to climate change.

In line with this, the principle of intergenerational equity within the Paris Agreement's preamble can be seen as linked to the protection of the right to life for future generations under Article 6 ICCPR. This implies that the Parties to the Paris Agreement, UNFCCC and the ICCPR have an obligation to implement climate policies that aim to prevent temperature increases above 1.5 °C, as failing to do so could foreseeably result in environmental conditions that threaten the lives of future generations. In this regard,

72 *Verein Klimaseniorinnen Schweiz and Others v. Switzerland* (n 47) 331.
73 United Nations International Covenant on Civil and Political Rights (n 45) 8–11.
74 ibid 8–12.
75 ibid.

the interdependence between international human rights obligations and environmental law becomes increasingly evident. This interpretation not only aligns with the objectives of the Paris Agreement, but also ensures that climate actions are firmly rooted in the protection of fundamental human rights, thereby advancing a holistic approach to climate justice. Consequently, the failure to adhere to the 1.5 °C limit could constitute a breach of the right to life, thereby further sustaining the argument that the 1.5 °C temperature goal is, in fact, legally binding.

This is also reflected in relevant scientific findings, which highlight significant differences in the impacts of a 1.5 °C temperature rise above pre-industrial levels compared to a 2 °C rise. Assuming that the rights of future generations can be protected in advance, it raises the question of how these rights would be affected by a temperature increase up to and beyond 1.5 °C above pre-industrial levels. In this sense, it is already predictable that exceeding the 1.5 °C threshold would have a substantial impact on the rights of future generations to life and respect for private and family life, even according to conservative scientific estimates.

By 2050, limiting global warming to 1.5 °C, as opposed to 2 °C, could result in significantly fewer people experiencing critical climate-related challenges. For instance, up to 270 million fewer people would be exposed to water scarcity globally, while up to 34 million fewer individuals may be vulnerable to increased flooding.[76] If warming reaches 2 °C, cities such as Karachi in Pakistan or Kolkata in India could face annual heatwave conditions similar to the deadly ones experienced in 2015.[77] These scenarios indicate a tipping point at warming over 1.5 °C in regards to the severity and frequency of heatwave impacts, which could lead to increased demand for cooling technologies, particularly in tropical and subtropical regions, placing further strain on energy resources and infrastructure.[78] Moreover, climate change is expected to have significant socioeconomic repercussions. By 2050, such changes in temperature and precipitation that can be linked to climate change are expected to cause global food prices to rise by as

---

76 Intergovernmental Panel on Climate Change (IPCC) (n 2) 213-214.

77 ibid 263.

78 Christopher B. Field and others (eds), *Climate Change 2014 Impacts, Adaptation, and Vulnerability: Working Group II Contribution to the Fifth Assessment Report of the Intergovernmental Panel on Climate Change* (Cambridge University Press 2014); Jinkyu Hong and Won Sup Kim, 'Weather Impacts on Electric Power Load: Partial Phase Synchronization Analysis' (2015) 22 Meteorological Applications 811; Intergovernmental Panel on Climate Change (IPCC) (n 2).

much as 84 %, exacerbating food insecurity.[79] Moreover, each one (unit) standard deviation increase in temperature or extreme rainfall, which is equivalent to roughly 0.13 °C in global annual temperature changes, is associated with an estimated 14 % rise in the frequency of intergroup conflict, with warming of 2 to 4 °C potentially leading to higher rates of violent conflict and socio-political instability.[80] Such impacts would disproportionately affect 'vulnerable populations' in the sense of groups that face 'sensitivity or susceptibility to harm and lack of capacity to cope and adapt', amplifying poverty and disadvantage worldwide.[81] Coastal flooding risks are also projected to rise, particularly in tropical regions and small islands, where extreme water-level events could double by 2050.[82]

By 2100, the impacts of global sea level rise will differ significantly depending on whether global warming is limited to 1.5 °C or ought to reach 2 °C. Regarding the scenario of limiting global warming to 1.5 °C above pre-industrial levels, the projected global sea level rise ranges from 0.26 to 0.77 meters, potentially exposing up to 10.4 million fewer people to the resulting effects compared to a warming of 2 °C, assuming no further adaptation measures are taken.[83] This smaller sea level rise at 1.5 °C would thus provide more time and opportunities for adaptation, helping to reduce the risk of flooding and other coastal impacts. Even so, the global sea level rise is expected to continue beyond 2100, indicating with high confidence that instabilities in the Greenland and Antarctic ice sheets could result in multi-meter rises over centuries to millennia.[84] The differences in sea level rise between 1.5 °C and 2 °C of warming will thus become increasingly significant after 2100, emphasising the long-term benefits of taking immediate action in order to limit warming and the severity of its effects accordingly. Adaptation strategies can further reduce certain risks, but the difference between 1.5 °C and 2 °C of warming will have profound implications for millions of people worldwide, particularly in coastal regions and small island nations.[85]

79 Intergovernmental Panel on Climate Change (IPCC) (n 2) 239.
80 Solomon M. Hsiang, Marshall Burke and Edward Miguel, 'Quantifying the Influence of Climate on Human Conflict' (2013) 341 Science 1235367.
81 Intergovernmental Panel on Climate Change (IPCC) (n 2) 245, 560.
82 ibid 235.
83 ibid 178.
84 ibid.
85 ibid.

Moreover, the consideration of the principle of intergenerational equity in the context of the legal interpretation of the Paris Agreement not only strengthens the argument for a binding 1.5 °C temperature goal but also underscores the necessity of proactive climate policies that prioritise the rights of future generations. The gradual shift in legal perspective emphasises that the failure to adhere to this threshold could constitute a breach of fundamental human rights, including the right to life and health for future generations as defined above. In this sense, the evolving jurisprudence highlights a growing recognition of the legal obligations that States owe to future generations in the context of climate change. Ultimately, surpassing the 1.5 °C threshold would significantly increase the likelihood of harmful outcomes for both the environment and humans in the future. When combined with the shown scientific data that outlines the severe difference in consequences, the goal must, as a result, be set at 1.5 °C in accordance with the future generations' rights under international human rights law.

IV. Conclusion

The concept of the rights of future generations has become an integral part of the discussion surrounding environmental protection. It is used as an argument to persuade States to take effective measures to mitigate the impact of climate change, since future generations will endure the most severe of consequences in the absence of adequate action. While it is the responsibility of States to act in accordance with the public interest and to keep it at the highest regard, the notion of public interest is not always construed the same. Those who have influence on today's policy-making might not always be motivated to consider the bigger picture and adapt a long-term thinking when their current interests hold more weight. When it comes to the environment and its protection, the interests of the current generation can seem to clash with what would be the best policy for future generations. However, from an objective perspective save from individual interests, what is beneficial for the future is usually in alignment with the general interest of the current generation. This is even more true as current generations have already started to experience the negative impacts of climate change.

The rights of future generations can be understood through the lens of intergenerational equity, which holds that current generations have a responsibility to utilise the resources available to them in a way that does not compromise the ability of future generations to meet their own needs.[86] This is based on the notion that each generation that has come and will arrive has in common the relationship they share with Earth. This common ground requires that each generation acts fairly and justly with a sense of responsibility towards the other. Whether this principle reflects only a moral-philosophical duty or whether it actually provides a legal right to future generations that can be claimed pre-emptively today and enforce certain legal obligations on the current generation is a controversial topic. It is clear that the principle of intergenerational equity and the concept of rights of future generations present some legal obstacles that must be dealt with. However, a strong case can be made in their favour in light of the international legal framework and recent court decisions.

The Paris Agreement symbolises a global unity in addressing climate change and provides a long-term vision to guide States in their policy-making. It has instigated a structured and collaborative approach to mitigate the impacts of climate change, spurring more awareness with the ultimate goal of protecting both current and future generations, which is also visible by its referral to intergenerational equity in the preamble. Based on this protective purpose, Article 2 of the Paris Agreement has set a goal to hold the increase in global average temperature to well below 2 °C and to pursue efforts to limit the temperature increase to 1.5 °C above pre-industrial levels. There have been some doubts as to which temperature goal was legally binding on States since the wording of the article does not necessarily make it clear. While 2 °C was considered a binding 'guardrail' from the beginning, 1.5 °C could also be understood as an aspirational objective due to the wording of the article. However, the principle of intergenerational equity and consideration of rights of future generations requires us to accept the 1.5 °C goal as legally binding and to take all necessary measures accordingly. This interpretation is in line with the general goals set out in the Paris Agreement's preamble, which must be taken into consideration based on Article 31 of the VCLT and is further supported by the relevant articles of UNFCCC, the ECHR and ICCPR. Recent decisions from the ECtHR, the UN Human Rights Committee, and some national courts together with the reports presented by the UNFCCC Subsidiary Body for Scientific and Technological Advice, the Intergovernmental Panel on Climate Change and

86 Weiss (n 27) 38–42.

relevant other bodies strengthen this conclusion. Furthermore, it is now also supported by the ICJ's Advisory Opinion on the *Obligations of States in respect of Climate Change*, according to which '1.5 °C has become the scientifically based consensus target under the Paris Agreement',[87] which from now on hardly allows for any other interpretation.

The Paris Agreement obliges States to '[pursue] efforts to limit the temperature increase to 1.5 °C above pre-industrial levels'. The fact that Article 2 of the Paris Agreement mentions 2 °C can neither be used as a basis to excuse nor justify any lack of effort by States in pursuing the 1.5 °C goal. It should also be emphasised that in addition to the binding nature of the 1.5 °C goal, States are obliged to take any necessary measures to keep global warming to a lower temperature. Any lack of effort to that end would be a breach of the States' contractual obligations under the Paris Agreement. As past and current efforts have been deemed 'insufficient for limiting warming to 1.5 °C with no or limited overshoot' by the IPCC amongst others,[88] the ICJ's recent advisory opinion underscores that 'the responsibility of a party may be engaged under the rules on State responsibility if there is any breach of the obligations' under the climate change treaty framework.[89]

In summary, these findings underline that future-proofing public law does not necessarily require the creation of entirely new legal instruments, but can also be done through a dynamic and forward-looking interpretation of existing frameworks in light of the latest scientific evidence and the evolving understanding of intergenerational justice. By interpreting existing obligations, such as those under the Paris Agreement, in a manner that integrates the rights of future generations and reflects current climate science, public law can remain effective and responsive to long-term global challenges.

87 *Obligations of States in respect of Climate Change (Advisory Opinion)* (n 56) para 224.

88 Intergovernmental Panel on Climate Change (IPCC), *Summary for Policymakers. In: Global Warming of 1.5 °C. An IPCC Special Report on Impacts of Global Warming of 1.5 °C above Pre-Industrial Levels in Context of Strengthening Response to Climate Change, Sustainable Development, and Efforts to Eradicate Poverty* (1st edn, Cambridge University Press 2022) para C.2.3 <https://www.cambridge.org/core/product/identifier/9781009157940/type/book> accessed 14 August 2025; H. Damon Matthews and Seth Wynes, 'Current Global Efforts Are Insufficient to Limit Warming to 1.5 °C' (2022) 376 Science 1404.

89 *Obligations of States in respect of Climate Change (Advisory Opinion)* (n 56) para 408.

Constitutional Identity: Against or in Favor of Human Rights?

Juan Alonso Tello Mendoza[*]

This paper examines the concept of 'constitutional identity' applied in recent European Court of Human Rights (ECtHR) decisions and its implications for human rights within the European legal framework. Initially developed within the European Union (EU) context under the 'national identity' category, constitutional identity is a legal tool for Member States to assert core constitutional principles against potential EU law overreach. This paper explores how the ECtHR has – apparently – adapted this doctrine, particularly in recent Latvian cases, to justify differential treatment of human rights under the European Convention on Human Rights (ECHR) while preserving a state's foundational constitutional values. The paper analyses the EU Court of Justice and the ECtHR case law and argues that constitutional identity balances the State's core constitutional elements with international human rights obligations when used under the margin of appreciation. Nevertheless, it warns of the doctrine's potential misuse to legitimise authoritarian practices. Ultimately, the paper proposes that if properly applied, constitutional identity can strengthen human rights protection within the European legal landscape by offering states limited discretion over constitutional matters without undermining the ECHR's integrity.

I. Introduction

The Treaty on the European Union (TEU) introduced the national identity clause[1] to safeguard member states' unique constitutional traditions from the EU's potential interference. While there is no consensus on the equiv-

---

* Assistant Professor of Constitutional Law, University of Barcelona.

1 Article 4.2 TEU: *The Union shall respect the equality of Member States before the Treaties as well as their national identities, inherent in their fundamental structures, political and constitutional, inclusive of regional and local self-government. It shall respect their essential State functions, including ensuring the territorial integrity of the State, maintaining law and order and safeguarding national security. In particular, national security remains the sole responsibility of each Member State.*

alence, this clause is often read as 'constitutional identity'. This clause's interpretation remains a significant contention among scholars and national and international judicial bodies, focusing on the scope of its protection, its potential impact on the primacy principle of EU law, and concerns over its possible misuse amid the current rule of law crisis. This debate, typically considered an EU issue, has started a new stage since the European Court of Human Rights (ECtHR) recognised 'constitutional identity' as a legitimate aim for justified differential treatment of the European Convention on Human Rights (ECHR), deserving a margin of appreciation. As expected, this doctrine has faced criticism for being seen as undermining human rights, encouraging arbitrariness, and legally supporting authoritarian regimes.

Given these considerations, it is worth exploring how the ongoing discourse surrounding national identity in the EU may influence upcoming deliberations within the Council of Europe (COE), and whether the enhanced use of 'constitutional identity' may contribute to future-proofing human rights protection. Consequently, I will first consider the debate on national and constitutional identity inside the EU. Second, I will develop the scope of what the ECtHR has pointed out on 'constitutional identity' in its decisions. Additionally, I will assess if incorporating this doctrine may contribute to better human rights comprehension and protection, before concluding with key findings.

II. National Identity: Two Competing Views at the EU

1. An Approach from the Literature

Considering the contributions made by *Cruz*[2] in this area, the original national identity clause was first introduced in the Maastricht Treaty of 1992[3] – probably more as a political value than a juridical one[4] – representing

2 cf Pablo Cruz, 'Identidad nacional y valores de la Unión Europea: límites a una interpretación extensiva del artículo 4.2 TUE' [2022] Revista de Derecho Político 245, 249–261.

3 Title I article F.1: *The Union shall respect the national identities of its Member States, whose systems of government are founded on the principles of democracy.*

4 cf Denys Simon, 'Article F. Commentaire' in Vlad Constantinesco, Robert Kovar and Denys Simon (eds), *Traité sur l'Union européenne, signé à Maastricht le 7 février 1992 : commentaire article par article* (Economica Paris 1995) 88–89.

the formalisation of an unwritten principle already established in community practice.[5] As is known, the European Convention body improved this formula and included it in Article I-5.1 of the frustrated Constitution for Europe of 2004. Later, the Lisbon Treaty of 2007 mainly reproduced this provision, as observed in the current Article 4.2 TEU.

In this context, the preparatory work for adopting the national identity clause, conducted by Working Group V of the European Convention, provides valuable insight into the drafting process. This group proposed two critical areas of national responsibility: the first, covering fundamental structures and essential functions of a member state (such as constitutional structure, national defense, or language), and the second, addressing basic public policies and social values (including taxation, education, or public health).[6] While most first-group matters were included in the final text, none from the second group were, reflecting a deliberate choice by the drafters. This exclusion, however, does not automatically imply a lack of EU legal protection. That is why there is still an ongoing debate within the EU. In fact, the multiple views could be synthesised into two main competing approaches:[7] a constitutional-legal notion[8] and a historical-cultural one[9]. Usually, the latter also includes the former.

Most scholars support the first perspective, based on a historical and textual analysis of Article 4.2 TEU, which now incorporates more precise and extensive content where the EU must maintain neutrality, moving beyond a generic declaration of national identity as it was in the Maastricht Treaty. As seen, that provision emphasises two principal components of the exclusive state responsibilities: fundamental constitutional structures (e.g., written or unwritten constitution, monarchy or republic, presidential or parliamentary system, centralised or decentralised governance, judicial

5 Agustín Menéndez, 'Una concepción alternativa de la identidad constitucional en el Derecho comunitario: de las excepciones idiosincráticas a la resistencia constitucional colectiva' [2013] Anuario de la Facultad de Derecho de la Universidad Autónoma de Madrid 561, 567.

6 Working Group V, Doc. 30, Revised Draft Report, 25/10/2002, p. 11.

7 cf Luke Spieker, 'Framing and Managing Constitutional Identity Conflicts' (2020) 57 Common Market Law Review 361, 368–369.

8 cf Gerhard van der Schyff, 'EU Member State Constitutional Identity' (2016) 76 Heidelberg Journal of International Law 167, 169.

9 cf Leonard Besselink, 'National and Constitutional Identity before and after Lisbon' (2010) 6 Utrecht Law Review 36, 42–43.

review of laws or legislative supremacy[10]) and essential state functions (e.g., territorial integrity, public order, or national security[11]). In addition, as *Weiler*[12] has asserted, fundamental rights are usually considered an integrated part of this clause. This view, thus, links national identity closely to constitutional texts as the repositories of foundational principles, structures, and functions. Therefore, it is not uncommon to observe how this comprehension is renamed as 'constitutional identity' insofar as it addresses the core elements of constitutions.[13] For some scholars, 'national identity' and 'constitutional identity' are seen as equivalent, whilst for others, the latter is just part of the former (a broader concept encompassing historical and cultural components).

With prevalent recognition in constitutional courts, the second perspective associates this clause with factors beyond constitutional frameworks, enclosing historical, cultural, social, and religious elements[14] to reflect a more cumulative understanding of a nation's political and social character. As seen, even though historical and cultural roots constitute essential criteria for understanding and interpreting the legal rules of society, with the changes introduced in the current wording of Article 4.2 TEU, the focus has narrowed the clause's scope to primarily legal considerations.[15] If that is the case, cultural and historical factors should be considered if clearly and previously included in the constitutional provisions. In that sense, how have courts applied this concept?

---

10 cf Luis Díez-Picazo, 'Observaciones sobre la cláusula de identidad nacional' in Marta Cartabia, Bruni de Witte and Pablo Pérez (eds), *Constitución europea y constituciones nacionales* (Tirant lo Blanch 2005) 439–440.

11 cf Sacha Garben, 'Collective Identity as a Legal Limit to European Integration in Areas of Core State Powers*' (2020) 58 Journal of Common Market Studies 41, 45.

12 cf Joseph H. H. Weiler, *The Constitution of Europe: 'Do the New Clothes Have an Emperor?' and Other Essays on European Integration* (CUP 1999) 102.

13 cf Dieter Grimm, 'Three Meanings of Constitutional Identity and Their Prospects in the European Union' [2024] Center for Advanced Studies, <https://www.blog.cas.uni-muenchen.de/topics/dissecting-democracy/three-meanings-of-constitutional-identity> accessed 19 August 2024.

14 cf Kriszta Kovács, 'The Rise of an Ethnocultural Constitutional Identity in the Jurisprudence of the East Central European Courts' (2017) 18 German Law Journal 1703, 1709–1710.

15 cf Pedro Cruz, 'La identidad constitucional de los estados miembros: dos relatos europeos' [2013] Anuario de la Facultad de Derecho de la Universidad Autónoma de Madrid 501, 504.

2. A Courts' Perspective

Applying the national identity clause involves an interrelationship between EU law and domestic law, which means there are implicit reciprocal mandates that influence and inform one another.[16] Nonetheless, it should not be understood as a permeable tool with analogous usefulness for both legal orders. As stated by *Grimm*, the 'Treaties mention "identity" only in connection with the member states, not the EU, and they do not speak of constitutional identity, but of national identity. The EU is obliged to respect it. This shows that the member states, as the authors of the Treaties, saw their identity endangered by the EU, not the other way round.'[17] In any case, the Court of Justice of the European Union (CJEU) and the constitutional courts understand this clause very differently.

As expected, the CJEU has approached national identity case-by-case,[18] focusing on specific areas such as language,[19] part-time judicial labor,[20] nationality,[21] name,[22] spouse's definition,[23] or state organisation,[24] often through preliminary rulings. These cases generally follow the Court's established framework of balancing national identity claims against the fundamental freedoms of the internal market, subject to a proportionality test. Perhaps, due to this particular focus, the CJEU has not needed to clearly state its preference for a constitutional-legal approach or a historical-cultural one in defining the national identity. Until now, criticism of this second perspective has commonly come from academia, not the CJEU, which has considered elements as 'language' (a cultural-historical feature) as an inherent component of the national identity clause. For instance, in the *Runevič-Vardyn* ruling, the CJEU supported a state linguistic policy insofar

16 cf Anita Schnettger, 'Article 4(2) TEU as a Vehicle for National Constitutional Identity in the Shared European Legal System' in Christian Calliess and Gerhard van der Schyff (eds), *Constitutional Identity in a Europe of Multilevel Constitutionalism* (CUP 2019) 12–16.

17 Grimm (n 13).

18 cf Miguel Azpitarte, 'Identidad Nacional y Legitimidad Del Tribunal de Justicia' (2017) 39 Teoría y Realidad Constitucional 413, 426–443.

19 Case C-202/11 *Las* [2013].

20 Case C-393/10 *O'Brien* [2012].

21 Case C-51/08 *Commission v. Luxemburg* [2011].

22 Case C-438/14 *Bogendorff von Wolffersdorff* [2016]; Case C-208/09 *Sayn-Wittgenstein* [2010].

23 Case C-673/16 *Coman and Others* [2018], paras 42-46.

24 Case C-51/15 *Remondis* [2016]; Case C-156/13 *Digibet and Albers* [2014].

as it responded to the Lithuanian national identity.[25] In any case, unlike constitutional courts, which often favor a broader interpretation of national identity, the above-mentioned CJEU cases have consistently limited their application by not endorsing the domestic courts' concept or recognising their exclusive power to declare it breached. Furthermore, the CJEU has rejected the idea that a violation of national identity could justify the non-application of EU law within national legal systems. Naturally, from the CJEU's perspective, accepting such an approach would undermine the principles of EU law primacy, effectiveness, and uniformity, which have been central to its jurisprudence. Instead, the CJEU has minimised the disruptive potential of national identity claims, allowing exceptions to applying EU law under certain, infrequent circumstances.

On the side of the constitutional courts, there is a different narrative. Its origins can be traced back to crucial rulings such as *Solange I*[26] by the German Federal Constitutional Court (GFCC) and the counter-limits (*controlimiti*[27]) doctrine established by the Italian Constitutional Court in the *Frontini* case.[28] Initially, the concerns were focused on fundamental rights, but later expanded to competences and national identity issues.[29] This concept gained further prominence during rulings concerning the Constitutional Treaty and the Treaty of Lisbon. Notably, the Spanish Constitutional Court's *1/2004*[30] declaration invoked national identity as a safeguard to ensure the primacy principle's compatibility with national law. However, it left room for constitutional intervention in exceptional circumstances. Similarly, the French *Conseil Constitutionnel* referred to national identity in its decision *2006/540 DC,* highlighting the limits on the transposition of EU directives if they go against specific principles of the French constitutional order, which are not protected in EU law.[31]

25 Case C-391/09 *Runevič-Vardyn* [2011] paras 84-89.

26 BVerfG, 29.05.1974 – 2 BvL 52/71.

27 A constitutional court's competence to question the application of EU law regarding measures that are likely to affect the core principles of the constitutional order.

28 Italian Constitutional Court, Decision N° 183/73. See also: Decisions N° 170/84, 232/89, and 238/2014.

29 cf Mattias Kumm and Víctor Ferreres, 'The Primacy Clause of the Constitutional Treaty and the Future of Constitutional Conflict in the European Union' (2005) 3 International Journal of Constitutional Law 473, 474–476.

30 DTC 1/2004, de 13.12.2004, paras 3-4.

31 Conseil Constitutionnel, Décision n° 2006-540 DC du 27 juillet 2006, para 19.

The GFCC has been more assertive in developing a national identity doctrine, particularly in the *Lisbon* case.[32] This decision linked national identity with the intangibility clause of the Basic Law (Article 79.3), which encompasses principles like human dignity, human rights protection, popular sovereignty, the rule of law, and the federal system. The Court has also claimed in that judgment the exclusive right to assess whether EU acts infringe on German national identity (which includes a constitutional-legal and a cultural-historical approach[33]), allowing for the non-application of EU law in such cases. However, the GFCC has balanced this purpose with a commitment to openness towards EU law. In subsequent rulings such as *Honeywell*[34] and *Gauweiler*[35], the GFCC has seemingly nuanced its position, bringing national identity control closer to *ultra vires* scrutiny and committing to seeking an opinion from the CJEU before declaring a possible violation. Considering this last sense, i.e., national identity as a part of the *controlimiti* doctrine, which supervises whether the EU goes beyond its conferred competences (*ultra vires* act) and thus has no binding effect, the GFCC has put it into practice for the very first time when refusing to comply with the CJEU ruling in the *Weiss* case.[36] Somehow, this resembles the *Landtovà* case[37] in the Constitutional Court of the Czech Republic, where a CJEU decision[38] was declared *ultra vires*, albeit for reasons unrelated to national identity and without sending a preliminary ruling to the CJEU.[39]

In 2018, Hungary introduced a national identity clause as part of a constitutional amendment. Following this, the Hungarian Constitutional Court analysed the question of whether local authorities must implement EU regulations that contradict fundamental rights or overreach the adjudicated competences. On that occasion, the tribunal articulated a dual judicial mechanism to safeguard national sovereignty and constitutional identity

32 BVerfG, 30.06.2009 – 2 BvE 2/08, paras 216-219.

33 ibid para 249.

34 BVerfG, 06.07.2010 – 2 BvR 2661/06.

35 BVerfG, 21.06.2016 – 2 BvR 2728/13, 2 BvR 2729/13, 2 BvR 2730/13, 2 BvR 2731/13, 2 BvE 13/13.

36 BVerfG, 05.05.2020 – 2 BvR 859/15, paras 115–119.

37 Constitutional Court of the Czech Republic, Judgment of 15.02.2012, Judgement file No. Pl. US 5/12.

38 Case C-399/09 *Landtová* [2011].

39 For a critical assessment, see Jan Komárek, 'Playing With Matches: The Czech Constitutional Court's Ultra Vires Revolution' [2012] Verfassungsblog.

against potential overreach by EU law,[40] drawing on the doctrine of other European constitutional courts, particularly the GFCC. The Hungarian court also emphasised that this mechanism is intended only in exceptional circumstances as a last resort, underscoring its commitment to dialogue and cooperation with the EU.[41] Finally, the court shed some light on the elements of constitutional identity.[42] Some of them have not produced problems at all, since they represent the same principles of other liberal democracies[43] ('freedoms, the division of powers, republic as the form of government, respect of autonomies under public law, the freedom of religion, exercising lawful authority, parliamentarism, the equality of rights, acknowledging judicial power, the protection of the nationalities living with us'[44]), while others have been criticised for their vague definition which includes Hungary's history, language, and culture.[45]

In the Polish case, a key feature is its conditional acceptance of the primacy principle. The judgment of the Polish Constitutional Court on the *Accession Treaty* case emphasised that its constitution holds supremacy over EU law, particularly in instances where the two are irreconcilable, recognising an *ultra vires* control if needed.[46] Most of the Member States do not accept an absolute notion of the EU primacy principle, at least when considering a collision with their constitutions (just a few of them allow so, e.g., the Netherlands, Cyprus, Ireland, or Estonia);[47] therefore, this is not the real problem with the Polish stand. The real issue here is that the Polish Constitutional Court does not limit the effectiveness of EU law to some inexcusable core elements of its *Magna Carta* (as other constitutional courts do) but considers the whole constitutional text as a potential limit. The Polish stance was further solidified in the *Lisbon* case, where the court introduced the concept of constitutional identity as a non-negotiable limit on transferring state competences to the EU, emphasising that Poland must

40 Hungarian Constitutional Court, Decision 22/2016 (XII. 5.) AB, para 54.
41 ibid para 46.
42 ibid paras 64-67.
43 cf Cruz (n 2) 265.
44 Hungarian Constitutional Court (n 40) para 65.
45 cf Dimitry Kochenov and Petra Bard, 'Rule of Law Crisis in the New Member States of the EU' (2018) 12.
46 Polish Constitutional Court, Judgment of 11.05.2005, K 18/04, sec. 11–13.
47 cf Monica Claes, 'The Primacy of EU Law in European and National Law' in Anthony Arnull and Damian Chalmers (eds), *The Oxford Handbook of European Union Law* (OUP 2015) 193–195.

retain its sovereignty on issues like the 'protection of human dignity and constitutional rights, the principle of statehood, the principle of democratic governance, the principle of a state ruled by law, the principle of social justice, the principle of subsidiarity, as well as the requirement of ensuring better implementation of constitutional values and the prohibition to confer the power to amend the Constitution and the competence to determine competences'.[48] For this court, the constitutional identity mandate originates from Article 90 of its constitution, aligning with Article 4.2 TEU, which also acknowledges the history, culture, and traditions of the Member States.

3. A European Constitutional Identity?

It has been correctly said that the national identity clause cannot be interpreted as an unconditional exception to the validity or application of EU law. Considering that, some scholars have argued that the values included in Article 2 TEU[49] constitute a 'European identity' that serves as a supranational counterbalance, preventing the misuse of national identity.[50] According to them,[51] the European Constitutional Identity (ECI) can also be deduced from the preamble and the amendment clause (48 TEU). Furthermore, it can be traced back to the 1973 Declaration of the Heads of State and Government, which aimed to define European identity based on shared values among Member States.[52] This notion, further developed through the Copenhagen criteria and subsequent treaty reforms, constitutes the core of the EU's legal framework, as demonstrated in the CJEU's *Kadi* case, which affirmed the supremacy of fundamental rights and principles in the EU order.[53] Currently incorporated by Article 2 TEU, these values

48 Polish Constitutional Court, Judgment of 24 November 2010, K 32/09, para 2.1.

49 Article 2 TEU: *The Union is founded on the values of respect for human dignity, freedom, democracy, equality, the rule of law and respect for human rights, including the rights of persons belonging to minorities. These values are common to the Member States in a society in which pluralism, non-discrimination, tolerance, justice, solidarity and equality between women and men prevail.*

50 Cf. Lucia S. Rossi, '2, 4, 6 (TUE)... l'interpretazione dell' "Identity clause" alla luce dei valori fondamentali dell'UE' (ITA 2018) 869–870.

51 For a detailed explanation, cf Pablo Cruz, 'La identidad constitucional de la Unión Europea: Una categoría jurídica en construcción' (2022) 70 Revista de Derecho Público 153, 158–162, 168–174.

52 Declaration of the Heads of State or Government, Copenhagen (14.12.1973), paras 1-3.

53 Case C-402/05 P *Kadi v. Council and Commission* [2008] paras 282 and 304.

serve as entry criteria for new members and as grounds for severe sanctions against those Member States that violate them.[54] Hence, those values could constitute a sort of European *controlimiti* against transgressions from other legal systems – national or international.[55]

In that spirit, some authors have considered the CJEU decisions about the Regulation 2020/2092 (Rule of Law Conditionality Regulation) as clear judicial support for the ECI thesis.[56] As is known, this regulation was created as a mechanism to limit, through a qualified majority of the Member States, the financial EU aid to countries that do not respect the rule of law. Hungary and Poland disagreed, claiming that it was intended to surreptitiously establish an alternative mechanism to replace the one provided for in Article 7 TEU – which requires unanimity of the Member States – in light of the experience of its apparent ineffectiveness. The CJEU did not uphold the Hungarian[57] and Polish[58] legal claims, highlighting in both decisions that '[t]he values contained in Article 2 TEU have been identified and are shared by the Member States. They define the very identity of the European Union as a common legal order. Thus, the European Union must be able to defend those values, within the limits of its powers as laid down by the Treaties.'[59] Additionally, the CJEU said: 'Article 2 TEU is not a mere statement of policy guidelines or intentions, but contains values which [...] are given concrete expression in principles comprising legally binding obligations for the Member States'.[60] Thus, the following scenario emerges: considering Article 4.2 TEU, constitutional courts have developed the national identity doctrine as a kind of *controlimiti* to restrain eventual transgressions caused by EU law. Similarly, by considering Article 2 TEU, the CJEU has recently developed the ECI doctrine to limit Member States' potential violations of EU law, including the misuse of their national identity.

---

54 Case C-896/19 *Repubblika* [2021], para 63.

55 cf Giacomo Di Federico, 'Il ruolo dell'art. 4, par. 2, TUE nella soluzione dei conflitti interordinamentali' [2019] Quaderni costituzionali 333, 333 et seq.

56 cf Pietro Faraguna and Tímea Drinóczi, 'Constitutional Identity in and on EU Terms' [2022] Verfassungsblog; María Roca, 'La Identidad Constitucional de La Unión Europea En La Jurisprudencia Del TJUE' [2024] Revista de Derecho Constitucional Europeo s 3.

57 Case C-156/21 *Hungary v. Parliament and Council* [2022], para. 159.

58 Case C-157/21 *Poland v. Parliament and Council* [2022], paras. 211–216.

59 *Hungary v. (...)* (n 57) para 127; *Poland v. (...)* (n 58) para 145.

60 *Hungary v. (...)* (n 57) para 232; *Poland v. (...)* (n 58) para 264.

Of course, while the national identity clause does not provide an unconditional exemption from the validity or application of EU law, it can also be argued that EU law is not infinitely effective if it significantly undermines the core constitutional elements of a state. That is why the national identity already existing in the community practice was later positively incorporated in the Maastricht Treaty, widened in the failed Constitution for Europe and consolidated in the Lisbon Treaty. Focusing strictly on the eventual collision of 'identities', if the national identity clause already functions as an exceptional 'limit', it seems odd that the new ECI doctrine may work as a 'limit to the limit'. In the abstract, there should be a confluence between both 'identities' insofar as the ECI built by the CJEU has its roots in the common constitutional traditions of the Member States.[61] Nevertheless, clashes are inevitable as EU integration advances, especially in controversial legal matters. Conflict should not be stigmatised but embraced as a natural consequence of the EU's complex and evolving integration process.

If that is the case, the advantages of creating the ECI as a responsive tool for the national identity execution remain under examination. It could be said that this new doctrine is reserved only for the misuse of national identity. In the same sense, it could be answered that national identity is only activated in the face of abuse coming from the EU. The potential for abuse is not restricted to just one side. However, this new doctrine has additional weaknesses: first, while the national identity is explicitly included in the TEU, the ECI is not. Second, even if the textual provision in the treaty would not be required to prove an 'identity', it is mandatory to specify at least its content. The problem is that if the scholarly claimed sources for ECI (2 TEU and the CJUE jurisprudence) are compared with those of national identity (4.2 TEU and constitutional courts jurisprudence), the nuclear components of the former and the latter are pretty much the same (the rule of law, democracy, and fundamental rights). Hence, this presents a situation in which European and constitutional judges may diverge in their interpretation of general values, going back to a longstanding question: who holds the ultimate authority to define these principles, that is, who has the last word? Third, the ECI thesis assumes that the EU treaties can be considered equivalent to a constitution. Is that possible?

61 Case C-62/14 *Gauweiler* [2015], Opinion of AG *Cruz Villalón*, para 61.

There is an open debate on that issue, with plausible arguments to support this idea because of some of the EU constitutional functions;[62] however, a skeptical perspective also has solid ground, given that the EU treaties lack some core elements of a constitution:[63] the symbolic effect (the 'constitutional moment' and the people's attachment),[64] the act of self-determination of the nation (instead of a hetero-determination through the Member States), the sovereignty (the EU has public authority but because it depends on others for its existence, purpose, and powers, it is not a sovereign political entity);[65] and the democratic decision-making[66] (with its correlated legitimacy). The EU's uniqueness lies in its position between nation-states and supranational organisations. It addresses transnational issues while preserving national control over critical decisions, ensuring democratic legitimacy. This hybrid model is a more promising basis for a European identity derived from its treaties than a purported constitution.

Furthermore, although it is wise to assert that any 'recourse to Article 4(2) TEU is only permissible insofar as it respects the values enshrined in Article 2 TEU',[67] a problem arises: who is to determine that finally? It has been rightly noted that the CJEU lacks direct jurisdiction over Article 2 TEU because Member States have opted to include a highly political instrument (Article 7 TEU) for addressing its violations.[68] However, it has also been asserted that this does not imply that the CJEU cannot utilise Article 2 TEU when evaluating the appropriateness and accuracy of a national court's claim regarding the constitutional identity of a Member State, while avoiding usurping power or challenging the federal balance within the

---

62 cf Paul Craig, 'Constitutions, Constitutionalism, and the European Union' (2001) 7 European Law Journal 125, 136–147.

63 cf Grimm (n 13); Dieter Grimm, 'Does Europe Need a Constitution?' (1995) 1 European Law Journal 282, 290–299.

64 cf Marco Dani and Agustín Menéndez, 'European Constitutional Imagination: A Whig Interpretation of the Process of European Integration?' in Jan Komárek (ed), *European Constitutional Imaginaries* (OUP 2023) 54–74.

65 cf Dieter Grimm, *The Constitution of European Democracy*, vol 1 (OUP 2017) 47.

66 cf Fritz Scharpf, 'De-Constitutionalisation and Majority Rule' (2017) 23 European Law Journal 315, 325–332.

67 Spieker (n 7) 396.

68 cf Núria González, *Secession and European Union Law* (OUP 2024) 169; Salvatore Fabio Nicolosi, 'The Contribution of the Court of Justice to the Codification of the Founding Values of the European Union' [2015] Revista de Derecho Comunitario Europeo 613, 643.

Union.[69] This valuable approach clarifies the analysed scenario, but some potential issues remain. As can be anticipated, there are instances in which a mere pronouncement by the CJEU may not only effectively dissuade but substantially supplant the political mechanism envisioned in Article 7 TEU – thereby shifting the intended balance of power and extending judicial authority into a domain that was explicitly designed to remain within the political discretion of the Member States.

That said, the ECI may also address legal controversies beyond an eventual Member State claim of the national identity clause. Given the legitimate and reasonable political and legal dispute on this issue, where conflicting interpretations converge on what the EU should be, or how its *sui generis* practice and nature should be reconciled with the activities of Member States, it may be strategically wise to create the ECI as an exceptional 'red line'[70] or barrier of containment – and rebalancing – against any flagrant abuse by a Member State.[71] In other words, although the foundations of the ECI may be questionable, its existence could serve as a convenient tool in cases of significant infringement of EU law. Particularly if, as experience teaches, 1) Member States are more likely to breach their international obligations than EU institutions, and 2) part of those obligations relate to some fundamental common values (Article 2 TEU) that Member States committed themselves to respect and cultivate.[72]

4. A Balance of the Legal Situation

As appreciated from the current debate's *status quo*, there are convergences among the national tribunals' approaches, but significant differences remain. Courts in Spain, France, and Italy have generally treated the power to protect national identity as hypothetical and exceptional. However, the GFCC has taken a more proactive stance, warning to use this power in specific cases, as finally happened in *Weiss*.[73] Hungary and Poland have adopt-

69 cf Luke Spieker, 'Breathing Life into the Union's Common Values' (2019) 20 German Law Journal 1182, 1210.

70 cf Piotr Bogdanowicz and others, 'A Potential Constitutional Moment for the European Rule of Law' (2018) 55 Common Market Law Review 983, 989.

71 cf González (n 68) 165–170.

72 cf Spieker (n 69) 1199–1213.

73 In any case, the problem was finally resolved. On May 5, 2020, in the context of a preliminary procedure regarding the European Central Bank's (ECB) bond-buying powers, the GFCC defied the EU's legal order by rejecting the *Weiss* decision

ed a constitutional-legal national identity perspective, like other Member States. The difference is that these countries have also incorporated a historical-cultural approach (as Germany did in 2009), opening a way for legal criticism, because that broad view may be easily misused for not complying with EU Law. Having said so, it is essential to remember that if the central criticism rests on the broad and uncertain scope of that approach, a potentially similar look could be taken for the 'fundamental rights' commonly included in the national identity notion or the 'values' incorporated in Article 2 TEU if the CJEU would be willing to apply the CEI. Thus, the main issue may not be the uncertainty of the norm, which is a common aspect of contemporary constitutional and international law, but the greater degree of ambiguity in the historical-cultural category and its non-legal status as a criterion for considering legal matters. If this is true, adding more precise historical and cultural characteristics to the constitutional provisions could be a tangible way to consider those factors in the legal interpretation and, thus, safeguard that perspective of national identity without needlessly raising the risk of breaching legal certainty in the EU. Finally, in most constitutional court jurisprudence, there is a usual warning to highlight that if an EU act or decision breaches the state's constitutional identity, it may be, *ultima ratio*, rejected. That explains why this notion is considered part of the *controlimiti* doctrine in the EU integration process.

On the other hand, for the CJEU, national identity is never an excuse (or right) to avoid the primacy of EU law; it is only a very exceptional authorised CJEU's deference to the Member States. Additionally, the CJEU has corroborated the existence of the ECI, supporting what some scholars have said about restricting the misuse of national identity.[74] While the plausibility of that thesis may be granted, it is equally important to acknowledge the valid counterarguments to the emerging doctrine. With this step, the

---

and dismissing the CJEU ruling as incomprehensible and *ultra vires*, urging EU institutions, especially the ECB, to provide further explanations. Subsequently, on May 8, 2020, the CJEU issued a press release stating that a judgment, including a preliminary ruling, is binding on national courts for decisions in main proceedings and that national courts must ensure the full effect of EU law. Despite the clash, EU institutions acknowledged the dispute. In June, at the first post-decision meeting, the ECB provided proportionality justifications that the German government deemed sufficient, thereby satisfying the GFCC and closing the matter–a conflict aptly termed a 'constructive misunderstanding'. cf Alegría Borrás and Núria González, 'Jurisprudencia Del Tribunal de Justicia de La Unión Europea (Abril-Junio)' [2020] Revista Jurídica de Cataluña 1115, 1121; González (n 68) 27 (footnote).

74 cf Roca (n 56) s 3.

CJEU has assumed a protagonist role in addressing the challenges facing the EU system. However, there is a potential long-term risk, as the current context reflects a political crisis rather than a judicial one. In this context, the debate between Kelsen and Schmitt on the role of constitutional courts becomes relevant. While Kelsen defended judicial review as a safeguard of constitutional order, Schmitt warned against courts overstepping their role in times of political crisis.[75] This tension underscores the need for institutional solutions beyond the judiciary[76] – much like what is currently unfolding, *mutatis mutandis*, in Venezuela.[77] Finally, because the legal certainty principle is crucial in the rule of law, there are more persuasive reasons to favor the constitutional-legal view of national identity than the historic-cultural one (unless those factors have been included in the constitution and work as an essential component). Anyway, potential issues persist.[78]

Last but not least, what should be finally understood by 'constitutional identity'? There are different views and no clear consensus.[79] It could be understood as a simple synonym of 'national identity' or, at least, as one of its comprehensions (a constitutional-legal concept). From a different vision, it could also be interpreted as a broader notion created by constitutional courts that sets some limits to European integration (*controlimiti*) if it clashes with essential principles or fundamental rights protected by the constitution (including the state's structure and functions explicitly protected in Article 4.2 TEU). This last notion better reflects the current debate. If that is the case, it seems the only way to change constitutional identity is through a constitutional amendment (except for eternity clauses) or, partially, through a TEU reform of Article 4.2. Thus, constitutional

---

75 For a more comprehensive overview of this well-known debate, see: Lars Vinx (ed), *The Guardian of the Constitution* (CUP 2015).

76 cf Alberto Gregorio, 'El Nuevo Régimen General de Condicionalidad Para La Protección Del Presupuesto de La Unión' [2022] Revista de Derecho Comunitario Europeo 11, 25.

77 OAS General Secretariat Rejects Ruling Issued by Venezuela's Supreme Court. August 23rd, 2024. Link: https://www.oas.org/en/media_center/press_release.asp?sCodigo=E-056/24.

78 E.g., if an Eastern European state potentially lacks historical-cultural constitutional provisions, should the historical impact of the Soviet Union's illegal occupation on its legal system be disregarded?

79 cf Enrico Albanesi, 'National Identity (under Art. 4(2) TEU) and Constitutional Identity (as Counter-Limits) Are Not the Same' in Martin Belov (ed), *Peace, Discontent and Constitutional Law* (1st edn, Routledge 2021) 108–126.

identity represents a legal argument for Member States to honestly justify a singular regulation that may be perceived as a TEU breach (this analysis does not consider an intended misuse of this legal tool). If the CJEU accepts it, there will be no problems at all. But if it does not accept it, there are two extreme remaining possibilities: the Member State is non-democratically forced to change its constitutional identity by implementing the CJEU decision, or, *ultima ratio,* a Member State's backlash is produced, e.g., by declaring a CJEU decision as *ultra vires.* Both are unwanted options, but are undoubtedly possible if judicial dialogue does not work.[80]

Nevertheless, it appears challenging to favor the latter pathway inside a supranational legal organisation with an integration purpose unless there are critical, good reasons to do so. That could be if that integration process commits an *ultra vires* act, e.g., when the Danish Supreme Court in the *Ajos* case[81] gave precedence to its national law over EU law after hearing the CJEU guidance and analysing the Danish EU Accession Act and its amendments, concluding that 'the ECJ did not have the competence or legal basis to give precedence to the unwritten principle prohibiting discrimination on grounds of age in a case where this was contrary to the national law'.[82]

III. Constitutional Identity: Two Competing Views at the COE

The extensive discussion of the national and constitutional identity within the EU system in the first section of this essay will serve as the theoretical foundation for the following analysis concerning the COE. Considering that both organisations share common roots regarding territory, countries, and European legal tradition (EU accession to the ECHR is an obligation incorporated in Article 6.2 TEU), it would be unwise to ignore the impact of the prolonged EU debate on the COE newborn debate, or even worse, to

80 The *Taricco* cases (2015 and 2017) initially showed promising signs of judicial dialogue between the Italian Constitutional Court (ICC) and the CJEU. However, a 2018 ICC judgment *de facto* contradicted the most recent CJEU decision, so an uncertain scenario is expected. cf Chiara Amalfitano and Oreste Pollicino, 'Two Courts, two Languages? The Taricco Saga Ends on a Worrying Note', [2018] Verfassungsblog.

81 For a comprehensive analysis, cf Helle Krunke and Sune Klinge, 'The Danish Ajos Case' (2018) 2018 3 European Papers 157; Mikael Madsen, Henrik Palmer and Urška Šadl, 'Competing Supremacies and Clashing Institutional Rationalities' (2017) 23 European Law Journal 140.

82 Supreme Court of Denmark. Case no. 15/2014, 6.12.2016, *Dansk Industri (DI) acting for Ajos A/S vs. The estate left by A,* para 3.

think that the latter discussion has little or nothing to do with the former one. But to what extent? To address this challenge, the analysis will first distinguish the EU from the COE. It will then examine the ECtHR's references to constitutional identity, followed by an analysis of the similarities and differences between the two frameworks. Finally, it will assess whether this emerging scenario is conducive to the protection of human rights.

1. An Approach from the Literature

This analysis highlights key distinctions between the EU and the COE to assess how the EU's 'identity' debate might be understood within a broader organisation with a different mandate. The EU, as a supranational entity, seeks deep integration across various domains, while the COE, an international organisation, focuses on promoting human rights, democracy, and the rule of law. Accordingly, Member States transfer sovereign competences to EU institutions, whereas COE members recognise specific competences. As a result, the EU legal order emphasises direct effect, uniformity, and primacy principles over subsidiarity (Article 5 TEU). In contrast, the COE framework prioritises the subsidiarity principle - particularly through the margin of appreciation - over uniformisation of human rights standards.

However, in practice, states sometimes behave as if those EU principles were applied to the COE legal framework.[83] That may explain why some countries have occasionally started to limit the precedence of the ECHR, as they do for EU law. Anyhow, it seems clear that EU law has also provided national judges with compelling reasons to reassess the effectiveness of the ECHR. As noticed by some scholars,[84] European integration has profoundly impacted the reception of law in national legal systems. The CJEU's supremacy and direct effect doctrines required national courts to prioritise EU law over conflicting national legislation. This shift led to significant transformations in national legal practices, compelling national judges to confront and often override traditional constitutional doctrines, such as the prohibition on judicial review of statutes, the principle of *lex posterior derogat legi priori*, and established concepts of the separation of

83 cf Giuseppe Martinico, 'Is the European Convention Going to Be "Supreme"?' (2012) 23 European Journal of International Law 401, 423–424.

84 cf Helen Keller and Alec Stone Sweet, 'Assessing the Impact of the ECHR on National Legal Systems', in Helen Keller and Alec Stone Sweet (eds), *A Europe of Rights* (1st edn, OUP 2008) 681.

powers. These structural challenges have also reappeared in the context of the ECHR.

Both European legal systems have doctrines that nuance and – sometimes – question the application of the principles above: 'national identity' concerning the EU direct effect, uniformity, and primacy principles and the 'European emerging consensus' respecting the COE subsidiarity principle (that is why this doctrine is seen as competing with the margin of appreciation). *Lato sensu*, from the Member State's perspective, national identity and the margin of appreciation are seen as doctrines that may adjust the application of their respective treaties to their domestic circumstances. Both doctrines were adopted through practice and later formalised through treaty provisions (Maastricht Treaty of 1992 and Protocol No. 15 of 2013 amending the ECHR, respectively). But, continuing from the Member State's perspective, there are some crucial differences between them. While the margin of appreciation is considered as self-restraining act from the international court, which recognises a deferential position to the local authorities (thus, it is not a prerogative for them), the national identity is viewed as a limit to the international court's action set by the national tribunal (thus, it sometimes works as a prerogative conferring them, *ultima ratio*,[85] the protection of its non-negotiable constitutional inheritance). While the margin of appreciation is based on the principle of subsidiarity, national identity relies on constitutional core elements that cannot be disregarded without breaching the foundations of the Member State itself. Finally, while the margin of appreciation may decrease in the face of a still-debated European emerging consensus doctrine, national identity seems only subject to change through a constitutional amendment or, partially, through an Article 4.2 TEU amendment.

From the supranational/international court perspective, national identity and the margin of appreciation are exceptional legal doctrines that do not constitute a state's excuse for violating the international obligations adopted. Therefore, each Member State cannot unilaterally determine the scope of these doctrines without the control of the international court. In this scenario, the international court decides on the Member State's claims of authority over these doctrines on a case-by-case basis. That being said, in the EU framework, the ECI doctrine has been created to have an external tool to limit national identity performance insofar as a) constitutional

85 cf Pablo Cruz, 'Identidad nacional y sistema del Convenio Europeo de Derechos Humanos: una dudosa analogía' [2020] Anales de Derecho 9, 12.

courts have not closed the door for potential *ultima ratio* backlash, and b) national identity, by definition, could only be moderated by an internal decision. Given this context, it is time to assess whether the ECtHR's notion of 'constitutional identity' aligns with the EU's concept of national identity or constitutes a separate idea.

2. An ECtHR's Perspective

It is important to remember that this is not the first time a constitutional court has set some doctrinal limits on ECtHR decisions. In 2004, the GFCC stated that in immigration law, the law on the protection of personality, and family law, there can exist boundaries for ECtHR case law prevalence.[86] Similarly, the UK Supreme Court has asserted that on rare occasions, it may question whether an ECtHR decision adequately accounts for specific elements of its domestic legal process.[87] In such cases, the British court may choose not to adhere to the Strasbourg ruling, offering a clear rationale for this choice and engaging in a constructive dialogue. The Austrian Constitutional Court has emphasised the option to depart from the ECtHR jurisprudence if following it would violate its constitution.[88] The Italian Constitutional Court decided that the ECHR holds a privileged position, yet it does not enjoy 'constitutional immunity'; thus, it must respect all constitutional norms.[89] As seen, there is a higher scrutiny than in the case of EU law, where the *controlimiti* usually addresses only core constitutional provisions rather than all of them.[90] The novelty is that, in recent years, even though it is not explicitly mentioned in the ECHR, the ECtHR has recognised the Member State's legal argument on constitutional identity. Previous judgments, such as *G.I.E.M. S.r.l.*[91] or *Mugemangango*,[92] only included justices' individual mentions. Nonetheless, the Latvian cases

86 BVerfG, 14. 10. 2004 – 2 BvR 1481/04 (*Görgülü* case).
87 *R v. Horncastle and Others [2009]* United Kingdom Supreme Court, para 11; *Manchester City Council v. Pinnock* [2010], para 48.
88 *Miltner* Austrian Constitutional Court VfSlg 11500/1987.
89 Italian Constitutional Court, Decisions 348 and 349/2007.
90 cf Francesca Biondi and Filippo Fontanelli, 'The Decisions No. 348 and 349/2007 of the Italian Constitutional Court' (2008) 9 German Law Journal 889, 915.
91 *G.I.E.M. S.r.l. and Others v. Italy* App no 1828/06 (ECtHR 28 June 2018). Dissenting Opinion of Judge *Pinto de Albuquerque*, para 10 (as a synonym of *controlimiti*).
92 *Mugemangango v. Belgium* App no 310/15 (ECtHR 10 July 2020). Concurring Opinion of Judge Wojtycek, para 4.

of *Savickis*,[93] *Valiullina*,[94] *Džibuti*,[95] and *Djeri*[96] made a significant difference.

In *Savickis*, the applicants were born in various regions of the former U.S.S.R. and later moved to the current Latvian territory. After Latvia regained its independence (1991), they were designated 'permanently resident non-citizens'. Upon retirement, unlike Latvian citizens, their years of service outside Latvia during the Soviet era were excluded from their pension calculations under the State Pension Law of 1996. In the *Andrejeva v. Latvia* case of 2009, the ECtHR ruled that this differential treatment between citizens and non-citizens violated Article 14 in conjunction with Article 1 of Protocol No. 1 of the ECHR. Following this ruling, several applicants applied to recalculate their pensions, but their requests were denied. In 2011, the Latvian Constitutional Court upheld the impugned provision, affirming its compatibility with the constitution and the ECHR. This national court distinguished this case, noting that, unlike *Andrejeva*, the current applicants had worked outside Latvian territory and, thus, lacked legal ties to Latvia. Considering mainly the doctrine of *State continuity* (as part of Latvian constitutional identity, as well as the Estonian and Lithuanian), which contemplates Latvia's non-successor status to the Soviet Union due to the unlawful occupation it suffered in 1940, the ECtHR recognised a broad national margin of appreciation and concluded that the differential treatment was based on objective and reasonable grounds. The joint dissenting opinion did not diminish the state's constitutional identity in specific cases but argued that it should not apply now. Moreover, it cautioned that this doctrine could be misused.[97]

A year later, in *Valiullina*, the ECtHR assessed whether legislative amendments enacted in 2018 to increase the proportion of subjects taught in the official language, Latvian, in public schools were disproportionate. The applicants, consisting of parents and children from Latvia's Russian-speaking minority, argued that these amendments significantly restricted the use of their mother tongue within the educational system. However, the Latvian Constitutional Court underscored, among other arguments, the negative impact of the Soviet occupation on the use of the Latvian language in society and the education system. The ECtHR affirmed that states possess

93 *Savickis and Others v. Latvia* App no 49270/11 (ECtHR 9 June 2022).
94 *Valiullina and Others v. Latvia* App no 56928/19 (ECtHR14 September 2023).
95 *Džibuti and Others v. Latvia* App no 225/20 (ECtHR 16 November 2023).
96 *Djeri and Others v. Latvia* App no 50942/20 and 2022/21 (ECtHR 18 July 2024).
97 *Savickis* (n 93). Joint dissenting opinion, para 24.

a broad margin of appreciation for the right to education regulation. At the same time, because the state's language is a central part of its constitutional identity, the ECtHR stressed that it is not its role to question the previous Constitutional Court's assessment of that issue unless it has been arbitrary. The reform allowed Russian-speaking students to continue learning their language and to preserve their cultural identity while ensuring that the education system functioned primarily in the official language. Thus, the ECtHR concluded unanimously that Latvia provided objective and reasonable justifications. Finally, the *Džibuti* and *Djeri* cases, also related to the 2018 amendments in the Latvian educational system – but now for private schools and preschool education, respectively – followed the same pathway as the *Valiullina* case, and no breach of the ECHR was found.

In sum, even though this is just an initial stage within the COE, with only four decisions related to Latvia, there are some common elements in those cases. First, the ECtHR explicitly recognised the constitutional identity doctrine as a valid but exceptional Member State argument to justifiably apply the ECHR provisions distinctly. Second, the claimed constitutional identity elements were not always in the Constitution but sometimes in ordinary Acts as well. That opens the doors to eventually finding a constitutional identity feature beyond the constitutional provisions. Third, the ECtHR's comprehension of constitutional identity is not reduced to a constitutional-legal approach. Instead, it seems to consider some components of the historical-cultural perspective insofar as provisions embrace them (e.g., the Pension Act being rooted in historical facts of the country's life or the 2018 amendments being anchored in an official language constitutional provision). Fourth, as Latvia requested, the ECtHR assessed constitutional identity as a legitimate aim for differential ECHR treatment under the margin of appreciation. Then, the ECtHR does not consider constitutional identity as a new autonomous doctrine but a novel motive within an already existing doctrine. If that is the case, and the constitutional identity is only a potential starting point for the margin of appreciation, a Member State's claim of constitutional identity will always be subject to posterior ECtHR control. Imagining that the ECtHR may admit a new doctrine whose last authority relies on the Member States is unthinkable. Nonetheless, is that also the Member States' standpoint?

3. A Constitutional Courts' Perspective

Given the early stage of this debate in the COE, any provisional answer should rely primarily on the EU's extensive experience. As seen, constitutional courts have commonly presented the constitutional identity doctrine as a tool to protect the inexcusable foundational elements of their constitutional order. In that sense, if an EU act or decision breaches those core contents, the Member State may consider such interventions non-legally binding as they are outside the adjudicated competence granted to EU institutions for the integration purpose (*ultra vires*). The constitutional identity components are habitually the states' structure and functions (Art. 4.2 TEU), the fundamental rights, and – depending on the country – some historical or cultural features. Is this the same concept being discussed within the COE? It appears so, as constitutional courts present those components as constitutionally essential for their legal orders, not anticipating in abstract an evident conflagration with the international obligations adopted by their states. In that vein, the state's structure and functions are not problematic. Since there is no integration purpose, those components will only be under the ECtHR scope if a singular arrangement is in breach of the ECHR obligations. For instance, it is difficult to imagine the ECtHR taking a stand on a state's fundamental structures (e.g., written or unwritten constitution, monarchy or republic, presidential or parliamentary system, centralised or decentralised governance, judicial review of laws,[98] church-state relation, or legislative supremacy). Conversely, it is anticipated that ECtHR rulings pertain to essential state functions (e.g., territorial integrity, public order, or national security[99]).

Nevertheless, the other components may be problematic in the new scenario since they are open-texture terms subject to controversy. As mentioned, historical-cultural features are not being considered for this paper unless they are explicitly integrated into the constitution. If so, the Member States' fundamental rights (or a constitutional court's interpretation thereof) compose the remaining element of the constitutional identity that might potentially limit the effectiveness of the ECHR (or an ECtHR interpretation thereof). This is not a new issue since Art. 53 ECHR has already

98 cf Núria González, 'La defensa europea de la independencia del Poder Judicial en el marco de la protección del Estado de derecho' [2022] Teoría y Realidad Constitucional 457, 465–466.

99 *Ireland v. the United Kingdom* App no 5310/71 (ECtHR 18 January 1978).

incorporated the so-called *pro homine* or *pro persona* principle. Thus, if there is a situation where a fundamental right of the constitution or a human right in another treaty offers better/more extensive protection than the ECHR, the former should prevail.[100] This assertion is not contested. The usual challenge is: who determines that, the ECtHR or the constitutional court? Then, the last-word battle arises again. Considering that the ECtHR has jurisdiction to interpret the ECHR (Art. 32), including Art. 53, this tribunal believes it already has the final say. Even though the *pro homine* principle is widely recognised in international human rights law,[101] it has not been created by the ECHR. Thus, it is also plausible for a Member State to claim such exceptional competence.

What seems novel about incorporating constitutional identity within the COE is that there could be a more robust legal argument to sustain that stance. That means, if truly needed, the constitutional court may give precedence to a domestic fundamental rights standard to avoid eroding a core element of its constitutional order, as may happen in the EU. But that approach seems unfeasible inside the COE insofar as it is a common stance for the ECtHR and the Member States to see constitutional identity as a new cause to operate the margin of appreciation. Therefore, it is a heteronomous doctrine, not an autonomous one, as it is in the EU. If the ECHR's preamble establishes that the states' enjoyment of the margin of appreciation is 'subject to the supervisory jurisdiction of the' ECtHR, then there is no legal ground for Member States to hold that, due to constitutional identity, they have the final say after an unsuccessful dialogue with the ECtHR. Anyhow, caution is warranted regarding this outcome, as the analysis treats the Latvian legal defense as representative of other European states by incorporating constitutional identity within the margin of appreciation. If that were not the case, and the constitutional courts' warnings from Germany, Austria, the UK, or Italy were still active, there would be an open window for defining constitutional identity as an exception to the ECtHR's supervision in case of a severe infringement of the constitutional

---

100 cf Wolfgang Däubler, 'Los derechos fundamentales en ordenamientos jurídicos de niveles múltiples' in Griselda Capaldo, Jan Sieckmann and Laura Clérico (eds), *Internacionalización del derecho constitucional, constitucionalización del derecho internacional* (Eudeba 2012) 138–139.

101 cf Mónica Pinto, 'El Principio pro Homine' in Martín Abregú, Christian Courtis and Germán J. Bidart (eds), *La Aplicación de los tratados sobre derechos humanos por los tribunales locales* (Del Puerto 1997) 163.

foundations. For instance, though the Italian defense in the *Lautsi* case[102] – on the role religious symbols play in the public square based on history and culture – was not structured precisely in terms of 'constitutional identity', considering its legal and political reaction, as well as the more than twenty COE's states that supported Italy,[103] it seems pretty plausible to believe that if the grand chamber had confirmed the first chamber's decision, a backlash would have been produced.

4. A Human Rights Perspective?

The key question is whether this new doctrine should be welcomed in the European System of Human Rights (ESHR). For those who viewed the states' intentions to constitutionalise the margin of appreciation in Protocol No. 15[104] with suspicion, this development may be seen unfavourably, especially now that a new legitimate aim – constitutional identity – could trigger that mechanism. The claimed reason is that constitutional identity serves as an empty concept, allowing authoritarian regimes to exercise political arbitrariness[105] and infringe upon their citizens' human rights[106] (as Russia has done to bypass the ECtHR rulings).[107] Indeed, there are reasonable concerns about that. Nonetheless, the potential mishandling by some actors (or, even worse, the implicit premise of states permanently willing to undermine the ESHR) seems insufficient to discard a legal doctrine, especially if the ECtHR has the authority to supervise it.

An abusive regime that is not willing to protect people's rights will find any excuse to do so, probably using constitutional identity as Russia in 2016,[108] any other doctrine, or even an old-fashioned paradigm of the absolute sovereigntist national state. Of course, that undeniable fact must be considered, but more as a warning to establish the proper doctrinal

102 *Lautsi v. Italy* App no 30814/06 (ECtHR 18 March 2011).

103 cf Grégor Puppinck, 'The Case of Lautsi v. Italy: A Synthesis' [2012] BYU Law Review 873, 886–887.

104 cf Federico Fabbrini, 'The Margin of Appreciation and the Principle of Subsidiarity' [2015] iCourts Working Paper Series 13–15.

105 cf Federico Fabbrini and András Sajó, 'The Dangers of Constitutional Identity' (2019) 25 European Law Journal 457, 467–469.

106 cf Sarah Ganty, Dimitry Kochenov and Ignatius Nugraha, 'Constitutional Identity vs. Human Rights' [2023] Verfassungsblog.

107 Constitutional Court of Russia, Judgment No 21-П/2015, 14 July 2015.

108 Constitutional Court of Russia, Judgment No. 12-P/2016, 19 April 2016, para 1.2.

safeguards than a motive to trash it. The Russian case is emblematic because it was unwilling to comply with the ECtHR rulings since 2000, with additional peaks with the *Chechen*[109] and *Magnitsky*[110] cases. The situation became worse after the Crimea annexation in 2014 and the invasion of Ukraine in 2022, which finally provoked Russia's expulsion from the COE. Invoking constitutional identity in that scenario was just a rhetorical excuse. As rightly asserted by *Mälksoo*,[111] the Russian Constitutional Court built its constitutional identity argument based on previous cases from Germany, Italy, and the UK. Nevertheless, those countries have not shown such behavior towards human rights and the COE. Thus, *prima facie*, the eventual actor's fault should not be confused with the eventual doctrine's shortcomings. The doctrine itself is not an imperative cause of the ECHR breach; therefore, its recognition is not a slippery slope.[112]

The second general objection relies on the doctrine's indeterminacy.[113] However, this is a common feature in doctrines working as a hinge between the international and national legal order. Undoubtedly, careful effort must be made to delimit and define the doctrines' contents and operative criteria. What seems conflicting is decrying the vagueness of national identity or the margin of appreciation while praising ECI or emerging consensus doctrines. All of them share that same weakness. Thus, all of them must be discarded or, instead, valued as imperfect but helpful theories to nurture the complex relationship between international human rights law and constitutional fundamental rights law. The latter pathway is preferable, particularly considering that national identity and the margin of appreciation have finally been incorporated into the TEU and the ECHR after several years of practice within the legal community.[114] If the current understanding of constitutional identity within the COE is just a new legitimate aim covered by the margin of appreciation, then there is no reason to be afraid.

---

109 *Isayeva v. Russia* App no 57950/00 (ECtHR 24 February 2005); *Bazorkina v. Russia* App no 69481/01 (ECtHR 27 July 2006); *Estamirov and Others v. Russia* App no 60272/00 (ECtHR 12 October 2006).

110 *Magnitskiy and Others v. Russia* App nos 32631/09 and 53799/12 (ECtHR 27 November 2019).

111 cf Lauri Mälksoo, 'Russia's Constitutional Court Defies the European Court of Human Rights' (2016) 12 European Constitutional Law Review 377, 388–394.

112 cf Ignatius Nugraha, 'Protection of Constitutional Identity as a Legitimate Aim for Differential Treatment' (2023) 19 European Constitutional Law Review 141, 150.

113 cf Fabbrini and Sajó (n 105) 467–469.

114 cf Shai Dothan, 'Standards of Review in International Courts' [2024] iCourts Working Paper Series 1, 4; Menéndez (n 5) 567.

As a possible button to activate the margin of appreciation, constitutional identity indirectly shares the advantages of such a doctrine. The margin of appreciation instructs the ECtHR to afford states a degree of discretion in formulating their policies without necessarily deeming them to be violating the ECHR unless a threshold is surpassed.[115] This doctrine allows for different case review standards to determine its width or narrowness:[116] a) the nature of the right involved; b) the existence of European consensus; c) how the policy procedure went through the legislature and whether national courts applied the proportionality assessment as the ECtHR does; and d) the potential harm of the ECtHR's social legitimacy for overstepping the democratically elected bodies' normative legitimacy. In that vein, the margin of appreciation has an advantageous impact on domestic law: a) from a procedural perspective, the consolidation of the separation of powers principle with its inherent institutional checks and balances; b) from a substantive perspective, the crystallisation of general and undetermined human rights principles inside particular and determined pluralist communities of human persons; in sum, the revalorisation of the political-democratic process for adopting decisions within the institutional-constitutional boundaries (constitutional democracy). Having said so, are there singular advantages coming from constitutional identity as such? Although not dissociated from the margin of appreciation benefits expressed before, there are two more reasons to support constitutional identity as a legitimate aim. At the domestic level, it is a helpful mechanism to avoid depoliticising human rights. In contrast, at the international level, it can compensate for the absence of traditional democratic structures.

a) Repoliticising Human Rights

If constitutional identity's purpose is to protect the core elements of the constitution, then it is safeguarding the most valuable foundations of that political community's order. That cannot be considered capricious. As mentioned earlier, the state's constitutional core elements within the COE framework are mainly fundamental rights. So, it could be the case that a constitutional court may consider it a threat to those rights if a particular

115 cf Eyal Benvenisti, 'Margin of Appreciation, Consensus, and Universal Standards' (1998) 31 Journal of International Law and Politics 843, 843, 845–846.

116 cf Dothan (n 114) 7–17.

ECtHR interpretation would be unreasonably far beyond the international obligations adopted in the ECHR or if a unique imperative understanding for a right would be provided, unjustifiably ignoring the open debate on that comprehension. Inside the national sphere, that international decision is an invitation to rethink the involved constitutional identity element so that it can be overthrown or reshaped. What seems unacceptable is to exclude a potential negative answer, even if it reflects a democratic principle's exercise through the national institutions (parliament) and procedures (a constitutional amendment).[117] In such a situation, the ECtHR's grand chamber may eventually modify or reaffirm the chamber's previous decision. In the latter case, there is always the unexpected but possible *ultima ratio* state action to depart from that judgment. This exceptional scenario needs more of a case-by-case assessment than a dogmatic solution since not only the ECtHR but also the Member State may have justified reasons to proceed that way. It is not recommended to assume *a priori* bad faith on any side.

The well-known *ABC v. Ireland* case[118] on abortion is a good example. Although it was not discussed in terms of constitutional identity, there was an explicit constitutional provision protecting the *nasciturus*' right to life (former Article 40.3.3 of the Irish Constitution) as well as a long legal tradition in that sense (national laws, courts decisions, constitutional amendments, etc.), strongly supported by a society majority (all that assumable as part of the Irish constitutional identity[119]). Considering the Irish legal and cultural context[120] and the absence of European consensus, the ECtHR recognised a broad margin of appreciation. For the sake of the example, if the ECtHR had held the right to abortion as part of a European consensus to the detriment of a margin of appreciation for Ireland to assess and balance the issue – as some justices suggested in the joint partly dissenting opinion – it seems clear that an essential feature of the Irish constitutional order would have been compelled to change but without and against its *demos*' participation. Furthermore, there is an additional problem since it is arguable whether that outcome is an international obligation enshrined in

117 I am not currently considering the alternative 'constitutional identity' debate, which limits substantive constitutional reforms and confers on constitutional courts an implicit judicial review competence to do so.

118 *A, B, and C v. Ireland* App no 25579/05 (ECtHR 16 December 2010).

119 cf Gary J. Jacobsohn, 'Constitutional Identity' (2006) 68 The Review of Politics 361, 384–394.

120 *A, B, and C v. Ireland* (n 118) paras 230-233.

Article 8 ECHR.[121] In other words, in a scenario like this, a human rights policy on a very contested issue would have been reached only through international judicial activity, subtracting the problem from the national political arena, where it should be democratically discussed, pondered, and decided (as it was in the Irish abortion referendum of 2018), or from the international political arena through the Member States' adoption of a new ECHR protocol. While some may fear this approach by considering that it contradicts the universal logic of human rights, 'subsidiarity serves to explain that the deference given to the states does not deny the universality of human rights, but simply allows the instantiation of universal principles according to the circumstances, culture, and history of each community'.[122]

In any case, this should not be a problem for the ECtHR since, in contrast to the Inter-American Court of Human Rights, which often adopts a more interventionist approach due to its substantive understanding of democracy, the ECtHR tends to exhibit greater deference, reflecting its adherence to a more formal concept of democracy.[123] That means that the ECtHR generally does not privilege a theoretical notion of human rights as a previous requirement to validate democratic decision-making, but prefers to validate a concrete human rights policy if it is an outcome of formal democratic decision-making. Similarly, empirical evidence indicates that the ECtHR increasingly references the margin of appreciation in discussions concerning the exhaustion of domestic remedies.[124] This shift may suggest a strategic margin of appreciation adaptation, transitioning from a general doctrine of deference to a more nuanced tool for assessing whether state-level processes warrant deference. This approach to human rights protection offers several benefits:[125] it conserves the ECtHR's resources, enabling it to focus on cases where deficiencies in domestic proceedings indicate a higher risk of serious violations. Additionally, it incentivises states to enhance their national legal processes to avoid adverse judgments. Being

121 cf Ángel Gómez-Montoro, 'Vida privada y autonomía personal o una interpretación "passe-partout" del artículo 8 CEDH' in Francisco Rubio Llorente and others (eds), *La constitución política de España* (CEPC 2016) s 5.

122 Soledad Bertelsen, 'The Margin of Appreciation Through the Lens of Subsidiarity' (Tesis doctoral, Notre Dame 2014) 270.

123 cf Yhasmin Montero, 'El Paradigma Entre La Democracia y La Interpretación Evolutiva de Los Derechos Humanos' [2024] Revista Costarricense de Derecho Internacional 88, 100–111.

124 cf Mikael Madsen, 'Rebalancing European Human Rights' (2018) 9 Journal of International Dispute Settlement 199, 199–203, 214.

125 cf Dothan (n 114) 13.

aware of the potential of constitutional identity flaws, there is good news when there is a chance to revalue the political component of human rights.

b) Rebalancing the System

The previous section addressed the recovery of the political factor in human rights substantiation. This section represents the other side of the coin in that it tries to equilibrate the relation between the long-term global-local and judicial-legislative debates. Among others, there are two reasons to consider that adjustment as positive. First, when facing a complex issue with strong competing views and no clear solution in the ECHR, the decision should be made by domestic democratic bodies, not the ECtHR. Similarly, if new challenges arise from exercising previously non-threatening freedoms, elected branches should be allowed to experiment and take risks in addressing them. The ECtHR will have the chance to assess if those pathways severely clash with the ECHR. As *Rush*[126] has noted on the freedom of expression when the U.S. Supreme Court struck down a Congressional ban on 'crush'[127] videos[128] and a California law that restricted minors' access to violent video games,[129] '[...] it is necessary for the judiciary to allow the legislature and the executive to take novel and perhaps unclear steps to address new challenges that will arise as a result of exogenous shocks to the political or constitutional system. While allowing such actions may create the possibility that the elected branches could act capriciously or threaten liberties, the judiciary has the capacity to respond.'

Mutatis mutandis, considering the Islamic veil cases,[130] it would have been an error for the ECtHR to adopt a uniform rule in a novel challenge started in Europe with the increasing Muslim immigration. Instead, the Member States adopted their own rules, evidencing the variety of answers, e.g., the case *SAS v. France* has proven how that issue can be directly linked

126 cf Mark Rush, '21st Century Speech Rights and the Paradigm Crisis of Constitutional Democracy (ICON-S Annual Conference)' (2024) 17–18.

127 Crush videos depict women harming small animals, often to cater to the sadistic sexual fetishes of viewers.

128 U.S. Supreme Court, *United States v. Stevens*, 559 US 460 (2010).

129 U.S. Supreme Court, *Brown v. Entertainment Merchants Association*, 564 US 786 (2011).

130 *Leyla Şahin v. Turkey* App no 44774/98 (ECtHR 10 November 2005); *S.A.S. v. France* App no 43835/11 (ECtHR 1 July 2014).

to a country's constitutional identity[131] (although France did not use those terms).[132] By banning the public use of the full veil, France invoked as part of its arguments the contradiction of that clothing with the national core values of 'liberty, equality, fraternity', as stated in the preamble of its Constitution. That illustrates how focusing on the constitution's preamble and amendment clauses can serve as a privileged way to identify constitutional values.[133] As is known, the ECtHR accepted that approach and recognised a wide margin of appreciation. If elected bodies must have primary authority in addressing new legal challenges, and if constitutional identity can guide those elected bodies to find a solution, then it is vital to value the latter positively.

The second reason addresses constitutional attachment. Disregarding constitutional identity may negatively impact the constitutional ideology[134] behind its delicate building. If ideologies contribute to creating identity,[135] constitutional ideology is attractive because of its role in constructing constitutional identity, providing meaning and value to people's lives, and being a link between the individual and the institutions. For instance, 'constitutional roles, such as citizen, judge, and legislator are, in significant part, ideological constructions, and it is our capacity to occupy constitutional roles that allow us to talk of constitutional identity, that is, the element of state members' identity that is constructed through their relationship with the state.'[136] Of course, constitutional identity is not static and may/must change. The best way to achieve this is not through a vertical international judicial decision but rather in the same way constitutional identity originally emerged: through a political-legal procedure in the domestic environment. Again, constitutional ideologies are vital in establishing consti-

131 cf Cruz (n 85) 18–19.

132 *S.A.S. v. France* (n 130).

133 cf Constance Grewe, 'Methods of Identification of National Constitutional Identity' in Alejandro Saiz Arnaiz and Carina Llivina Alcoberro (eds), *National constitutional identity and European integration* (Intersentia 2013) 39.

134 Barber defines constitutional ideology '*as an analytical tool, one which builds on the standard way of viewing constitutions as sets of rules, but which treats these rules as grounded in social groups and combining to form a worldview, a model of reality contained within the constitutional order that conditions discourse within constitutional institutions*', Nicholas Barber, 'What is constitutional ideology?' (2024) 22 International Journal of Constitutional Law 34–35.

135 Cf. Jack Balkin, *Cultural Software: A Theory of Ideology* (YUP 2003) 18.

136 Barber (n 134) 12.

tutional attachment, enabling identification with the constitutional order,[137] i.e., ideological concepts or symbols that ground the stories that render the constitutional order understandable and attractive to its people.[138] Hence, there is another reason to ponder the constitutional identity carefully.

After all, this new trend may correspond to what *Lustig* and *Weiler*[139] have named the third wave within the contemporary world. In synthesis, after two global waves (constitutional revolutions and the emergence of international law), there is a third one that works as a reaction, being an attempt of domestic courts to address the lack of rule of law, democracy, and identity in transnational governance. If one were to distill the substantive normative core of the constitutional revolution – the first wave – to its fundamental elements, it would center on the protection of individual autonomy and equality. The international aspect of this core – the second wave – plays a crucial role in resisting nationalism's excesses. While these are undeniably noble aspirations, the conspicuous absence of social and collective considerations is striking. This contributes to cultural homogenisation across societies and the flattening of identity.

As both scholars continue, the concept of identity is often vaguely defined and can appear as a rhetorical device to soften the assertive use of sovereignty. However, it may also reflect a genuine shift in constitutional thought. According to the authors, an alternative interpretation of the Lisbon jurisprudence[140] addresses the democratic deficit issue by evolving toward a focus on identity. This shift is evident in the EU treaties, which have recently emphasised protecting 'national identity' as a core value. Traditionally, constitutional provisions, particularly in human rights, have protected individuals against collective interests. But this new approach reinterprets such provisions as cultural and identitarian markers of the collective, which constitutional courts are now tasked to safeguard. The prominence of the national identity clause underscores its significance, representing a third wave in constitutional thinking. As *Lustig* and *Weiler* suggest, this development subtly detaches human rights protection from its classical liberal framework – where the individual is pitted against the state, at least in the most extreme interpretation of liberalism – and reconfigures

137 cf Martin Loughlin, 'The Constitutional Imagination' (2015) 78 The Modern Law Review 1, 2–5, 15.

138 cf Barber (n 134) 12–13, 34–35.

139 cf Doreen Lustig and Joseph H. H. Weiler, 'Judicial Review in the Contemporary World' (2018) 16 International Journal of Constitutional Law 315, 340–341, 357–358.

140 It refers to the body of case law developed in response to the Treaty of Lisbon.

it as an expression of national identity. This reimagination of rights justifies an alternative interpretation or rejection of international legal norms, favoring domestic conceptions of fundamental rights.

As they finally state,[141] the emergence of the third wave in international governance can be viewed as a self-corrective mechanism within the system, though 'international purists' often see it as deviating from the norm. This shift, however, appears inevitable from a normative perspective. Traditional democratic theories, grounded in *demos*, nation, and state concepts, offer limited applicability to international governance, where no '*global demos*' exists. Thus, this shift requires a crucial reevaluation of democracy's core elements and exploring alternative mechanisms for legitimacy that can compensate for the absence of democratic structures at the international level. If the rule of law is the cornerstone of a pluralist democracy, the third wave is inevitable and potentially beneficial. Nonetheless, this is contingent upon national judges playing a prudent role by recognising the international legal order's benefits as an *acquis* and ensuring that these advantages are not gained at the expense of disenfranchising people and peoples.

IV. Conclusion

As *Martinico*[142] underscores, though constitutional provisions regarding the status of EU and ECHR norms vary, an increasing number of national judges have started applying the structural principles of EU law, such as primacy and direct effect, to the ECHR. However, at the same time, they have constrained the interpretative authority of ECHR norms by constitutional principles often referred to as *controlimiti*. This phenomenon could be understood differently as a rapprochement between EU law and the ECHR, an expected reaction of constitutional courts due to the ECtHR's abandonment of its margin of appreciation,[143] or a self-correcting mechanism of the global legal system (third wave).

Without discrediting the other explanations, the latter is the most accurate interpretation describing why there was an increasing demand for national identity within the EU and a margin of appreciation inside the COE during the last two decades, in which process the constitutional courts

141 cf Lustig and Weiler (n 139) 370–371.
142 cf Martinico (n 83) 423.
143 cf Wojciech Sadurski, 'Partnering with Strasbourg' (2009) 9 Human Rights Law Review 397, 397.

played a protagonist role. As is known, both doctrines were also enshrined in the TEU and the ECHR, respectively. Nevertheless, what sparked this research was the recent incorporation by the ECtHR of 'constitutional identity' as a potential legitimate aim for differentiated treatment of the ECHR through the margin of appreciation. The debate within the COE remains in its early stages, and further contributions from the ECtHR and Member States are needed to clarify this emerging doctrine. Drawing on the EU's long-standing discussion of national identity, I have outlined its possible contours and how it may offer a pathway toward future-proofing human rights protection. While concerns remain, there are reasons to believe that, if properly applied, constitutional identity may represent an improvement for the ESHR.

Future-proofing the Freedom of Expression Online

Tavini Nanayakkara[*]

Given the pervasive use of social media platforms to engage in speech in the online sphere, coupled with the need to ensure it remains a conducive place for expression for future generations, this article focuses on how this sphere may be future-proofed. As a result of the unique dangers faced by future generations due to their scarcity of attention, generational anxiety, potent digital technology such as dark patterns, privacy violations through micro targeting and deepfakes, and overt reliance on social media, there are greater chances for distortion of the marketplace of ideas for future generations that may want to make the digital world their abode. To mitigate this, I suggest the online space be regulated by a consortium of stakeholders including the state, social media platforms, and users through several recommendations. These include the prevention of monopolies and oligarchies of social media companies, freedom for social media companies to decide on their censorship policies coupled with their mandatory disclosure. Apart from what social media companies may be required to do, I also recommend initiative on the part of consumers in social media spaces to take matters into their own hands through ascribing a higher brand value to platforms that respect online speech. I recommend that governments take action to protect children and equip them before they enter the online space along with a call to decentralise the lives of children and adults from the digital space. Finally, I call upon present generations that engage in speech online to conduct themselves in a manner that set a good example for future generations in how to use the online space to engage in expression. These mechanisms would allow for hope for the continuation of the freedom of expression online amidst the more pronounced and unique harms that will be faced by future generations in the digital world.

* Lecturer at the Department of Private and Comparative Law, Faculty of Law, University of Colombo.

I. Introduction

The marketplace of ideas is an age-old concept that has been successfully defended time and again. Assuming its continued relevance and reverence, this article analyses whether the online space shows signs of decline and danger for free speech. A main intermediary that allows for free speech is social media which plays a major role in public and private conversations online. This article asks the central question of how expression in the online space may be rendered future-proof. It contains a descriptive and normative analysis.

This article is divided into six main parts. Following the introduction in Part I, Part II defines 'future-proofing' and 'social media'. Part III addresses the question of whether online expression should be regulated in order to render it future-proof. I argue that social media platforms should be regulated in order to protect and promote an online marketplace of ideas, in great part due to certain characteristics of future generations and the emerging online space that makes them especially vulnerable. These include users' dwindling attention spans, higher levels of anxiety, potency of technology in perpetrating online harms through dark patterns, privacy violations and deepfakes as well as users' overt reliance on social media to obtain information. In Part IV, I ask the question of who should regulate the online space. I argue that it should be a combination of the state, social media platforms, and consumers, both present and future, that should create an informal consortium that would allow regulation, market forces, and individual action to achieve an effective online space for free speech. Finally, in Part V, I put forward seven suggestions for how the online space may be managed by these varied stakeholders to allow free speech to thrive for years to come. Part VI concludes.

This study is limited to the extent that there may be an inherent illegitimacy in making normative suggestions for future generations as opposed to leaving it to be decided by said generations. Nevertheless, it presents a study on the importance of taking action, both formally through regulation and informally through social and cultural means in order to render the digital sphere future-proof, especially given the dangers it holds with the improvement of technology and unique vulnerabilities of future generations.

II. Definitions of 'Future-proofing' and 'Social media'

To answer the question of whether online expression should be regulated at all, it is important to first define some of the key terms that will be dealt with in this article. In the sub-sections that follow, I define what I consider to be future-proofing within this article, and what I refer to as social media platforms.

First, as for future-proofing, this has been defined elsewhere as 'the process of anticipating the future and developing methods of minimising the negative effects while taking advantage of the positive effects of shocks and stresses due to future events'.[1] While future-proofing is by no means novel in many contexts such as design, environmental protection and technology, its use in the digital context, especially with regard to expression is underexplored. In this article, I pay special attention to future generations and how the online sphere may be made a fertile ground for conversation, debate, discussion and dissent for prospective inheritors of this space.

Second, I turn to recognised definitions of platforms and social media platforms. *Grafanaki* clarifies what is meant by online *platforms*. She points out that it was social media companies that started using the term to describe the services they were providing.[2] Following *Grafanaki's* lead, I limit the use of the term platforms '...to the original use of the term, i.e. to social media platforms that handle predominantly expressive content'.[3] *Haidt* states that there are four major characteristics of social media that qualify them to be placed in this category: ability to create user profiles to share personal information and interests, creation of user-generated content to share with audiences, networking and interacting through 'liking, commenting, sharing or direct messaging'.[4] *Haidt* considers networking to include befriending users and joining groups, among other activities and the act of interacting to include the communications that take place among users. Regardless of the overlap between these categories, these activities are reasonable characteristics of social media platforms. Some examples of

---

1 See 'Principles of Future-proofing: Research on Future-proofing the Built Environment, http://principlesoffutureproofing.com' as cited in Sofia Ranchordás and Mattis van 't Schip, 'Future-Proofing Legislation for the Digital Age' (2019) 36 University of Groningen Faculty of Law Research Paper https://ssrn.com/abstract=3466161.

2 Sofia Grafanaki, 'Platforms, the First Amendment and Online Speech Regulating the Filters' (2018) 39 Pace L Rev 111, 115.

3 ibid.

4 Jonathan Haidt, *The Anxious Generation, How the Great Rewiring of Childhood is Causing an Epidemic of Mental Illness* (Penguin Press 2024), part III.

social media platforms are Facebook, Instagram, X (formerly Twitter) and TikTok.

I choose to discuss social media platforms for their enduring nature. The inception of social media can be seen from around the early 2000s, and different platforms have managed to capture varied generations' allegiances. Much like MySpace and Facebook were for generation X,[5] Instagram for millennials[6] and TikTok for GenZ,[7] though the popular and most relatable platform may change by generation, the creation of communities online that engage in expression in these spaces has been an enduring trend since the turn of the millennium. Signs of continuation of this trend abound.[8]

These social media platforms are private entities that, as *Gillespie* states, '...provide storage, navigation, and delivery of the digital content of others.'[9] Therefore, social media platforms play a key role in shaping the conversations of the modern day and show no signs of relinquishing this power. In fact, interestingly, the etymology of 'platform' is shown to be 'a "raised, level surface" designed to facilitate some activity that will subsequently take place.'[10] *Gillespie* highlights the discursive and versatile nature of the term 'platform' as one that can reconcile potentially overlapping interests between the different stakeholders that sites like YouTube attempt to appeal to – everyday users, advertisers, major media producers, and policymakers.[11] *Balkin* opines that social media facilitates public participation, organises

5 Katie Caron, 'How different generations use social media' [2020] Home Accents Today https://www.homeaccentstoday.com/furniture-lighting-and-decor/how-different-generations-use-social-media/#:~:text=(22%20percent).-,Gen%20X,their%20favorite%20social%20media%20platform ('95% of generation X uses Facebook'), accessed 19 July 2025.

6 Jennifer Dublino, 'Instagram Marketing Strategies that Actually Work for Millennials' [2025] business.com https://www.business.com/articles/engaging-millennials-instagram-marketing/, accessed 21 Nov 2025: 'Instagram has become the essential platform for reaching millennials because it aligns perfectly with how this generation discovers, researches and connects with brands'.

7 'TikTok Statistics – Updated May 2024' [2024] Wallaroo https://wallaroomedia.com/blog/social-media/tiktok-statistics/#:~:text=Gen%20Z%20–%2060%25%20of%20TikTok,the%20largest%20generation%20of%20all ('60% of TikTok users are Gen Zers'), accessed 31 Aug 2024.

8 Alison Zeller, 'The Future of Social Media (2025-2027)' [2025] Exploding Topics https://explodingtopics.com/blog/future-of-social-media, accessed 25 Aug 2025.

9 Tarleton Gillespie, 'The Politics of "Platforms"' (2010) 12 New Media & Soc'y 347, 348.

10 ibid 350.

11 ibid.

public conversation and curates public opinion.[12] Given these claims of elevation of the fabled town crier by social media, capturing generations of occupiers who turn to different platforms to express themselves, this sphere remains an important point of discussion when it comes to expression.

III. Should Online Expression be Regulated to Render it Future-proof?

With the above definitions in mind, I move to answer the main question I ask in this part which is whether regulation is necessary in order to render online expression future-proof. While it is trite that there is a need to presently regulate the online sphere in order to combat crimes such as child abuse, bullying and harassment, the question that is asked here is more specific.

In the present context, I refer to whether there should be an epistemic authority that is tasked with the responsibility to ensure that the online sphere remains fertile ground for expression and if such an authority should exist, the nature of such an authority and which actions it should take to accomplish such a goal. In answer to the first question, I put forward the argument that there should be regulation in the online sphere. While this might, at first sight, be seen to go against the time-honoured concept[13] of the marketplace of ideas, this is not necessarily so. In the suggestions I put forward in this article, I find a middle ground between regulation and the marketplace of ideas to the effect that some regulation may actually promote a marketplace of ideas online that would allow social media platforms to be safe and nurturing spaces in which future generations can engage in conversation with each other.

In the sub-section that follows, I 1. briefly recapitulate the importance of the marketplace of ideas to guarantee free speech online and 2. analyse the unique challenges faced by future generations online which would require specific attention to be paid towards future-proofing the online space.

12 Jack M. Balkin, 'How to Regulate (and Not Regulate) Social Media' (2021) 1 J Free Speech L 71, 75.

13 I refer to the concept of the marketplace of ideas as time-honoured because it is one that has stood the test of time, albeit with some dissent, and is still held in high esteem by various scholars. See the following footnote for some relevant scholarship.

1. Importance of Future-proofing Expression on Online Platforms through Promoting a Marketplace of Ideas

Given the convincing work done by scholars on the importance of the marketplace of ideas,[14] I restrict this section to providing only a brief account of the concept.

As *Patty* writes, referring to many other writers, the freedom of speech is often defended on the ground that it is essential to the progress of the being[15] as well as a healthy democracy.[16] He refers to the declaration of the Supreme Court of the United States of America (US), which has stated that the primary purpose of the First Amendment to the US Constitution was 'to preserve an uninhibited marketplace of ideas in which truth will ultimately prevail',[17] especially through viewpoint diversity.[18] *Patty* adds to this by referring to the insight of *Mill*, who has written one of the seminal texts on the freedom of speech, which, apart from the capacity of the marketplace of ideas to reveal certain important truths, also recognises that truth can be subjective and humans fallible.[19] Therefore, the co-existence of all ideas is important, regardless of whether one thinks they are right or wrong.

The online marketplace of ideas is all the more important as it elevates the status of a town crier standing on a soap box.[20] Given the vast reach and speed with which expression online can spread, social media makes the

---

14 John S. Mill, *On Liberty* (Batoche Books 1859); Michael Patty, 'Social Media and Censorship: Rethinking State Action Once Again' (2019) 40 Mitchell Hamline L J Pub Pol'y & Prac 99; Eugene Volokh, 'In Defense of the Marketplace of Ideas/Search for Truth as a Theory of Free Speech Protection' (2011) 97(3) Virginia Law Review 595; Dawn C. Nunziato, 'The Marketplace of Ideas Online' (2019) 94(4) Notre Dame Law Review 1519.

15 Patty (n 14) 100.

16 Brian Miller, 'There's No Need to Compel Speech. The Marketplace of Ideas Is Working' (4 Dec 2017) Forbes https://perma.cc/VXP4-ZXEY. For a highly critical discussion of the analogy of the marketplace of ideas, see Paul H. Brietzke, 'How and Why the Marketplace of Ideas Fails' (1997) 31 Val. U. L. Rev. 951 as cited in Patty (n 14) 100.

17 Jacquelyn E. Fradette, 'Online Terms of Service: A Shield for First Amendment Scrutiny of Government Action' (2013) 89 Notre Dame Law Rev. 947, 948 (quoting *Red Lion Broadcasting Co. v. F.C.C.*, 395 U.S. 367, 390 [1969]) as cited in Patty (n 14).

18 See Nathan Honeycutt, 'Political Intolerance Among University Faculty Highlights Need for Viewpoint Diversity' (21 Nov 2016) Forbes https://perma.cc/96NR-URD3 as cited in Patty (n 14) 101.

19 Mill (n 14) Ch 2.

20 Patty (n 14).

soap box taller and the town crier louder. Except, sometimes, the people of the square may not even see the town crier and the message may spread to numerous other town squares as well. In fact, social media has been used to orchestrate turning points in entire democracies over the past two decades. Some examples are the storming of the US Capitol on 6 January 2021, following the tweets of President *Trump*,[21] the mobilisation of entire populations during the historic protests in Sri Lanka that held the government accountable for its mismanagement of the country that resulted in the economic crisis in 2022,[22] as well as, allegedly, for counter revolutions to the Arab springs.[23]

These real-life events demonstrate that the power of social media platforms to spread messages far and fast is undeniable. However, there are important considerations to keep in mind regarding such unbridled power that these platforms hold. In the section that follows, this article zooms in on the unique challenges faced by future generations online that would require the power of social media platforms to be kept in check through various measures.

2. Unique Challenges Faced by Future Generations

In this section, I point to four main challenges that have not affected past generations, not even the generations that first entered the online space to the extent that they may potentially harm future generations. I refer to the extreme scarcity of attention that current younger generations and future generations are bound to suffer online due to the intense and constant flow of information; the development of conditions of anxiety that increasingly plague young adults; dangerous technology that can manipulate and mislead online users, such as dark patterns, privacy violations, and microtargeting as well as deepfake technology. Finally, I also refer to the overt reliance of users on social media to receive information. These characteristics that are unique to the younger users that currently call social media home and are bound to be more pronounced in future generations

21 Brian Duignan, 'January 6 U.S. Capitol Attack' [2024] Britannica https://www.britannica.com/event/January-6-U-S-Capitol-attack, accessed 31 Aug 2024.

22 'Freedom on the Net 2022' [2022] Freedom House https://freedomhouse.org/country/sri-lanka/freedom-net/2022, accessed 31 Aug 2024.

23 Haythem Guesmi, 'The social media myth about the Arab Spring' [2021] Aljazeera https://www.aljazeera.com/opinions/2021/1/27/the-social-media-myth-about-the-arab-spring, accessed 31 Aug 2024.

require immediate attention of law and policy-makers when deciding on how free speech online may be promoted best while mitigating these harms.

a) Attention Scarcity

Studies in the field of environmental law refer to the scarcity of natural resources and expounds the importance of inter-generational equity in order to advance the idea of using natural resources for the benefit of present generations while preserving enough for future generations.[24] The study of the online space and online conversations are inherently reversed. In the information age of today, '[i]nformation has become abundant; in fact, we are drowning in it'.[25] As opposed to this, what is actually scarce is the ability of consumers to absorb the vast amounts of data in a meaningful manner and to ensure their attention is diverted to the right sources. *Grafanaki* points out how the term 'attention economy'[26] has even made its way into pop culture.[27]

This brings us to the most worrisome aspect of online expression that leaves us apprehensive about the ability of social media to remain conducive spaces for genuine, honest and unmanipulated conversation. Given

24 Some cases of the International Court of Justice that have dealt with the concept of intergenerational equity are Maritime Delimitation in the Area between Greenland and Jan Mayen (Den. v. Nor.), 1993 I.C.J. 41 (June 14); Pulp Mills on the River Uruguay (Arg. v. Uru.), 2010 I.C.J. (Apr. 20); Legality of the Use by a State of Nuclear Weapons in armed Conflict, Advisory Opinion, 1996 I.C.J. 227 (July 8).

25 See Herbert A. Simon, 'Designing Organizations for an Information Rich World' in Martin Greenberger (ed), *Computers, Communications, and the Public Interest* (Johns Hopkins Press 1997) 37, 40-41 as cited in Grafanaki (n 2) 124.

26 See Tim Wu, *The Attention Merchants: The Epic Scramble to Get Inside our Heads* (Knopf 2016) as cited in ibid.

27 Charles M. Blow, 'Trump's Attention Economy' (4 Jan 2018) N.Y. Times https://www.nytimes.com/2018/01/04/opinion/trump-attention-economy.html; Mathew Ingram, 'The Attention Economy and the Implosion of Traditional Media' (12 Aug 2015) Fortune http://fortune.com/2015/08/12/attention-economy/; Andrew Keen, 'The "Attention Economy" Created by Silicon Valley Is Bankrupting Us' (30 July, 2017) TechCrunch https://techcrunch.com/2017/07/30/the-attention-economy-created-by-siliconvalley-is-bankrupting-us/; Robert Safian, 'How to Stand Out in the Attention Economy' (3 Oct 2017) Fast Company https://www.fastcompany.com4/0473876/how-to-stand-out-in-the-attention-economy' as cited in Grafanaki (n 2) 125; 'New Economics for Sustainable Development, Attention Economy' United Nations Economist Network https://www.un.org/sites/un2.un.org/files/attention_economy_feb.pdf, accessed 19 July 2025.

the fact that platforms are not welfare enhancing and are, for the most part, mercenary, their goal is to simply 'keep users *on* the platform'[28] [emphasis as in original text]. Their business models have no consideration for quality or truth, and in fact, lower quality content that is easier to consume, they realise, has the potential to allow for greater viewership.[29] As *Grafanaki* makes clear, algorithms transport users to the kinds of content they would like to reach as it is impossible for consumers to comb the online spaces to find content they prefer to consume on their own. When algorithms lead consumers to certain content and users spend more time on the platforms that host said content, the platforms become more attractive to advertisers. In this case, advertisers may be more forthcoming in spending money to advertise on these platforms to capture the attention of consumers. Since a majority of platforms' revenue comes from advertising, the better the reputation of the platform in keeping consumers engaged and satiated, the more money advertisers will be willing to spend on the platform in order to advertise their content.[30] Once social media became monetised, its primary target customer became the advertiser,[31] the employee became the content creator and the end goal of the product became the capture of the social media user's attention. It is now less about connecting people and more about earning revenue at the cost of the 'social'.[32]

Simply, the better equipped a social media platform is to garner the attention of consumers and make them want to remain on the platform, the more lucrative it may be for advertisers to advertise on such platforms in return for payment to the platform. Given that advertisements are one of the major sources of revenue for platforms, this is an important aspect. In fact, *Grafanaki* points out further how journalists feel 'pressure to write *click-bait* articles that "pander to readers' worst impulses,"[33] [emphasis as in original text] and are "[t]oo-good-to-check" stories' as opposed to those

---

28 Grafanaki (n 2) 125.

29 See Eli Pariser, *The Filter Bubble: What the Internet is Hiding from You* (Penguin Books Ltd. 2011) 68; Cass R. Sunstein, *#Republic: Divided Democracy in the Age of Social Media* (Princeton Univ. Press 2017) 65 as cited in Grafanaki (n 2) 125.

30 Grafanaki (n 2) 125.

31 Matt D'Avella, 'Why everyone is quitting social media' [2025] YouTube https://www.youtube.com/watch?v=zN-rElTzR_4, accessed 19 July 2025.

32 ibid.

33 Grafanaki (n 2) 127.

that are well reported as the former have a higher chance of grabbing the attention of readers.[34]

The manner in which this sinister digital environment impacts the online space is that, click-bait, overly exaggerated, unverified content which have the sole aim of grabbing the attention of users online is not well placed to create a marketplace of ideas. Such a system would produce a drastically compromised online space for future generations to engage in speech on. They would have distorted views, grossly imperfect information and short attention spans which carry the potential to rid them of the ability to have worthwhile conversations online. The fight for attention has the potential to create noise that would silence honest, meaningful and contemplative discussion, not only for future generations, but current generations online as well.

b) An 'Anxious Generation' in 'Dopamine Nation'

The level of attention scarcity that is discussed in the section above and its associated harms for online speech are further compounded when the mindsets of future generations are considered. Some glaring characteristics of the mental state of future generations that would make matters worse for their ability to engage in meaningful speech online are heightened levels of anxiety and dopamine addiction which I turn to now.

> *'When we gave children and adolescents smartphones in the early 2010s, we gave companies the ability to apply variable-ratio reinforcement schedules all day long, training them like rats during their most sensitive years of brain rewiring. Those companies developed addictive apps that sculpted some very deep pathways in our children's brains.'*[35]

This impassioned quotation is from *Haidt's* work on present younger generations, in other words, as he puts it, the 'anxious generation'.[36] In this work, *Haidt* points to the profound changes that occurred in the 2010s in terms of how children were raised which he calls 'the great rewiring'.[37] They became

34 Timothy B. Lee, 'Mark Zuckerberg is in Denial about how Facebook is Harming our Politics' (10 Nov 2016) Vox http://www.vox.com/new-money/2016/11/6/13509854/facebook-politics-news-bad as cited in Grafanaki (n 2) 127.

35 Haidt (n 4).

36 ibid.

37 ibid.

addicted to their phones which affected the development of their social, emotional and cognitive abilities.[38] He speaks of how this has led to 'social deprivation, sleep deprivation, attention fragmentation [similar to what is discussed in the section above] and addiction.'[39] I focus on addiction and how it has made younger generations more anxious, vulnerable and at danger of being manipulated online, which would sabotage an effective marketplace of ideas.

When small actions, followed by invoking feelings of pleasure, are repeated, causing the release of dopamine, this creates new neural pathways in the brain.[40] Social media designers learned the formula of creating strong habits in users through four steps. First, you invite the user to leave the work they are currently attending to through a trigger received on their phone. Second, you activate a desire to engage in a certain action, through the trigger, which is linked to an earlier feeling of pleasure. Third, the action will be allowed to lead to pleasure, but as a variable reward. This is important because a dopamine hit has been found to be even more effective when the user is not *always* rewarded but only *sometimes.* Finally, and very importantly, investment. This is where social media allows the user to make the action internal. Since they would have included personal aspects within their social media accounts, users would have an internal motivation to keep returning to the action.[41]

While some may make the argument that this is simply clever business, the (im)morality of the *modus operandi* of social media comes in when we consider the target audience – children and adolescents. This is because, as *Haugen* presented in his work, the teenage brain is not completely developed.[42] In fact, it is only about 80 % mature. The remaining 20 % of development yet to occur sits in the frontal cortex. At this time, teenagers rely on 'emotions, memory and learning, and the reward system reigns supreme.'[43] There is evidence that Facebook and other social media designers aim to take advantage of this vulnerability in getting young persons hooked to their platforms.[44]

38 ibid, part III.

39 ibid, chapter 6.

40 Haidt (n 4).

41 These four steps are extracted from and explained in detail in Haidt (n 4) under 'Harm #4: Addiction'.

42 Haidt (n 4).

43 ibid citing a presentation by several employees of Facebook.

44 ibid.

Lembke, who has engaged in extensive research into addiction, shows how the regions in the brain, which deal with pain and pleasure, overlap.[45] Therefore, once a person seeks pleasurable activity, the brain automatically balances this with pain.[46] However, if one were to chase pleasurable activity and enjoy 'the chase' of the pleasurable reward, our brain would send an increased amount of pain to reach equilibrium.[47] Repeated chasing would then provide less pleasure than it did on the previous occasion until finally, the drug or addiction stops being pleasurable and causes more pain than pleasure.[48] She refers to how the only way to rid oneself of elevated levels of dopamine is to stay off the dopamine-inducing activity which is inherently unpleasant and would require a week or more of withdrawal to return to the default state. She also points out that 'the universal symptoms of withdrawal from any addictive substance are anxiety, irritability, insomnia, and dysphoria'.[49]

Therefore, the average platform-addicted anxiety-ridden child and adolescent of today would inherently seek, absorb and respond to speech online in a uniquely vulnerable manner. Given their fragile mental state, they could be easily influenced in negative ways and thereby manipulated. Given this lack of safety for speech and ideas online, it is all the more important that the exchange of ideas remains effective so that vulnerable children may not be unduly influenced by one idea but rather be exposed to many that would allow them to exercise some judgment before settling on one perspective. More and the right information at the right time can make all the difference in how their lives may be shaped.

c) Potency of Technology

Another aspect that requires special consideration in the online space is the potency of technology that is used today. Compared to the kinds of dangers that past generations have faced, we encounter unique dangers in today's digital world. I will demonstrate these dangers through some of the

---

45 Anna Lembke, *Dopamine Nation. Finding Balance in the Age of Indulgence* (Dutton 2021).

46 ibid.

47 ibid.

48 ibid.

49 Lembke (n 45) and referred to in Haidt (n 4).

most manipulative technologies in use which are dark patterns, violations of privacy and microtargeting as well as deep fakes.

(1) Emergence of Dark Patterns

Although there is a lack of agreement on how to define dark patterns,[50] *Lugari* and *Strahilevitz* put it simply that 'dark patterns are user interfaces whose designers knowingly confuse users, make it difficult for users to express their actual preferences, or manipulate users into taking certain actions'.[51]

A common example of a dark pattern would be an instance in which you may be browsing the internet and arrive on a page. On the page, you find an 'X' that allows you to close an advertisement to view the content. When you press on it, you are led to a page that hosts the website connected to the advertisement. There is a small button at the bottom labelled 'close' that would take you several minutes to find in order to finally close the advertisement and to get to the content that you were looking for.[52] This can be found with regard to various other tactics where platforms would make it difficult for users to choose the cookies they allow, lead to hidden costs, and resort to forced registration of users.

A demonstrative example of dark patterns is the case of the Publishers Clearing House (PCH). After being charged by the Federal Trade Commission of the US for manipulating its customers, the PCH entered into an $18.5 million settlement with its customers.[53] The case centred around the dark patterns that had been utilised by the PCH in order to mislead consumers into entering their sweepstakes by leading them to believe that they had to purchase a good in order to win or that such a purchase would

50 Arunesh Mathur, Jonathan Mayer and Mihir Kshirsagar, 'What Makes a Dark Pattern... Dark? Design Attributes, Normative Considerations, and Measurement Methods' CHI '21, May 8–13, 2021, Yokohama, Japan.

51 Jamie Luguri and Lior Jacob Strahilevitz, 'Shining a light on dark patterns' (2021) 13 Journal of Legal Analysis.

52 This example is taken from 'Dark Patterns' The Decision Lab https://thedecisionlab.com/reference-guide/design/dark-patterns, accessed 30 Aug 2024.

53 'FTC Takes Action Against Publishers Clearing House for Misleading Consumers About Sweepstakes Entries' [2023] Federal Trade Commission https://www.ftc.gov/news-events/news/press-releases/2023/06/ftc-takes-action-against-publishers-clearing-house-misleading-consumers-about-sweepstakes-entries, accessed 24 Aug 2024.

at least increase their odds of winning.[54] The website would also display that sweepstake entries were incomplete when, in fact, they were not. They would charge surprise shipping and handling fees.[55] Consumers would also be provided with misrepresentations that their orders are 'risk free' and sent deceptive emails. PCH is even said to have sold users' personal data to third parties while its policies stated that this would not be the case.[56]

While some of these actions are explicitly illegal, the subtle manipulations that online platforms resort to by using words, phrases, deals and alerts that would push a consumer to make a choice that he would not have originally made are less amenable to existing legal rules. The existence of this culture requires greater attention to be paid to protecting the online space in order to make sure individuals that resort to dark patterns to mislead users of social media do not pervade into platforms in which expression takes place.

(2) Violations of Privacy and Micro-targeting

Another online harm that would make users of online spaces particularly vulnerable is violations of privacy and being 'micro-targeted' through such violations. A prime example of the covert and pronounced nature of this phenomenon can be illustrated through the infamous Cambridge Analytica scandal.

Foreseeing the extraordinary potential that Facebook holds to get insight into their users' interests and preferences from the 'likes' placed by an individual on a post, the pages they browse, the length of stay on a single post, to the friends they maintain, the Chief Executive of Cambridge Analytica, *Alexander Nix* signed on with lecturer *Aleksandr Kogan* for a private commercial venture.[57] Kogan and his company Global Science Research de-

54 ibid.
55 ibid.
56 ibid.
57 Carole Cadwalladr and Emma Graham-Harrison, 'How Cambridge Analytica turned Facebook 'likes' into a lucrative political tool' [2018] The Guardian https://www.theguardian.com/technology/2018/mar/17/facebook-cambridge-analytica-kogan-data-algorithm, accessed 31 Aug 2024.

veloped a personality quiz on an app called 'thisisyourdigitallife' in 2013.[58] Cambridge Analytica paid people to take this quiz and paired their answers with their Facebook accounts to create extremely valuable and infiltrating profiles. Although the paid test-takers signed a terms and conditions in order to agree to share personal information, this was argued to be a violation of privacy as the collection of data was used for a commercial purpose which Facebook's rules did not allow. This led to the creation of a database of US voters whose political persuasions and personality traits could be analysed through an algorithm.[59] Armed with this knowledge, individual voters could be targeted through messages that could appeal to them, which is a political approach known as 'micro-targeting'.[60] This scandal has been said to have affected the very democratic process of electing the President of the US.

While the Cambridge Analytica scandal was a large-scale example of micro-targeting with national ramifications, everyday examples of micro-targeting are plenty. For example, in a much smaller situation that took place over a decade ago, a young girl was sent coupons related to baby clothes and cribs from Target. When the father of the recipient contacted Target to hold them responsible for sending inappropriate advertisements, he was later made aware that, unbeknown to him, his daughter was pregnant.[61] This level of micro-targeting can be achieved through the high-volume of purchaser information that is collected and mined by companies which would give them clues to some of the most private details of a person. Such keen potential of technology to obtain deeply personal information, most even unknown to those closest to the data subject and for it to be wielded as a weapon to further certain commercial interests of social media platforms is deeply troubling.

The potential for micro-targeting is even more clearly evinced by an example where a TikTok user once posted a video with evidence that when she and her partner had looked at the same post at the same time, they

58 Sam Meredith, 'Facebook-Cambridge Analytica: A timeline of the data hijacking scandal' [2018] CNBC https://www.cnbc.com/2018/04/10/facebook-cambridge-analytica-a-timeline-of-the-data-hijacking-scandal.html, accessed 19 July 2025.

59 ibid.

60 Cadwalladr and Graham-Harrison (n 57).

61 Kashmir Hill, 'How Target figured out a teen girl was pregnant before her father did' (16 Feb 2012) Forbes https://www.forbes.com/sites/kashmirhill/2012/02/16/how-target-figured-out-a-teen-girl-was-pregnant-before-her-father-did/, accessed 31 Aug 2024.

would see different comments appear at the top of the comments section of the post.[62] The comments that would show up on top would be those most relatable to the user based on the judgment of the algorithm. This may be problematic, as the comment section informs the user of dominant narratives and may influence the way she views the situation. The manner in which comments therefore show up in posts for different persons according to their tastes although they have not adjusted it to be so would pave the way for echo chambers and polarisation of groups' ideals. This is yet again an automatic micro-targeting to feed information to users in such a way that they are told what they want to hear as opposed to creating a conglomerate of ideas to choose from, transforming a marketplace of ideas to a 'place' of 'one idea'.

(3) Deepfakes

Artificial Intelligence (AI) carries with it enormous potential to transform the online space. Especially, AI image and video creating possibilities allow for creators online to, at less cost, time and energy, produce realistic digital products. Unfortunately, such enormous potential, absent policing, carries with it room for misuse. This section refers to one such example.

A digital manoeuvre that demonstrates how deceptive and alarming new technology can be are deepfakes. Coined by an anonymous user on Reddit, 'deepfakes' is an amalgam of the words 'deep learning' and 'fakes'.[63] Simply, deepfakes are a kind of technology that allows actual people's appearance or voice to be superimposed onto another real or fictional being. While disinformation and fake news are by no means a new phenomenon and existed in analogue forms as well, the harms that would be created by deepfakes online are especially severe.

Given the believability of and ease with which deepfakes may be generated in modern times,[64] they have the potential to distort narratives that take place online through the spread of false information. Pretty soon,

62 'Apparently different comments show up on videos based on the user' [2024] reddit https://www.reddit.com/r/TikTokCringe/comments/1d14916/apparently_different_comments_show_up_on_videos/, accessed 31 Aug 2024.

63 Jan Kietzmann et al., 'Deepfakes: Trick or treat?' (2019) On the Horizon.

64 'The disturbing trend of state media use of deepfakes' [2023] The Conversation https://theconversation.com/the-disturbing-trend-of-state-media-use-of-deepfakes-203368, accessed 30 Aug 2024.

generations of users may be made to live in a climate where they could not be assured of the veracity of any image or video as they could be easily manipulated.[65] There are technological measures that can be developed further in order to detect a manipulated image or video as well as to preclude manipulation through technological protection measures.[66] However, this technology is still in the process of being developed and faces the inherent challenge of ensuring that it stays up to date with new developments in technology that would make it more and more difficult to identify a deepfake.

An example of the nefarious use of deepfake technology is the use of an AI international news anchor by the government of Venezuela.[67] Venezuela used an AI news anchor to report favourably on certain actions taken by the government, as if done by international media outlets. This type of activity carries with it two main harms. For one, it provides a pretence of validation for the activities of the government, on the part of the international community.[68] Second, when sources could be said to originate from outside one's country and in favour of the actions of a government, it could change the direction of internal sentiments of the people of the country. By adding validation to actions hitherto unaccepted, it could gain traction and distort the marketplace of ideas and even tip the scales in a different direction than in which the conversation may have travelled had it not been manipulated by the use of AI.

d) Overreliance of Younger Generations on Social Media to Obtain Information

Another important aspect that makes younger and future generations more vulnerable to be misled online in the information they receive which would impact the conversations they engage in, is their *dependence* on social

65 Grafanaki (n 2) 131–2.

66 For an example see Shawn Shan et al., 'Glaze: Protecting Artists from Style Mimicry by Text-to-Image Models' [2023] https://www.researchgate.net/publication/368362026_GLAZE_Protecting_Artists_from_Style_Mimicry_by_Text-to-Image_Models, accessed 1 Dec 2025, which speaks of the use of a style cloak named Glaze, which creates disturbances in images making it difficult for generative AI to be trained on the images.

67 The Conversation (n 64).

68 ibid.

media as *the* source to get their information.[69] Previously, reliance was placed on newspapers that provided high-quality fact-checked content with reputations that would suffer if false information was circulated.[70] One of the topics people are most likely to search for on Facebook are 'news and current affairs'.[71] As was shown under section (a), the main aim of social media is to keep users on the platform as opposed to providing them with verified high-quality content. Therefore, this puts at risk generations of social media users that turn to social media and only social media to obtain information, which would in turn be the source of the conversations they engage in online.

With these unique and pronounced online harms in mind, I turn to who should regulate expression online to mitigate and, if possible, eliminate said harms.

IV. Who should Regulate Expression Online?

With the conclusion reached in the previous sub-section that there is a need for social media platforms to be regulated, this sub-section turns to the question of who should be the epistemic authority that carries out such regulation. I consider whether it should be state actors, social media companies themselves or a different stakeholder. I conclude that it should be a combination of state actors, social media platforms and social media users.

1. State Actors as Sole Regulators of Online Expression: Doubts of Impartiality

State actors may not be suitable to be the sole regulators of speech online for several reasons. Out of them, I argue, the most potent is their vested

69 See Patty (n 14) 103–105 for a comprehensive discussion on the importance of social media for political discussion; Grafanaki (n 2) 113.

70 I concede, however, that even among newspapers there has been 'yellow journalism' which refers to a style of over-sensationalised reporting. For more details see Richard L. Kaplan, 'Yellow Journalism' in Wolfgang Donsbach (ed), *The International Encyclopedia of Communication* (2008).

71 Katherine Haan and Kiran Aditham, 'Is social media the new Google? Gen Z turn to Google 25% less than Gen X when searching' [2024] Forbes https://www.forbes.com/advisor/business/software/social-media-new-google/, accessed 31 Aug 2024.

interest in promoting messages favourable to their public image and impeding information that they feel cast them in a bad light. This political bias, which might stifle the freedom of expression, can be shown best through a case study of Sri Lanka.

Sri Lanka enacted its Online Safety Act[72] in 2024. This Act was enacted to 'provide safety from prohibited statements made online' among other purposes.[73] Prohibited statements include statements that are false,[74] amount to contempt,[75] wantonly give rise to provocation to cause a riot,[76] disturb a religious assembly,[77] outrage religious feelings,[78] lead to online cheating,[79] circulate false reports with the intent to cause mutiny or an offence against the state etc.[80] and communicate statements to cause harassment.[81]

While the legislation, on its face, might be defended, its possibility to stifle speech in problematic ways for the benefit of legislative actors can be seen through certain statements captured in the Hansard following its second reading in parliament. Based on some statements made by Members of Parliament (MPs), the legislation appears to be driven by frustrations faced by MPs due to statements made online that they feel are disparaging of their reputations, which have led to their family members being denied medication and opportunities to pursue education.[82] However, the willingness to pick and choose which speech they find to be conducive, and which not, has the potential to drastically impact the freedom of expression.

In 2022, one of the largest socio-political mobilisations of citizens took place in Sri Lanka that resulted in the resignation of the then-President.

72 No. 9 of 2024.
73 Preamble: 'to establish the online safety commission; to provide safety from prohibited statements made online; to prevent the use of online accounts and inauthentic online accounts for prohibited purposes; to make provisions to identify and declare online locations used for prohibited purposes in Sri Lanka; to suppress the financing and other support of communication of prohibited statements and for matters connected therewith or incidental thereto'.
74 Section 12.
75 Section 13.
76 Section 14.
77 Section 15.
78 Section 16.
79 Section 17.
80 Section 19.
81 Section 20.
82 Parliamentary Debates (Hansard) 24.01.2024 Vol 310 No 2, 194-6.

During the reading of the Online Safety Bill in parliament, MPs blamed the success of the historic protests on the work of 'cowards' hiding behind fake accounts.[83] With regard to an unrelated incident, an MP spoke of his efforts to pursue someone who had posted a disparaging statement about him online.[84] Reference was also made to comedian *Natasha Edirisooriya* against whom a case was filed[85] to convict her for certain statements supposedly made by her against Buddhists during a comedy show.[86] One may opine that the compounded message these statements made in parliament convey is a need to silence certain speech that the legislature finds to be unsuitable. This would inherently go against the marketplace of ideas in which a problematic statement may be countered by another statement, leading to debate that would finally allow the public to land on the truth or, rather, their perception of what the truth is, which is considered to be a cornerstone of democracy.[87]

In response to the enactment of the Online Safety Act, Meta, Google, Apple and Amazon threatened to exit the country. The legislation also received condemnation of the United Nations Human Rights Council and various other international organisations.[88] However, despite these threats and disapprovals, the Online Safety Act stands enacted today. While the implementation of the Act remains to be seen, it carries the possibility for the state to utilise the legislation for benevolent purposes but, unfortunately, also leaves potential for governments to censor the public's speech in order to only spread messages they deem appropriate.

Therefore, this case study illustrates that to place the power to regulate expression online solely in the hands of the state could prove dangerous and undesirable.

2. Social Media Companies as Sole Regulators of Expression Online: Clash with Profit-maximisation and Vested Interests

Much like states, social media too is not free of political bias due to competing interests, coupled with 'strong economic pressures related to preserving

83 ibid 203.
84 ibid 194-5.
85 This was referred to in parliament and was endorsed, ibid 197.
86 See Bail Application, Colombo High Court Case No HCEBA/1335/2023 05.07.2023.
87 Mill (n 14).
88 Hansard (n 82) 200.

relationships with advertisers'.[89] *Patty* points to three reasons why allegations of censorship on social media platforms should raise serious concerns. For one, the power social media companies hold is exceptional and represents a major concentration of control over a significant amount of speech. Second, he points out that it is reasonable to conclude that many systems that have been put in place to regulate content on these platforms have been programmed to be politically liberal. Third and finally, because these platforms are private, their actions were pointed out to be generally outside the scope of protections granted in constitutions.[90]

In fact, numerous allegations have been raised against social media companies for leaning towards one ideology when it comes to censoring as opposed to another and programming its algorithms to block content belonging to opposing ideologies from consumers.[91] Therefore, much like governments of countries, social media too does not appear to be immune to the service of various political biases, ideological prejudices, and other vested interests.

3. Solution: A Combined Effort

This section puts forward a list of stakeholders that I argue would need to build a nuanced web of accountability for social media platforms in order to ensure it remains a space for continued conversation for future generations, regardless of its content. To leave the online space completely unregulated is not a feasible option as it could be a breeding ground for dangerous crimes, especially perpetrated against the young. However, in a similar vein, to leave the regulation of expression online to governments may also be problematic as it may leave space for governments to censor messages, which they deem harmful to their public image, and promote those, which advance their standing among their potential electorate. Unfortunately, social media companies, too, do not appear to be immune to these interests. As a predominantly money-oriented industry, the allegiance of social media companies lies with those channels that provide them the greatest revenues through advertising their products or services, as well as,

89 Patty (n 14).
90 ibid.
91 This is one of the key arguments that was made in *Prager Univ. v. Google LLC,* No 17-CV-06064-LHK, 2018 WL 1471939 (N.D. Cal. Mar. 26, 2018) analysed in Patty (n 14) 118–121.

at times, ones that align with their ideological biases. What remains are the users of platforms. Users of social media would have the most organically aligned interests in ensuring that the online space retains its character as a place where ideas can thrive. However, users would have little chance to ensure this takes place if they stand alone.

I argue that states, social media platforms, and their users should all come together in order to ensure that expression that takes place online continues to be one where ideas can be discussed without fear or favour. I argue that this may be done best through seven key methods in the part that follows.

V. How Should Social Media be Regulated and Managed to Optimise Free Speech Online for Future Generations?

Further to the suggestion put forward in Part IV which would include a consortium of stakeholders in regulating and promoting a marketplace of ideas online, the sections that follow put forward seven suggestions on how this may be implemented: (1.) preclusion of the creation of monopolies of social media companies through competition law, (2.) allowance for different social media platforms to decide on their censorship policies, (3.) introduction of regulations for mandatory public disclosure of censorship measures of social media platforms, (4.) educating the public so that social media platforms respecting the freedom of expression carry greater brand value in the market, (5.) government regulation on exposure of children to technology, (6.) platform self-regulation and, finally, (7.) good conduct of present users of online spaces to set a good example for future generations.

1. Preclusion of the Creation of Monopolies of Social Media Platforms by State Regulation

One effective solution to entrench free speech online would be to ensure that consumers have a place filled with choices in order to engage in speech online. To this end, governments could enact competition law to ensure that a monopoly of expression is avoided. This would be desirable because a monopoly or even an oligarchy would carry the risk of consumers having little choice to 'walk away' even if the predominant platform has problematic forms of censorship.

Balkin recommends a 'sort of social media federalism', where there would be many small social media platforms, space for new startups to enter the market and he even goes as far as to recommend that functions relating to platforms, which are currently performed by the same company, should be separated.[92] One example would be a situation in which one company engages in advertising and another company in the delivery of content on the same platform.[93] While one might argue that this may be expecting too much of platforms, the current manner in which the online space functions may constitute a good example of the diversity that I suggest to retain for the sake of future generations. It provides users with a wide array of platforms in which they may engage in speech online. The main platforms are Facebook, Instagram, Reddit, TikTok, X, LinkedIn, Pinterest and YouTube, which allow for different kinds of expression depending on the preference of the user. It is this availability of alternatives that keeps each platform accountable and mindful about the fact that problematic behaviour on its part may motivate consumers to abandon its services and pick another. A recent example of this would be how X 'went offline' in Brazil – the country with the fifth largest population in the digital world – following *Elon Musk's* refusal to comply with the laws of the country.[94] Due to this, the Supreme Court of Brazil blocked the platform.[95] This resulted in users opting to use a rival network, Bluesky, which reported 500,000 new users within two days.[96]

In fact, X's decreased popularity following the shutdown of certain journalists' accounts by *Musk* (although later reinstated)[97] and his statements during the riots in the United Kingdom[98] may constitute proof that no social media company is and should be indestructible. Consumers should

92 Balkin (n 12) 91.

93 ibid.

94 Tom Phillips, 'X goes offline in Brazil after Elon Musk's refusal to comply with local laws' [2024] The Guardian https://www.theguardian.com/technology/article/2024/aug/31/x-offline-brazil-elon-musk, accessed 31 Aug 2024.

95 ibid.

96 ibid.

97 Nikki McCann Ramirez and Charisma Madarang, 'Elon 'free speech' Musk un-suspends accounts of journalists who criticized him' [2022] RollingStone https://www.rollingstone.com/music/music-news/elon-musk-twitter-journalists-banned-1234648351/, accessed 31 Aug 2024.

98 Grace Gollasch, 'X reputation falls to lowest level since Musk takeover' [2024] MarketingWeek https://www.marketingweek.com/x-reputation-falls/, accessed 27 Oct 2024.

have the power and agency to walk away and resort to alternatives if they find the platform's conduct unacceptable. Furthermore, apart from laws to prevent monopolies, arrangements of state support for online social media startups have the potential to increase choices for consumers and further the marketplace of ideas.

2. Social Media Platforms to Decide their Own Censorship Schemes

Leading from the above suggestion of having a variety of platforms in the market, another potential solution would be that these platforms carry with them different environments that consumers can choose in order to express themselves. This would be desirable because in order to create a lively online space for speech we would need different platforms 'with many different affordances, and many different ways for individuals to participate in and make culture.'[99] This goes beyond merely having 'diverse and antagonistic sources of information' to 'diverse affordances, value systems, and innovations'.[100] Accordingly, in line with the suggestion above, the regulation of the state would only go so far as to preclude the creation of monopolies and, to the extent possible, oligarchies. It should refrain from mandating how different platforms should regulate expression online.

While a completely uncensored environment would be most conducive for a marketplace of ideas, this may be too much to ask of social media companies. The next best option would be to allow the different social media companies to decide not only on their schemes of censorship but also on the different affordances and value systems[101] that they wish to create. This would allow for the option for users to gravitate towards the platform they feel most connected to. However, it is important to point out that this carries with it the possibility of creating echo chambers and polarisation of discourse between the platforms that are chosen by users.[102]

99 Balkin (n 12) 80.

100 ibid.

101 By value systems I refer to the goals and ideas that a platform would deem important. Values may range from brutal honesty, to providing uplifting content to individuals, revealing scandals and holding people to account and providing people with vocational opportunities. Each platform may have different values in mind and have conversations that promote those goals.

102 See Amy Mitchell et al., 'Political Polarization & Media Habits', Pew Research Ctr.: Journalism & Media, (21 Oct 2014) https://perma.cc/ATE3-U48G as cited in Patty (n 14) 136.

Nevertheless, this still leaves the option open for users to visit different platforms should they want to be exposed to different ideologies.

3. Mandatory Disclosure of Censorship Schemes through State Regulation

The suggestion to allow social media companies to censor and function as they please as long as there are enough platforms for users to choose from, through safeguards in competition law, can be further strengthened with the possibility for users to make an informed choice on the platform through governments enacting laws that require mandatory disclosure of the censorship schemes and value systems of the platforms. In fact, sometimes, social media companies themselves seem to be taking the lead on this with *Elon Musk's* voluntary move to reveal former censorship measures taken by pre-*Musk* leadership.[103] Known as the 'Twitter files', *Musk* declared that he plans to reveal former censorship activities to the public in order to ensure transparency and to transform X into a haven for free speech.[104] However, unfortunately, there is also some sentiment that what is being revealed as Twitter files is nothing novel, that they are small excerpts chosen by journalists who have been handpicked by *Musk*, with the excerpts being released to the public without context.[105]

Nevertheless, this move was revealed to be very desirable for users of X. A mandatory disclosure would allow for users to understand to what extent their content may be shielded or promoted on a specific platform and choose where to express themselves accordingly. Especially when it comes to children, due to mandatory disclosures, parents would be able to understand the safest options for their children, based on children's evolving capacities.[106]

An important aspect to keep in mind is that, when it comes to disclosures, while the complicated coding that allows for censoring may be released to the public, the relevant code should also be disclosed in a simple

---

103 Bruce Golding, 'Elon Musk warns evidence of Twitter censorship "may have been deleted"' [2022] New York Post https://nypost.com/2022/12/08/elon-musk-vows-to-release-everything-on-twitter-censorship/, accessed 31 Aug 2024.

104 ibid.

105 Shannon Bond, 'Elon Musk is using Twitter Files to discredit foes and push conspiracy theories' [2022] NPR https://www.npr.org/2022/12/14/1142666067/elon-musk-is-using-the-twitter-files-to-discredit-foes-and-push-conspiracy-theor, accessed 29 Aug 2025.

106 Article 5 of the UN General Assembly, *Convention on the Rights of the Child*, United Nations, Treaty Series, vol 1577, p 3, 20 Nov 1989.

manner that can be understood by users who may not be technologically proficient to an advanced degree, but have a basic functional knowledge of the relevant technology in order to make an informed decision of the platform they would want to choose.

4. Attribution of a Higher Brand Value by Users to Expression-respecting Platforms

We now arrive at the role that should be played by the users of social media to safeguard the space online which they use to express themselves. As a first step, social media users should be educated on the importance of safeguarding expression online. Secondly, users need to stand together in the importance they attribute to the aspect of respect for free speech online and attach greater brand value to platforms that allow for the functioning of a marketplace of ideas. Exercising the freedom to leave platforms that do not allow for their freedom of expression and actively seeking out platforms that respect speech would signal to platforms that speech-respecting platforms are valued by users. Such action would compel social media platforms to demonstrate an interest in guaranteeing user speech online, due to the importance placed on this aspect by users and their willingness to attach a low brand value to platforms that fail to respect speech online.

5. Legislative Regulation on Exposure of Children to Technology

The suggestions above centre around what can be done to protect the digital space itself in order to allow future generations to engage in speech in it. Now, if we turn to the individual or the member of a future generation that would use this space, there are steps that can be taken by governments to ensure that these prospective members, i.e. children, are protected from the harms of the digital sphere if they were to engage in speech in it.

Perhaps, one of the most advisable solution to protect future generations in their engagement of free expression online would be to delay the opportunity to participate in the intense and vigorous marketplace of ideas until they are better equipped to safely and independently function in such a space. While this may be paternalistic and distrustful of children's ability to appropriately conduct themselves online, there are evidence-based findings of psychologists of the pitfalls of premature and extensive exposure to the digital world.[107]

Haidt recommends that the best way to protect future generations of children from the harmful mental health effects of social media is to bring back play-based childhoods instead of phone-based childhoods. A study published in JAMA Pediatrics has shown that 'excessive screen time in a child's first year [may result in] lower cognitive skills later in life' as their attention and executive functions will be lowered.[108] Therefore, exposure that occurs too soon and in considerable amounts can impact meaningful engagement that a member of the future generation is able to conjure up in later life. This would result in the marketplace of ideas becoming weak and unproductive due to its prospective members' lower cognitive skills and inability to have focused, well-reasoned and meaningful conversations.

To this end, apart from parental screen controls, content filters, and supervised use that can be resorted to for the sake of children as they begin to use online spaces, governments could mandate that certain portions of a child's life be spent without the use of smartphones. Government-mandated prohibitions of access to smart devices during school hours would be a step in the right direction. *Haidt* refers to this as 'phone-free schools'.[109] Secondly, setting a reasonably high age limit to create social media accounts, coupled with the responsibility being placed on tech companies to ensure that age verification is carried out, would allow for greater safety for children to grow up online. Thirdly, increased promotion of the recommended extent of screen time for children of various ages would also be helpful in navigating how much use is too much use of the online space.[110]

---

107 This was discussed previously under section III(2)(b) citing Haidt (n 4).

108 Becca Stanek, 'How much screen time is too much for kids' [2023] Forbes Health https://www.forbes.com/health/family/how-much-screen-time-kids/, accessed 31 Aug 2024.

109 Haidt (n 4). Sri Lanka is a good example of an adverse attitude to access to and use of phone in schools. In fact, such use has been banned in both public and private schools. See Circular 0044/2025 'Banning the use of an access to personal mobile phones by pupils during the school day' gov.ie (12 June 2025) https://gov.ie/en/department-of-education/circulars/banning-the-use-of-and-access-to-personal-mobile-phones-by-pupils-during-the-school-day/#:~:text=The%20circular%20informs%20primary%20schools,guidance%20on%20implementing%20this%20requirement, accessed 19 July 2025.

110 Stanek (n 108): For children under 2 years, screen time should be very limited; for 2–5 years, 1 hour per day; for 5–8 years, monitor usage; for 9+ years, media usage

Children who have been protected from the perils and deceptive aspects of the online space at a young age can grow to become adults who have engaged in three-dimensional, real-world experiences and have matured into well-rounded adults who would be able to better manoeuvre their way in whichever digital platform they may find themselves in. While there are many different aspects that would create an impact on the mental health of a child and adult, social media has been shown to be one that may carry some weight. Therefore, in the event the mental well-being of children is zealously guarded, especially with regard to what they are exposed to on social media, in the most formative years of their life, it would leave open a greater possibility to have children's upbringing enriched through experiences enjoyed off screens, thereby giving them a better chance to turn into well-matured adolescents and adults who can be themselves and engage in meaningful conversations online.

6. The Need for a Fundamental Shift: Users' Self-regulation on Platforms

Taking the cue from the previous suggestion, while the responsibility to ensure that children are not introduced to the digital world too soon and at unsustainable levels is placed on the parent, the government, and the social media platform, I also suggest that, along with children's evolving capacity, children should be provided the opportunity to self-regulate.

However, this could only come about through a fundamental shift that would decentralise current lives from the world online. The digital world has now become an alternative reality for many whose lives revolve around TikTok trends, dangerous pranks and consuming carefully curated content that by no means reflect real lives. It is only if children are removed from this alternative reality and brought back into the real world filled with toil, trouble, slow moments and boredom, that we can confidently pass on the ability to children to control themselves and hold future generations accountable when they are engaging in varied kinds of speech online. Similar to how children are given greater responsibility and autonomy as they grow older to make their own choices, we must make children aware that they are being trusted with a very potent resource, which is the online space, and that their conduct will have an impact on their futures, to some

---

should become a conversation. See Haidt (n 4) for discussion on age limits and screen time.

extent mould the kind of people they grow into and the way in which they exchange ideas with their fellow humans online.

Through educating children about the perils and pitfalls of social media, how it can be used intelligently, and trusting adolescents to handle the responsibility for their conduct online would build more confident, well-adjusted and self-assured online users. Through learning the right skills and mindset, they would be able to avoid abuse and exploitation through dangerous tactics of manipulation that social media platforms resort to. This would help to cure, or at least control, the sometimes unhealthy and toxic nature of the digital sphere and lead to a healthier relationship between future generations and the online space that would hold said generations in good stead in navigating this complex domain.

7. Setting an Example: Duty of Present Generations of Users towards Future Generations of Online Users

While all six suggestions above centre on the *protection* of *future* generations, I also turn to how the *use* of the online space by *current* generations can be done in a manner that sets an example for future generations. In order for the suggestions above to be effective, current generations which are of age, full capacity, and engage in speech online, must be mindful of their actions, words, the ideas that they spread, speak their truth, and use the marketplace of ideas for its intended purpose which is to engage in conversation with their fellow co-citizens in a respectful manner. To excuse current generations from online behaviour that is harmful to free speech would be to exempt entire generations from the responsibilities that should have been imposed on them long ago. To only impose responsibilities on future generations to ensure the online space remains conducive for speech would be inadequate. It is only if current generations mindfully protect the online space and leave it in a condition in which future generations can engage in speech online that free speech may thrive in the digital sphere for years to come.[111]

111 In fact, since recently there has been found to be a trend of people leaving social media and pursuing interests offline due to its increasingly unattractive nature: Jordan, 'Social media is dead and everyone really is leaving now' Spirited Earthling [2025] https://www.spiritedearthling.com/media-self-care/social-media-is-dead-and-everyone-really-is-leaving-now, accessed 31 Oct 2025. If more and more online

All seven suggestions mentioned above need to be cumulatively accomplished in order to ensure a marketplace of ideas online, which would allow future generations to have free conversations about diverse topics. The responsibilities enunciated above fall on platforms, the state, as well as current and future users of the online space. The third revision to the United Nations Declaration on Future Generations includes the need to create inclusive and equitable access to knowledge as well as generations that are imbued with critical thinking skills that will hold them in good stead.[112] To this end, it is important that regulation and other socio-cultural tools at the disposal of governments, platforms, as well as the users of today and tomorrow are brought together in order to build a better, safer and more vibrant online space for expression.

VI. Conclusion

While the debate surrounding the freedom of expression and how best to facilitate it, given competing interests, has been one that is age-old, even with regard to the online space, this article addressed a previously unaddressed dimension which is how best to safeguard expression online for the benefit of future generations. It paid special attention to the trends that can be seen in the digital generations which may be more pronounced in the future to come. I maintain that future generations that will be engaging in speech online will be particularly vulnerable due to heightened levels of scarcity of attention, anxiety, dangerous and manipulative technology as well as dependence and overreliance on getting information from any source online without double checking for their veracity. Addressing these harms will have to be multi-faceted, and collective action can be taken on

users were to turn away from the online space due to its toxicities, it would dampen the digital marketplace of ideas.

112 Declaration on Future generations, REV3 https://www.un.org/sites/un2.un.org/files/sotf-declaration-on-future-generations-rev3.pdf, accessed 31 Aug 2024 ('36. Ensuring inclusive and equitable access to knowledge, science and information, while promoting innovation, critical thinking and life-skills to create generations of citizens that are agents of positive change and transformation' and '30. Harness the benefits of existing, new and emerging technologies and mitigate the associated risks through effective, inclusive and equitable governance at all levels, scaling up collaboration to bridge the digital divides within and between developed and developing countries, increasing capacity building efforts in the field of science, technology and innovation, and promoting the transfer of technology on mutually agreed terms.').

the part of the state, social media platforms, and consumers by minimising the dangers these aspects would have for the ability of future generations to have informative, and meaningful conversations online. Some solutions that this article puts forward are: the preclusion of social media platform monopolies and oligarchies; allowing for social media platforms to decide on their speech policies; mandatory disclosure of said policies and algorithms in a simple and understandable manner; educating users on the importance of respecting free speech online and building a culture in which companies that respect free speech carry a higher brand value in the market; regulation of children's exposure to social media; children's and adolescent's self-regulation; and, finally, ensuring that the use of the online sphere by current generations sets a conducive example for future generations to follow.

The European 'Regulatory Turn' towards Big Tech Platforms through the Lens of Digital Constitutionalism

*Giulia Taraborrelli**

This paper will draw connections between the development of internet regulation, the theoretical foundations of digital constitutionalism, and the recent 'regulatory turn' endeavoured by the European Union, as evidenced by the Digital Markets Act and the Digital Services Act, both approved in 2022. The research will examine how internet and platform regulation have emerged and have been shaped over the past decades, and what the similarities and differences between US and EU approaches to the issue are. Special emphasis will be placed on the freedom of expression in the digital environment, which serves as a key test for the extent to which rights and freedoms are being compromised by platform dynamics. Finally, the paper will examine Europe's new constitutional approach to internet and platform regulation, which marks a step forward in a complex strategy to manage the digital environment while preserving European democratic values and fundamental rights.

I. Introduction

The progressive diffusion of new technologies and the resulting socio-economic metamorphosis have inspired the conceptualisation of our age as the subject of the 'fourth industrial revolution',[1] which differs from the previous revolutions for having questioned the place traditionally attributed to fundamental liberties and to the state.

In a relatively short period of time, the novel dynamics driven by the Internet have had a disruptive impact on the sphere of rights and freedoms of users, while simultaneously giving rise to a complex relationship between public and private authority within cyberspace. The gradual concentration of power in the hands of a few digital platforms developed by large

* PhD student, Faculty of Political Science, La Sapienza University of Rome.

1 Luciano Floridi, *The Fourth Revolution: How the Infosphere Is Reshaping Human Reality* (OUP 2014).

technology companies (hereafter Big Tech companies) has resulted in the evolution of these entities into organisations of unprecedented scale and influence, largely due to their immense capabilities and reach.[2] A favourable regulatory regime, characterised by a lack of constraints and a significant number of incentives, has enabled digital platforms and new online services to become vertically integrated networks with oligopolistic or monopolistic tendencies, leaving society and public authorities with an inevitable slow reaction to, and anticipation of, this new context.[3]

The transition of large multinationals operating in the digital sector from economic power to a *para-public* – albeit formally private – nature has been attributed to their unprecedented global influence.[4] The emergence of these multinational corporations is related to the pervasiveness of the digitisation process and to the enormous amount of user-generated data, as well as the development of increasingly sophisticated algorithmic systems to collect and process it.[5] The distinction between the digital environment and seemingly analogous phenomena is attributable to the fact that the economic model of major technological corporations is founded on the establishment of extensive online communities, which function as a surrogate public sphere. This model has profound implications for the regulation of information on a global scale and the exercise of the freedom of expression.[6] Digital platforms wield considerable economic influence that extends far beyond the market, profoundly impacting the evolving reality of the public sphere and fundamental rights. Such a dynamic can be characterised as 'multidimensional in its nature and universal in its extent', thereby prompting a re-evaluation of the role of the state order in the digital realm.[7]

---

2 Kean Birch and Kelly Bronson, 'Big Tech' (2022) 31 Science as Culture 1.

3 Luisa Torchia, *Lo stato digitale. Una introduzione* (Il Mulino 2022) 13.

4 Luca Belli and Jamila Venturini, 'Private ordering and the rise of terms of service as cyber-regulation' (2016) 5 Internet Policy review 1.

5 Marijn Janssen and George Kuk, 'The challenges and limits of big data algorithms in technocratic governance' (2016) 33 Government Information Quarterly 371.

6 Miguel Poiares Maduro and Francisco de Abreu Duarte, 'Regulating Big Tech Will Take Pluralism and Institutions' [2021] Euronews <https://www.euronews.com/2021/10/07/regulating-big-tech-will-take-pluralism-and-institutions-view> accessed on 10 June 2025: 'Previous monopolists were not involved in the regulation of speech, nor in the dissemination of knowledge that shapes public opinion. But for Big Tech companies, fostering a large community – similar to a public sphere – is key to the business model'.

7 Luisa Torchia, 'Poteri pubblici e privati nel mondo digitale' (2024) 1 il Mulino, Rivista trimestrale di cultura e di politica 14, 20-21.

In the light of this context, this research aims at analysing whether the recent European regulatory efforts in the digital field are effectively contributing to the protection of fundamental rights. Additionally, this paper will investigate if such regulatory efforts prove successful in creating a future-proof framework, adequate to inspire other regulations globally, and effectively change the course of action of Big Tech companies.

The research paper is structured as follows: the first section will attempt to reconstruct the reasons behind the development of Internet regulation and the theoretical foundations of digital constitutionalism, tracing the evolution of these concepts from the late 20th century to the present day. The discrepancy between the United States (US) and the European Union (EU) approaches to this issue will be discussed, highlighting their initial alignment and their subsequent divergence. Secondly, the research will examine the impact of digital platforms on the global freedom of expression, focusing on the main threats to pluralism on the Internet. It will also consider the role of content moderation and the exercise of quasi-legislative and quasi-judicial functions by digital platforms. Thirdly, the paper will address the European Union's 'regulatory turn', which is trying to set new rules and standards for digital platforms, thus, circumventing the establishment of a model of self-regulation based on the exercise of private power. The research will also address the consolidation of Europe's global leadership in the regulation of the digital phenomenon and the avoidance of fragmentation within European Member States' initiatives in the management of the relationship between platforms and users. Eventually, after analysing some of the regulatory issues that public authorities need to address, the essential conclusion evidenced by the essay is that a proactive regulatory approach is vital and required to safeguard the democratic and pluralistic sphere in the digital environment, as well as to develop a sustainable and lasting European policy strategy.

II. The Need for Regulation and the Rise of Digital Constitutionalism

This section provides an account of the evolution of the scholarship surrounding the regulation of Internet and digital platforms. The development is charted from the early utopias that viewed cyberspace as a free and unregulated domain, and which exerted a significant influence on the US approach to online intermediaries in the late 1990s. The US Government's decision to promote competition and withhold responsibility for platforms has been mirrored by the EU's endeavours to regulate privacy and e-commerce, resulting in Big Tech becoming significant market and social entities. The relationship between major technology companies and public authorities is nowadays arguably without precedent, raising significant concerns about the balance of power and the respect of citizens' fundamental rights in democratic societies. This situation has prompted a scholarly response that calls for regulatory intervention in cyberspace, with the aim of reintegrating political considerations and perspectives into the governance of the Internet, leading to the development of the body of literature known as 'digital constitutionalism'.

1. Early Visions of the Internet

In the early 1990s, dominant ideas saw cyberspace as an unregulated domain, free from any external interference from national authorities or legal constraints, fuelling over time market optimistic perceptions and an aversion for regulation.[8] It has been suggested that the Internet operates within a self-regulatory framework that transcends the conventional boundaries of law and government regulation: such a framework, which may be described as a *Lex Informatica*, constitutes the technological capabilities and system design choices that shape the online environment.[9] As a result, the idea emerged that national authorities could not, by their very nature, regulate such a digital world that has no physical territory or specific population.[10]

From a constitutional perspective, the functioning of cyberspace has been associated with the liberal vocation of the Internet, leading to the need to protect the right to participate in virtual society from potential undue state influence.[11] This necessity reinforced the argument that if na-

8 Marco Betzu, 'Poteri pubblici e poteri private nel mondo digitale' (2021) 2 La Rivista. Gruppo di Pisa 1; Elettra Bietti, 'A Genealogy of Digital Platform Regulation' (2023) 7 Geo. L. Tech. Rev. 1.

9 Joel R. Reidenberg, 'Lex Informatica: The Formulation of Information Policy Rules through Technology' (1997) 76 Texas Law Review 533; Lawrence Lessig, *Code. Version 2.0* (Basic Books 2006).

10 Against the idea that cyberspace will, or should, resist all governmental regulation, see Jack L. Goldsmith, 'Against Cyberanarchy' (1998) 65 Chicago Law Review 1199, who aimed to explain in general terms how traditional tools of jurisdiction and choice of law apply to cyberspace transactions.

11 About the view of the Internet as a new channel of communication that promised to overcome the problem of concentration of power in traditional media, Jack M. Balkin, 'Old-School/New-School Speech Regulation' (2014) 127 Harvard Law Review

tional governments can undermine the Internet and its freedom, then the time has come, not for restrictive regulation, but rather for the opposite, hence the requirement of constitutional guarantees of Internet freedoms, an 'Internet Bill of Rights'.[12] Such an approach, which has been successful until recently,[13] can be linked to the theory of a *freedom of information*, developed by the Italian doctrine in 1981, whose ideological matrix lies in the conception of a new liberalism, understood as the yeast of a liberal civilisation promoted by the technological revolution, and which developed on the basis of a new dimension of the right to personal freedom.[14]

A first attitude towards technology within the Western world at the end of the last century considered the digital environment as a vehicle for economic growth and a novel space for freedom of expression, as opposed to the means of censorship perpetuated by traditional media.[15] The conspicuous proliferation of digital platform monopolies over the past two decades can be attributed to the initial optimism surrounding decentralised networks that characterised the early Internet utopias. If originally freedom was the prevailing norm, later such utopias diverged into an enclosed

---

2296; Marianne I. Franklin, *Digital Dilemmas: Power, Resistance, and the Internet* (OUP 2013).

12 Stefano Rodotà, 'Una Costituzione per Internet?' (2010) 3 Politica del diritto 177. About the issues raised by an 'Internet Bill of Rights', see Giovanna De Minico 'About the Regulation of Internet: Constitutional Issues, Models and Challenges' (2017) 3 Osservatorio sulle fonti 1. For a broad perspective about the significant number of Internet bills of rights have emerged around the world, Edoardo Celeste, *Digital Constitutionalism. The Role of Internet Bills of Rights* (Routledge 2022).

13 Lex Gill, Dennis Redeker and Urs Gasser, 'Towards Digital Constitutionalism? Mapping Attempts to Craft an Internet Bill of Rights' (2018) 80 International Communication Gazette 302 argue: 'The idea of an "Internet Bill of Rights" is by no means a new one: in fact, serious efforts to draft such a document can be traced at least as far back as the mid-1990s. Though the form, function and scope of such initiatives has evolved, the concept has had remarkable staying power, and now— two full decades later—principles which were once radically aspirational have begun to crystallize into law. [...] we propose a unified term to describe these efforts using the umbrella of "digital constitutionalism" and conduct an analysis of thirty initiatives spanning from 1999 to 2015'.

14 Vittorio Frosini, 'La protezione della riservatezza nella società informatica' in Nicola Matteucci (ed), *Privacy e banche dei dati* (Il Mulino 1981); Tommaso E. Frosini, 'Il diritto costituzionale di accesso a Internet' (2011) 1 Rivista dell'Associazione italiana dei Costituzionalisti 1.

15 David R. Johnson and David Post, 'Law and Borders: The Rise of Law in Cyberspace' (1996) 48 Stanford Law Review 1367; John P. Barlow, 'A Declaration of Independence of Cyberspace' (1996) Electronic Frontier Found <https://www.eff.org/cyberspace-independence> accessed 10 June 2025.

economy, controlled by a few private actors, and endowed with only fragile safeguards for individuals.[16] To understand the reasons behind this reversal, it is necessary to examine the legal mechanisms that have laid the foundations for the extent of the powers gained by major technology companies, primarily based in the US, both in economic and social terms.

2. The US Approach to Media

The US Telecommunications Act (1996) broadly encouraged competition in traditional electronic media, voice telephony, and data services. Over time, it allowed technological companies to flourish without the typically imposed constraints, such as price controls, restrictions on access to infrastructure and services, and limitations on market position and growth.[17] The mix of steady deregulation and the permission of ever-increasing concentration proved to be crucial in facilitating the development of the emerging technological companies from start-ups to global platforms, and thus, justifying their sustained expansion both in terms of investment and market size.[18]

Another fundamental piece of the puzzle is the American approach to online intermediaries, based on the provisions of Section 230 of the Communication Decency Act (1996)[19] – known as 'the twenty-six words that created the Internet'[20] – and Section 512 of the Digital Millennium Copyright Act (1998)[21]. The peculiarity of the American legal framework is rooted in a general scepticism towards regulation and an explicit opposition to any form of content-based regulation that might distinguish between material legitimately accessible in cyberspace and material accessible in

16 Debra Howcroft and Brian Fitzgerald, 'From Utopia to Dystopia: the twin faces of the Internet' (1998) 2 Information Systems: Current Issues and Future Changes, Proceedings of IFIP WG8 1.

17 S. 652 – Telecommunications Act of 1996, 104th Congress (1995-1996); Joseph D. Kearney and Thomas W. Merrill, 'The Great Transformation of Regulated Industries Law' (1998) 98 Columbia Law Review 1323.

18 Torchia (n 3) 14; Harold Feld, 'The case for the Digital Platform Act: Market structure and regulation of digital platforms' [2019] Roosevelt Institute <https://rooseveltinstitute.org/wp-content/uploads/2020/07/RI-Case-for-the-Digital-Platform-Act-201905.pdf> accessed 10 June 2025.

19 Communication Decency Act, 47 U.S.C., Section 230.

20 Jeff Kosseff, *The Twenty-Six Words That Created the Internet* (Cornell University Press 2019).

21 Digital Millennium Copyright Act, 17 U.S.C., Section 512.

the real world, allowing digital actors to evolve as media channels without legal accountability.[22] On the one hand, Section 230(c)(1) of the Communication Decency Act provides a safe harbour of immunity from liability for providers and users who publish information provided by third-party users, as it states: 'No provider or user of an interactive computer service shall be treated as the publisher or speaker of any information provided by another information content provider'. Furthermore, Section 230(c)(2) establishes the *Good Samaritan rule*, which ensures protection from civil liability for operators of interactive computer services in the good faith removal or moderation of third-party material they deem 'obscene, lewd, lascivious, filthy, excessively violent, harassing, or otherwise objectionable, whether or not such material is constitutionally protected'. Section 512 of the Digital Millennium Copyright Act, on the other hand, provides liability limitations for four types of online service providers, shielding them from financial liability for copyright infringement based on the actions of their users in exchange for cooperating with copyright owners to remove infringing content expeditiously and meeting certain conditions.[23] By recognising that online intermediaries are not involved in creating content, they can be allegedly exempted from liability for transmitting or hosting unlawful third-party content, promoting freedom of expression and the development of the digital environment – at least on the surface.

3. Online Intermediaries Regulation in Europe

Turning to the other side of the Atlantic, the European model for regulating online intermediaries was shaped by the aforementioned US provisions, at least prior to the binding effects of the Charter of Fundamental Rights of the European Union – which was formally proclaimed in *Nice* in December 2000 and became legally binding with the entry into force of the Treaty of

22 Oreste Pollicino, 'Di cosa parliamo quando parliamo di costituzionalismo digitale?' (2023) 3 Quaderni costituzionali 569, 578. See also Rebecca Tushnet, 'Power without Responsibility: Intermediaries and the First Amendment' (2008) 76 George Washington Law Review 986; András Koltay, 'The Protection of Freedom of Expression from Social Media Platforms' (2022) 73 Mercer Law Review 523, 541-543.

23 U.S. Copyright Office, 'Report on Section 512 of Title 17: Resources on Online Service Provider Safe Harbors and Notice-and-Takedown System', May 21, 2020, <https://www.copyright.gov/512/> accessed 10 June 2025; Thomas S. E. Hilton and Ingrid C. Ulstad, 'An Ethics Analysis of the Digital Millennium Copyright Act' (2004) 5 Issues in Information Systems 495.

Lisbon in December 2009.[24] At the end of the last century, the influence of the United States led the EU to develop a paradigm of 'digital liberalism' that was firmly based on the protection and the strengthening of Europe's fundamental economic freedoms.[25]

As evidenced by the Data Protection Directive (1995)[26] and the e-Commerce Directive (2000)[27], the EU's primary objective was to harmonise its internal market. It was assumed that a bottom-up approach to the Internet would have a more favourable impact on the EU's economic development, would avoid the imposition of excessive restrictions on the free movement of information society services and data between Member States, and thus would ultimately stimulate technological innovation.[28] The Data Protection Directive set out obligations concerning the processing of personal data. It enshrined the principle of consent and limited the ability to process personal data freely by requiring data controllers to comply with specific legal bases.[29] In comparison, the e-Commerce Directive exempted Internet service providers from liability for the unlawful conduct of third parties and prohibits Member States from imposing measures that would require the platform to exercise a general duty of supervision over the content posted by users. However, according to the e-Commerce Directive, hosting providers are not to be held liable for information or content stored by their users, unless they fail to remove or disable access to the unlawful information or content without undue delay in accordance with a «notice and takedown» procedure once they become aware of the unlawful nature of the information or content stored.[30] While both initiatives have the merit

24 Charter of Fundamental Rights of the European Union, 2000/C 364/01.

25 Giovanni De Gregorio, *Digital Constitutionalism in Europe. Reframing Rights and Powers in the Algorithmic Society* (Cambridge University Press 2022) 41.

26 Directive 95/46/EC of the European Parliament and of the Council of 24 October 1995 on the protection of individuals with regard to the processing of personal data and on the free movement of such data.

27 Directive 2000/31/EC of the European Parliament and of the Council of 8 June 2000 on certain legal aspects of information society services, in particular electronic commerce, in the Internal Market.

28 Thomas Hoffmann and Sander Sagar, 'Intermediary liability in the EU digital common market – from the E-commerce directive to the digital services act' (2021) 34 IDP 3.

29 Peter Hustinx, 'EU Data Protection Law: The Review of Directive 95/46/EC and the General Data Protection Regulation' in Marise Cremona (ed), *New Technologies and Eu Law* (OUP 2017) 123-173.

30 Lilian Edwards (ed), *The New Legal Framework for E-Commerce in Europe* (Hart 2005).

of attempting to regulate a novel phenomenon while preserving economic interests, by converging with the US model, digital liberalism has inevitably facilitated the emergence of dominant oligopolistic digital platforms.

4. A New Relationship between Public and Private Authorities

Large digital platforms have amassed considerable influence around the world because of the growing number of users and their associated data, coupled with the considerable discretion they have in moderating content and the lack of robust accountability mechanisms. Even assuming that Big Tech companies are economic actors whose main activity is the sale of services or goods, either directly or as intermediaries between service and goods providers and buyers, they have developed new and unprecedented traits, especially when compared to traditional entrepreneurial economic power: their own social and political influence.[31] Large digital platforms are, in effect, a tool for community building and for individual and collective communication, being now a substantial layer of public discourse and affecting public opinion.[32] Among the many nuances highlighted by scholars, it can be stated that while digital platforms hold potential to facilitate greater freedom of expression and participation within the public sphere, they can also contribute to the polarisation of views and the surveillance of individuals, inevitably affecting the pluralist dimension of society, with far-reaching consequences in terms of disruption of market dynamics.[33]

The rise of digital platforms has led to a significant dilution of the traditional boundaries between public and private authority, particularly in the political and economic spheres. The restriction of freedom of expression online has evolved to the stage of including not only sanctions by public authorities, but also the influence of private censorship, which is essentially almost entirely under the control of the platforms themselves. The use of advanced technologies, including artificial intelligence systems, has undoubtedly benefitted digital platforms in many ways, from enhancing

31 Torchia (n 3).

32 Miguel Poiares Maduro and Francisco de Abreu Duarte (n 6).

33 Cathy O'Neil, *Weapons of math destruction: how big data increases inequality and threatens democracy* (Penguin Books 2017); Shoshana Zuboff, *The Age of Surveillance Capitalism. The fight for a human future and the new frontier of power* (Public Affairs 2019).

efficiency to cutting marketing costs, with negative consequences for data governance and user privacy.[34]

The notion that large technology companies could amass vast influence was inconceivable in the late 1990s and early 2000s. The evolving role of the major digital platforms shows that they are no longer merely economic entities but have also become extremely pervasive private powers, competing with public institutions. In this context, it is becoming increasingly evident that the fundamental rights and democratic values that underpin our society face an uncertain future. The aforementioned digital development justifies the shift that has occurred in the European approach in recent years, which led to a growing divergence from US regulatory perspectives and the emergence of the scholarly discourse on digital constitutionalism, defined as an 'ideology that aims to establish and guarantee the existence of a normative framework for the protection of fundamental rights and the balancing of powers in the digital environment'.[35]

5. Digital Constitutionalism

At first glance, the concept of digital constitutionalism can be perceived as a complex strategy designed to integrate political considerations and perspectives back into the governance of the Internet, while at the same time providing a clear basis for political debate on the Internet based on fundamental rights and democratic principles.[36] The effort to delineate the limits of private authority within society gives rise to a particular interpretation of the function of constitutional law in its dual objective of safeguarding fundamental rights and containing the rise of power over citizens' rights.

34 Ahmed Bounfour, *Platforms and Artificial Intelligence* (Springer International 2022).

35 Edoardo Celeste, 'Digital Constitutionalism: A New Systematic Theorisation' (2019) 33 International Review of Law, Computers & Technology 76, 88; see also: Kinfe Yilma, 'Digital privacy and virtues of multilateral digital constitutionalism—preliminary thoughts' (2017) 25 International Journal of Law and Information Technology 115; Oreste Pollicino, *Judicial Protection of Fundamental Rights on the Internet. A Road Towards Digital Constitutionalism?* (Hart 2021); Giovanni De Gregorio, 'Digital Constitutionalism across the Atlantic' (2022) 11 Global Constitutionalism 297.

36 Nicolas P. Suzor, *Lawless: The Secret Rules That Govern Our Digital Lives* (Cambridge University Press 2019) 173: 'digital constitutionalism requires us to develop new ways of limiting abuses of power in a complex system that includes many different governments, businesses, and civil society organisations'.

To illustrate the main points surrounding the definition of digital constitutionalism, some commentators have suggested that it is synonymous with a form of *social constitutionalism* and is exemplified by numerous initiatives worldwide to define kinds of 'Internet Bills of Rights'.[37] Other authors, noting the growing interest of EU institutions in digital platforms, have proposed digital constitutionalism as a new phase of European constitutionalism: a strategy that focuses on safeguarding fundamental rights and democratic values was devised to mitigate the internal market imprint of the EU.[38] Sensitivity to the protection of the fundamental values within the EU has been observed also at a national level, as evidenced by the adoption by some Member States of an approach in line with the European consensus, as exemplified by developments in Germany and France.[39] Other scholars have described digital constitutionalism as an evolutionary process of constitutionalisation within the digital environment. This process, which according to them should have originated at the societal level, should have involved the formulation of new constitutional principles designed

37 Claudia Padovani and Mauro Santaniello, 'Digital Constitutionalism: Fundamental Rights and Power Limitation in the Internet Eco-System' (2018) 80 International Communication Gazette 295; Mauro Santaniello et al., 'The language of digital constitutionalism and the role of national parliaments' (2018) 80 International Communication Gazette 320.

38 As Giovanni De Gregorio argues in *Digital Constitutionalism in Europe* (n 25) 4: 'As the expression suggests, digital constitutionalism is composed by two souls. While the first term ("digital") refers to technologies based on the Internet such as automated technologies to process data or moderate content, the second ("constitutionalism") refers to the political ideology born in the eighteenth century where, according to the *Lockean* idea, the power of governments should be legally limited, and its legitimacy depends upon complying with these limitations. Despite this chronological gap, the adjective "digital" entails placing constitutionalism in a temporal and material dimension. Digital constitutionalism indeed refers to a specific timeframe, precisely the aftermath of the Internet at the end of the last century. Moreover, from a material perspective, this adjective qualifies constitutionalism, moving the focus to how digital technologies and constitutionalism affect each other. Merging the expressions "digital" and "constitutionalism" does not lead to revolutionising the pillars of modern constitutionalism. Instead, it aims to understand how to interpret the (still hidden) role of constitutional law in the algorithmic society'. About European digital constitutionalism, see also Luciano Floridi, 'The European Legislation on AI: a Brief Analysis of its Philosophical Approach' (2021) 34 Philosophy & Technology 215.

39 About the German case, see Netzwerkdurchsetzungsgesetz, 1 September 2017. About the French case, see Loi organique et loi ordinaire du 22 décembre 2018 relatives à la manipulation de l'information, 22 December 2018.

to mitigate the changes to the constitutional balance brought by digital technologies.[40]

Despite arguments that digital constitutionalism is an inappropriate label,[41] criticisms of its underlying conceptual framework,[42] and that it is inchoate, gradualist and fundamentally hortatory,[43] it is safe to state that the significance of digital constitutionalism lies in its ability to study, through the lens of the digital world, a reasoning on the dual nature of the concept of a constitution – not only as a Bill of Rights, but also as a frame of government. In sum, rather than focusing exclusively on new rights, digital constitutionalism fully embraces an examination of the dynamics that are eroding the pillars of modern constitutionalism.[44]

---

40 Celeste (n 35).

41 Massimo Luciani, 'Relazione conclusiva al Convegno del Gruppo di Pisa Il diritto costituzionale e le sfide dell'innovazione tecnologica' (2021) 3 La Rivista. Gruppo di Pisa 1, 7, which refers to a 'constitutionalism without adjectives'. According to the author, the reason for this doctrinal preference lies in the desire to preserve the traditional categories of constitutionalism. Therefore, the theorisation of a true and proper digital constitutionalism is a gamble of doubtful utility in terms of the dogmatic framing of problems; our categories should therefore remain intact even in the face of challenges such as technological innovation or the apparent dissolution of the territory.

42 Angelo Jr Golia, 'The Critique of Digital Constitutionalism' (2022) 13 Max Planck Institute for Comparative Public Law & International Law (MPIL) Research Paper <https://papers.ssrn.com/sol3/papers.cfm?abstract_id=4145813> accessed 10 June 2025, 30: 'to address the challenges posed by new technologies, [digital constitutionalism] should embrace a more explicitly critical discourse, radically questioning several assumptions of liberal, state-centred constitutional theory. In this sense, [digital constitutionalism] should be framed as a theory for the digital age and, more broadly, as an opportunity for a long-overdue reckoning of modern constitutional theory with its inner contradictions'.

43 Yilma Kinfe, 'Reimagining Digital Constitutionalism' (2025) 14 Global Constitutionalism <https://ssrn.com/abstract=5242148> accessed 10 June 2025. The author interestingly addresses criticism stemming from many works, mainly from Petros Terzis, 'Against Digital Constitutionalism' (2024) 3 European Law Open 336; Róisín Costello, 'Faux Ami? Interrogating the Normative Coherence of Digital Constitutionalism' (2023) 12 Global Constitutionalism 326; Jane Pereira and Clara Iglesias Keller, 'Digital Constitutionalism: Contradictions of a Loose Concept' (2022) 13 Revista Direito e Práxis 2649. Against the same opinions, Edoardo Celeste, 'Conceptual Approaches to Digital Constitutionalism: A Counter Critique' in Indra Spiecker, Laura Mendes and Ricardo Campos (eds), *Digital Constitutionalism. A Normative and Institutional Framework for Conflict Solving under Construction* (Nomos 2025).

44 For an overview of the perspectives of digital constitutionalism – the liberal, the societal and the global – see Francisco de Abreu Duarte, Giovanni De Gregorio and Angelo Golia, 'Perspectives on Digital Constitutionalism' in Bartosz Brozek, Olia

III. Freedom of Expression in the Digital Economy

1. Content Moderation

The key test for assessing the impact of the private power held by large digital economy corporations on constitutional principles – and thus the relevance of a constitutional approach to digital policy – lies in how online freedom of expression is currently protected in Western democracies. The notion of neutrality, formerly assumed to be an intrinsic attribute of digital platforms, has been openly challenged, raising concerns about the role of these platforms in contemporary society.[45] In the landscape of what has been called 'Big Data Capitalism',[46] a small oligopoly of private companies, predominantly based in the US, holds a leading role in the governance of the global communications space.[47] In addition to their function as infrastructure technology providers, digital platforms are the primary intermediaries of information across the world, transcending national boundaries. The ability of media organisations to influence public opinion is a crucial factor in the success or failure of democratic systems; the same holds true for the aforementioned digital platforms, which have the power to shape public opinion and, as a result, the balance between the media market and the pluralistic public sphere.[48]

A full understanding of the extent to which platforms are impacting the right to freedom of expression, in a way that once was reserved to the State authority alone, can be achieved by considering three key factors: (a) the

---

Kanevskaia and Przemyslaw Palka (eds), *Handbook on Law and Technology* (Edward Elgar 2023).

45 Emily Taylor, 'The Privatization of Human Rights: Illusions of Consent, Automation and Neutrality' (2016) 24 Global Commission on Internet Governance Paper <https://www.cigionline.org/static/documents/gcig_no24_web_2.pdf> accessed 10 June 2025, 14; Anupam Chander and Vivek Krishnamurthy, 'The Myth of Platform Neutrality' (2018) 2 The Georgetown Law Technology Review 400.

46 Christian Fuchs, 'Karl Marx in the Age of Big Data Capitalism. Digital Objects' in David Chandler and Christian Fuchs (eds) *Digital Objects, Digital Subjects: Interdisciplinary Perspectives on Capitalism, Labour and Politics in the Age of Big Data* (University of Westminster Press 2019).

47 Jack M. Balkin, 'Free Speech is a Triangle' (2018) 118 Columbia Law Review 2011.

48 Natali Helberger, 'The political power of platforms: How current attempts to regulate misinformation amplify opinion power' (2020) 8 Digital Journalism 842-854; Isabella De Vivo, 'Il potere d'opinione delle piattaforme online: quale ruolo del "regulatory turn" europeo nell'oligopolio informativo digitale?' (2024) 2 Federalismi 45.

logic behind content moderation, (b) the use of self-regulation, and (c) the supervision over said self-regulation.

a) The Logic behind Content Moderation

Content moderation can be defined as the set of governance mechanisms that structure participation in an online community with the aim of facilitating collaboration between users and preventing the commission of abuses.[49] Contrary to the initial argument that moderation is a neutral activity, it appears that it is coessential to the activity of digital platforms.[50] The technological companies that own said platforms are driven by the goal of maximising profit, pursued through the processing of content and the collection of data with the ultimate aim of attracting customers to advertisements. If social media platforms employ content moderation as a tool for achieving their business purposes, then it can be argued that content moderation does not reflect democratic values and has instead resulted in the establishment of the so-called 'attention economy'.[51] Content moderation for profit reflects the underlying logic of what has been termed as *digital capitalism* or even *information capitalism*.[52] Such moderation allows online platforms to engage in surveillance and governance as manifestations of their power and financial gain from online discourse, all while operating

49 James Grimmelmann, 'The Virtues of Moderation' (2015) 17 Yale Journal of Law and Technology 42. For an analysis of the intersection between content moderation and digital constitutionalism, see Edoardo Celeste et al., *The Content Governance Dilemma. Digital Constitutionalism, Social Media and the Search for a Global Standard* (Palgrave Macmillan 2023).

50 Taron Gillespie, *Custodians of the Internet: platforms, content moderation, and the hidden decisions that shape social media* (Yale University Press 2018) 21: 'Moderation is not an ancillary aspect of what platforms do. It is essential, constitutional, definitional. Not only can platforms not survive without moderation, they are not platforms without it'.

51 Tim Wu, *The Attention Merchants: The Epic Scramble to Get Inside our Heads* (Knopf 2016).

52 Nick Srnicek, *Platform Capitalism* (Polity Press 2016); Julie E. Cohen, *Between Truth and Power: The Legal Constructions of Informational Capitalism* (OUP 2019). About the manipulation of the public sphere in a capitalistic economy, see Nancy Fraser, 'Rethinking the Public Sphere: A Contribution to the Critique of Actually Existing Democracy' (1990) 25/26 Social Text 56.

without accountability due to the immunity of online intermediaries from liability for hosting third-party content.[53]

b) The Use of Self-regulation

The capacity of digital platforms to establish the parameters within which users can articulate their online perspectives renders content moderation not just a mere set of technical rules, but rather an integral component in defining the benchmark for safeguarding freedom of expression within the digital domain. The tools used by intermediaries to manage, or better, govern content are not laws created by a democratically elected parliament. Rather, they are rules set out in a variety of contractual documents, variously referred to as *terms of service* (ToS), *conditions of use*, or *community standards*, for instance. These documents are, in their formal designation, agreements between private parties, but they display attributes that align them more closely with regulatory sources. Firstly, ToS apply to millions of people, thereby giving the phenomenon a threatening dimension. This is particularly true in the case of the monopolistic position held by major platforms on the web and the fact that users nowadays are almost unable to express their thoughts outside the most widespread platforms.[54] Secondly, ToS are usually not open to negotiation between the user and the platform, which results in a fundamental imbalance of power: so, while the organisations that own the platforms hold gigantic economic and contractual power, users are left in an appalling inequality, as they are obliged to accept non-bargainable terms in order to use such platforms, which nowadays completely overlap with the public sphere, as emphasised by the US Supreme Court in the *Packingham v. North Carolina* case.[55] As a result of this distinctive feature of the phenomenon, a considerable number of

53 De Gregorio (n 25) 167.

54 Taina Bucher, 'Want to Be on the Top? Algorithmic Power and the Threat of Invisibility on Facebook' (2012) 14 New Media & Society 1164.

55 Tomer Shadmy, 'The New Social Contract: Facebook's Community and Our Rights' (2019) 37 Boston University International Law Journal 307; Madeleine Burnette-McGrath, 'Packingham v. North Carolina' (2019) 44 Ohio Northern University Law Review 117.

attempts have been made to draw parallels between these agreements and constitutional charts.[56]

Anyhow, the absence of democratic legitimacy inherent in the ToS is evident. Although they have a significant and far-reaching impact on how users can exercise their rights online, ToS are an inadequate means of articulating the users' rights and platforms' responsibilities, also considering that, in some cases, the internal guidelines for content moderation are unknown.[57] The terms and conditions of major platforms are typically structured to afford providers considerable discretion and to minimise their liability. This approach effectively circumvents the possibility of external legal standards being applied to governance processes. Therefore, digital platforms exercise a quasi-legislative power in parallel with that of the relevant public authority, yet, without being subject to the same obligations regarding constitutional guarantees. This scenario gives shape to what has been called the 'rule of the platform',[58] which is at odds with the public interest, especially when the economic freedoms of corporations are transformed into illegitimate forms of power.[59]

c) The Supervision over Self-regulation

In addition to their role in moderating content, service providers are also responsible for performing quasi-judicial functions, which in some cases resemble to the role of courts. Indeed, digital platforms are granted complete autonomy in the application of their own rules governing the circulation of ideas, thereby creating a form of private censorship.[60]

---

56 Edoardo Celeste, 'Terms of Service and Bills of Rights: New Mechanisms of Constitutionalisation in the Social Media Environment?' (2018) 33 International Review of Law, Computers & Technology 122; Nicolas P. Suzor, 'Digital Constitutionalism: Using the Rule of Law to Evaluate the Legitimacy of Governance by Platforms' (2018) 4 Social Media + Society 1.

57 Suzor (n 36) 167; Kate Klonick, 'The New Governors: The People, Rules, and Processes Governing Online Speech' (2018) 131 Harvard Law Review 1598.

58 Orly Lobel, 'The Law of the Platform' (2016) 101 Minnesota Law Review 87.

59 Oreste Pollicino, 'Digital Private Powers Exercising Public Functions: The Constitutional Paradox in the Digital Age and its Possible Solutions' [2021] European Court of Human Rights, <https://prd-echr.coe.int/documents/d/echr/Intervention_20210415_Pollicino_Rule_of_Law_ENG> accessed 10 June 2025.

60 Gian Luca Conti, 'Manifestazione del pensiero attraverso la rete e trasformazione della libertà di espressione: c'è ancora da ballare per strada?' (2018) 4 Rivista dell'As-

Digital platforms have built their own judicial apparatus, of which Facebook's Oversight Board is a paradigmatic example.[61] Such body can be likened to an internal court, with the task of issuing reasoned and binding decisions on the content published by users on the social network. The Board thus represents a private model of rights protection as an alternative to the State's. Decisions are taken in accordance with the principles and values established by the platform, which, as stated above, are heavily influenced by the platform's business model and are formulated in a rather unclear and evasive manner.[62] In this context, it is evident that the principle of rule of law, which should be the guiding principle for fundamental rights both online and offline, faces significant challenges in the digital environment.[63] Moreover, when the right to freedom of expression is violated, other democratic values are undermined: a society can only be defined as democratic if individuals can express their opinions and ideas without undue restrictions.[64]

2. Content Moderation and Freedom of Expression across the Atlantic

In the light of this intricate landscape, in which the management of online content is largely left to the unilateral decisions of the platforms, and with a clear lack of specific guarantees for the users, several initiatives have been introduced globally to standardise the content moderation process.[65] However, a prevailing fragmentation of legal responses still remains unaddressed at the global level. We witness, in effect, a notable discrepancy

---

sociazione italiana dei Costituzionalisti 200; Matteo Monti, 'Privatizzazione della censura e Internet platforms: la libertà d'espressione e i nuovi censori dell'agorà digitale' (2019) 1 Rivista italiana di informatica e diritto 35.

61 Valentina Cavani, 'Nuovi poteri, vecchi problemi. Il costituzionalismo alla prova del digitale' (2023) 1 Diritto pubblico comparato ed europeo 223.

62 Kate Klonick, 'The Facebook Oversight Board: Creating an Independent Institution to Adjudicate Online Free Expression' (2020) 129 Yale Law Journal 2418.

63 Robert Spano, 'The Rule of Law as the Lodestar of the European Convention on Human Rights: The Strasbourg Court and the Independence of the Judiciary' (2021) 27 European Law Journal 211.

64 De Gregorio (n 25) 19.

65 Two illustrative examples are the Manila Principles on Intermediary Liability and the Best Practices (2015), and the Santa Clara Principles on Transparency and Accountability in Content Moderation (2018).

between the approaches adopted by both sides of the Atlantic regarding the protection of the freedom of expression on digital platforms.[66]

The US legal system assumes that freedom of expression is a prominent fundamental right and should be protected by all means on the basis of the First Amendment.[67] This stance is supported by the consistent approach of the Supreme Court, which since the first relevant ruling on the subject, *Reno v. ACLU*,[68] has placed significant emphasis on the uniquely libertarian nature of the Internet phenomenon, deploying the metaphor of a 'free marketplace of ideas'.[69] In addition, in the mentioned *Packingham v. North Carolina* case,[70] the Supreme Court reinforced such an idea of the Internet

66 See Matteo Monti, 'The Unity of Opposites in the Regulation of Social Media Platforms: Content Moderation Between the EU Digital Services Act and the US First Amendment Theories' [2024] EUI LAW Working Paper 2024/7, <https://ssrn.com/abstract=4834433 or http://dx.doi.org/10.2139/ssrn.4834433> accessed 10 June 2025; João P. Quintais et al., 'From the DMCA to the DSA: A Transatlantic Dialogue on Online Platform Regulation and Copyright' [2024] <https://ssrn.com/abstract=4860225> accessed on 10 June 2025. For a general comparison between the European and the US' conception of freedom of expression, see Brittan Heller and Joris van Hoboken 'Freedom of expression: A comparative summary of United States and European law' [2019] Transatlantic Working Group <https://ssrn.com/abstract=4563882> accessed 10 June 2025.

67 First Amendment to the Constitution of the United States: 'Congress shall make no law respecting an establishment of religion, or prohibiting the free exercise thereof; or abridging the freedom of speech, or of the press; or the right of the people peaceably to assemble, and to petition the Government for a redress of grievances'.

68 *Reno v. American Civil Liberties Union* [1997] 521 U.S. 844. The Communication Decency Act (CDA) introduced criminal penalties for online speech deemed 'indecent' or 'patently offensive', with penalties of up to two years of imprisonment and/or fines of up to $250,000. These provisions were designed to prevent online content from being accessed by minors. The ACLU argued that the censorship provisions were unconstitutional because they criminalised speech protected by the First Amendment, and because the terms 'indecent' and 'patently offensive' were unconstitutionally vague. The Supreme Court ruled that the CDA placed an unacceptably heavy burden on protected speech that threatened to have a significant impact on a large segment of the Internet community. The Court also highlighted that the interest in promoting free speech in a democratic society outweighs any theoretical but unproven benefit of censorship.

69 *Abrams v. United States* [1910] 250 US 616, 624.

70 *Packingham v. North Carolina,* [2017] 582 U.S. 98. The Supreme Court ruled that a *North Carolina* law was unconstitutional because it made it a crime for a registered sex offender to use social media sites where children could be members. A registered sex offender took the case after being convicted under the law for a Facebook post in 2010. The Supreme Court reached its decision because the law was overly broad to achieve the government's aim of preventing child abuse.

by ruling that 'while in the past there may have been difficulty in identifying the most important places (in a spatial sense) for the exchange of views, today the answer is clear. It is cyberspace — the "vast democratic forums of the Internet" in general, and social media in particular'.

The divergence between European standards and the US' approach to freedom of expression seems to be the consequence of a vertically oriented interpretation of the right to said freedom. According to the US system, the right to freedom of expression can only be restricted in relation to public power, but not in relation to entities that cannot be considered state actors or that do not perform public functions.[71] As a direct result, online platforms are not required to comply with First Amendment guarantees and are also shielded from liability for content posted by users, without any legal framework able to translate constitutional rights into statutory provisions.

In contrast, the European perspective advocates for the same degree of protection for the freedom of expression as that afforded to other fundamental rights.[72] It is further argued that all rights must be reconciled with each other in a way that safeguards human dignity.[73] This harmony is achieved through a multilevel balancing of rights enshrined in the Charter of Fundamental Rights of the European Union, the European Convention on Human Rights, and national constitutions.[74]

---

71 In the case of *Manhattan Community Access Corp. v. Halleck* [2019] 587 U.S. ___, the Supreme Court effectively precluded the possibility of extending the state action doctrine by determining that private entities, specifically cable television companies operating public access channels, do not function as a public actor (in this case, the city of *New York*) and are therefore not subject to the same obligations regarding the protection of free speech rights.

72 Oreste Pollicino and Marco Bassini, 'Free Speech, Defamation and the Limits to Freedom of Expression in the EU: A Comparative Analysis' in Andrej Savin and Jan Trzaskowski (eds), *Research Handbook on EU Internet Law* (Edward Elgar 2014); Vincenzo Zeno-Zencovich, *Freedom of Expression: A Critical and Comparative Analysis* (Routledge 2008).

73 Mattias Kumm and Alec D. Walen, 'Human Dignity and Proportionality: Deontic Pluralism in Balancing' in Grant M. Huscroft, Bradley W. Miller and Grégoire Webber (eds), *Proportionality and the Rule of Law: Rights, Justification, Reasoning* (Cambridge University Press 2014).

74 Ingolf E. A. Pernice, 'The Treaty of Lisbon: Multilevel Constitutionalism in Action' (2009) 15 Columbia Journal of European Law 349; Oreste Pollicino and Graziella Romeo, *The internet and constitutional law: The protection of fundamental rights and constitutional adjudication in Europe* (Routledge 2016).

In the perspective of the multifaceted and constantly evolving challenges of cyberspace, a purely reactive regulatory approach cannot be considered sufficient to effectively protect the flow of information from abuses within the EU. Instead, it has been argued that a proactive approach, guided by the principles of digital constitutionalism, is required to foster the development of a global democratic public sphere while reinforcing the human-centric perspective that has always been at the core of European values.[75]

IV. The European 'Regulatory Turn': A New Constitution-oriented Phase?

1. The First Steps of the European Digital Single Market Strategy

As argued so far, the absence of regulation has allowed the freedom of online platforms to be transformed into a quasi-legal environment in competition with State authority.[76] This threatening tendency is addressed by the European 'regulatory turn', which proposes a 'third way towards hard law' in terms of data standards, privacy, and content moderation.[77] This step constitutes the heart of the transition to what has been hailed as a new and third Internet era, that of the 'regulated Internet'.[78] This shift has resulted in the characterisation of the European approach as 'reactive' – as opposed to the US 'omissive' approach –, which has been shaped by a period of notable activism of the European Court of Justice (ECJ). For

75 De Gregorio (n 25) 23.

76 Oreste Pollicino, 'La prospettiva costituzionale sulla libertà di espressione nell'era di Internet' (2018) 1 Medialaws 48.

77 Christoph Busch, 'The P2B Regulation (EU) 2019/1150: Towards a "Procedural Turn" in EU Platform Regulation' (2020) 9 Journal of European Consumer and Market Law 133; Philip Schlesinger and Martin Kretschmer, 'The changing shape of platform regulation' [2020] <https://blogs.lse.ac.uk/medialse/2020/02/18/the-changing-shape-of-platform-regulation/> accessed 10 June 2025; Mauro Santaniello, 'Sovranità digitale e diritti fondamentali: un modello europeo di Internet governance' (2022) 1 Rivista italiana di informatica e diritto 49.

78 Terry Flew, *Regulating Platforms* (Wiley 2021); Luciano Floridi, 'The End of an Era: from Self-Regulation to Hard Law for the Digital Industry' (2021) 34 Philosophy and Technology 619.

instance, as highlighted by the *Schrems*[79] and *Google Spain* rulings,[80] the ECJ sought to impose new obligations and procedures on platforms to protect fundamental rights.

Since 2015, the EU has taken concrete steps in the context of its Digital Single Market Strategy to tackle the issue of liability of online platforms. This Strategy acknowledged the relevance of the digital economy and the diversity and rapidly changing nature of platform ecosystems, leading to new policy and regulatory challenges.[81] In this framework, some of the jurisprudence from the ECJ case law were codified and new constraints have been introduced for online platforms operating in Europe in terms of transparency and accountability in content moderation and data processing.[82]

79 The *Schrems* judgments are rulings adopted by the ECJ with the objective of reorganising the agreements between the EU and the US regarding the processing of personal data. On 6 October 2015, the *Schrems I* ruling (C-362/14) resulted in the annulment of the pre-existing *Safe Harbor treaty*, which permitted US companies to process the personal data of their European users on US servers. Subsequently, on 16 July 2020, the *Schrems II* ruling (C-311/18) led to the annulment of the US-EU Privacy Shield and the recognition of the legality of Standard Contractual Clauses.

80 *Google Spain SL v. Agencia Espanola de protección de Datos*, C-131/12, 13 May 2014. In 2010, *Costeja González* complained to Spain's Data Protection Agency about *La Vanguardia* newspaper, Google Spain, and Google Inc. *González* wanted the newspaper to remove or alter the record of his 1998 proceedings so that the information would no longer be available online. He also asked Google Inc. or Google Spain to remove or hide the data. The Agency dismissed the complaint against the newspaper because it was legally justified. On appeal, the National High Court of Spain stayed the proceedings and presented several questions to the ECJ concerning the applicability of the EU Directive 95/46 (protection of personal data) to the Internet search engines. The Court ruled that search engines are controllers of personal data because they collect, store, and share it. It also ruled that search engines can be required to remove personal information from third-party websites, though this should be balanced against the public interest in accessing that information.

81 Communication from the Commission to the European Parliament, the Council, the European Economic and Social Committee and the Committee of the Regions Online Platforms and the Digital Single Market Opportunities and Challenges for Europe, COM(2016) 288 final.

82 Oreste Pollicino and Giovanni De Gregorio, 'A Constitutional-Driven Change of Heart: ISP Liability and Artificial Intelligence in the Digital Single Market' (2018) 18 The Global Community Yearbook of International Law and Jurisprudence 237.

The path towards cyberspace governance then continued with the issuing of the General Data Protection Regulation (GDPR),[83] which represented a significant shift in the *constitutionalisation* of personal data protection within the EU, and a major turning point in the global evolution of privacy protection.[84] The European project for 'digital sovereignty'[85] was born and developed as a necessary alternative to the dichotomy that distinguishes the US liberal model, based mainly on industry self-regulation, from the authoritarian models, such as those of Russia and China, which have prioritised the control over the market and platforms.[86] Unlike the United States and China, it is widely recognised that Europe does not play a significant role in the production of technology or in the ownership of major digital communication platforms and systems. Consequently, the European approach has focused on altering the competitive landscape from one being solely based on technology to one being defined by regulatory frameworks.[87] The EU's strategy is to establish itself as a leader in the regulatory creation and to set the European model as a global reference point to be adopted in other geopolitical regions, in a process known as

83 European Parliament and Council Regulation (EU) 2016/679 on the protection of natural persons with regard to the processing of personal data and on the free movement of such data and repealing Directive 95/46/EC [2016] OJ L119/1.

84 About the evolution of EU Data Law, see Michèle Finck, 'The Maturation of European Data Law: From Fundamental Rights to Economic Rights' in Jeremias Adams-Prassl et al. (eds), *The Internal Market Ideal: Essays in Honour of Stephen Weatherill* (OUP 2024).

85 The term 'digital sovereignty' was first employed by Commission President *Ursula von der Leyen* during her State of the Union Address on 16 September 2020 and has since become a commonplace concept, appearing with regularity in several recent official EU documents. About the concept of digital sovereignty, see Stephane Couture and Sophie Toupin, 'What Does the Notion of "Sovereignty" Mean When Referring to the Digital?' (2019) 21 New Media & Society 2305; Edoardo Celeste, 'Digital Sovereignty in the EU: Challenges and Future Perspectives' in Federico Fabbrini, Edoardo Celeste and John Quinn (eds), *Data Protection beyond Borders: Transatlantic Perspectives on Extraterritoriality and Sovereignty* (Hart 2021); Milton Mueller, 'Against Sovereignty in Cyberspace' (2020) 22 International Studies Review 779.

86 Yun Wen, *The Huawei Model: The Rise of China's Technology Giant* (University of Illinois Press 2020); Eva Claessen, 'Reshaping the Internet – The Impact of the Securitisation of Internet Infrastructure on Approaches to Internet Governance: The Case of Russia and the EU' (2020) 5 Journal of Cyber Policy 140; Matthew S. Erie and Thomas Streinz, 'The Beijing Effect: China's "Digital Silk Road" as Transnational Data Governance' (2021) 54 New York University Journal of International Law and Politics 1.

87 Giusella Finocchiaro, 'La sovranità digitale' (2022) 3 Diritto pubblico 809.

the *Brussels effect*.[88] This strategy aims at establishing a form of European digital sovereignty that is both external, in relation to the other two global players, and internal, in relation to the EU Member States, thus preventing internal fragmentation.[89] The Brussels effect hence shall cause the rules of the EU to spill over into other jurisdictions through the regulation of technological companies – in a *de facto* effect – and shall allow for harmonisation of legislative changes by jurisdictions outside the EU – in a *de jure* effect.[90]

The power of these legal approaches has proven effective in indirectly shaping the Terms of Service of multiple social media platforms: European regulation has in effect been impactful in ameliorating the way in which Big Tech companies collect, manage, and store users' personal data. For instance, between 2016 and 2018, companies like Meta, Google, and Microsoft have started to implement a single global privacy policy that aligns with the principles of the GDPR.[91] Also, it is worth noting that the language used by major platforms appears to have been influenced by the European Code of Conduct on countering illegal hate speech online.[92] International technological companies have adopted a common definition of *hate speech* to determine which content to remove from their platforms, thereby adhering to European standards and overshadowing the principles of the First Amendment of the US Constitution regarding the freedom of expression.[93]

88 Anu Bradford, *The Brussels Effect: How the European Union Rules the World* (OUP 2020).

89 As evidenced by the explanatory memorandum to the European Commission's proposal for a regulation on artificial intelligence, the Union's interest is to preserve the EU's technological leadership: proposal for a regulation of the European Parliament and of the Council laying down harmonised rules on artificial intelligence (Artificial Intelligence Act) and amending certain union legislative acts (com/2021/206 final).

90 Bradford (n 88).

91 Kimberly A. Houser and Gregory Voss, 'GDPR: The End of Google and Facebook or a New Paradigm in Data Privacy?' (2018) 25 Richmond Journal of Law & Tech 1.

92 The European Code of Conduct on countering illegal hate speech online was adopted in May 2016 by the Commission with Facebook, Microsoft, Twitter and YouTube. From 2018 to 2022 many digital platforms announced their participation to the Code of Conduct (e.g. Instagram, Snapchat, Dailymotion, and Twitch). On 20 January 2025, the Commission announced the integration of a revised Code of conduct: <https://commission.europa.eu/strategy-and-policy/policies/justice-and-fundamental-rights/combatting-discrimination/racism-and-xenophobia/eu-code-conduct-countering-illegal-hate-speech-online_en> accessed 10 June 2025.

93 Paolo Cavaliere, 'Digital platforms and the rise of global regulation of hate speech' (2019) 8 Cambridge International Law Journal 282.

Interestingly enough, as evidenced by the Directive on Copyright and Related Rights in the Digital Single Market,[94] the Directive on Audiovisual Media Services,[95] and the Regulation on the Dissemination of Terrorist Content Online,[96] the gradual introduction of new procedural obligations demonstrates the European Commission's intention to enhance legal accountability of private actors operating in the cyberspace.

2. The European Regulation of Digital Markets, Services and Artificial Intelligence

The introduction of procedural obligations for platforms has also been the chosen approach in the context of the recent Digital Services Act (DSA, 2022),[97] which addresses the way online service providers implement content moderation decisions. This regulatory framework, building on the e-Commerce Directive,[98] provides a range of new obligations and due diligence duties for providers of services which transmit or store data on behalf of users (Intermediary Service Providers). These obligations are differently tailored according to the nature of the services provided and the size of the provider, making the DSA tiered and cumulative, so that a very large online platform or search engine must comply with the highest degree of obligations.[99] Notably, the territorial criterion of application – adopted as

94 Directive (EU) 2019/790 of the European Parliament and of the Council of 17 April 2019 on copyright and related rights in the Digital Single Market and amending Directives 96/9/EC and 2001/29/EC.

95 Directive (EU) 2018/1808 of the European Parliament and of the Council of 14 November 2018 amending Directive 2010/13/EU on the coordination of certain provisions laid down by law, regulation or administrative action in Member States concerning the provision of audiovisual media services (Audiovisual Media Services Directive) in view of changing market realities.

96 Regulation (EU) 2021/784 of the European Parliament and of the Council of 29 April 2021 on addressing the dissemination of terrorist content online.

97 Regulation (EU) 2022/2065 of the European Parliament and of the Council of 19 October 2022 on a Single Market for Digital Services and amending Directive 2000/31/EC (Digital Services Act).

98 Directive 2000/31/EC of the European Parliament and of the Council of 8 June 2000 on certain legal aspects of information society services, in particular electronic commerce, in the Internal Market.

99 Some of the obligations include rules that organise the process of notification, evaluation, removal and contestation of content (arts. 16 to 21); providers are also bound to issue annual or bi-annual transparency reports about how they conduct content moderation (arts. 15 and 24); VLOPs and VLOSEs have further disclosure obligations

well in the Digital Markets Act (DMA, 2022),[100] which addresses issues related to the protection of competition in an environment characterised by the dominance of oligopolistic and vertically integrated platforms – is not based on the place of establishment or residence of the service provider. Instead, it refers to the place of establishment or residence of the recipient of the service if it is in the EU, thus widening the protection provided by the Act.[101] The DMA has established clear, harmonised rules to tackle the challenges posed by the business practices of online platforms, regulating them on an economic level and mitigating the potential adverse consequences of gatekeeping practices, aiming at promoting a favourable business environment while simultaneously safeguarding the interests of users and, ultimately, society as a whole.

While the DSA introduced multiple obligations relating to content removal and risk assessment systems, some of the aspects that generated the greatest perplexity within the scholarship is the asymmetry in the obligations imposed on large platforms versus smaller ones. The rules designed for large platforms aim to rebalance the power that size brings with it, while minor digital service providers are subject to a regime of substantial exemption from regulatory obligations.[102] Moreover, the DSA has not yet shifted from a bottom-up to a top-down logic, because major online platforms retain the power to implement moderation policies, determining what content is allowed and what is removed, driven by content-dependent normative goals as fairness and transparency, which are filtered by the platforms' self-regulation and have thus gained legitimacy by the DSA.[103] Contributing to the debate, some scholars have argued that the European legislator has limited itself to implementing mainly procedural measures,

(art. 42), must provide access to data to researchers to study risks and mitigation strategies on their services (art. 40) and must appropriately train their staff, including content moderators, and monitor risk management within companies (arts. 34,35, 42(2)(b)).

100 Regulation (EU) 2022/1925 of the European Parliament and of the Council of 14 September 2022 on contestable and fair markets in the digital sector and amending Directives (EU) 2019/1937 and (EU) 2020/1828 (Digital Markets Act).

101 Regulation (EU) 2022/2065, art. 2.1; Regulation (EU) 2022/1925, art. 1.2.

102 De Gregorio (n 25) 213.

103 Moritz Schramm, 'Platform Administrative Law. A Research Agenda' [2024] <https://ssrn.com/abstract=4898542> accessed on 10 June 2025, 5.

without establishing the necessary substantive rules to define which forms of expression are prohibited.[104]

Despite the criticism and its shortcomings, the DSA, by introducing specific measures to increase transparency and accountability of online platforms, has been considered a valid horizontal framework and a 'paradigmatic example of European digital constitutionalism'.[105] The regulatory approach chosen by the EU is not limited to the removal of harmful content, as it also incorporates efforts to apply content moderation procedures of social media platforms to guarantee users' rights.[106] The DSA provides a viable approach to tackle the power of Big Tech corporations while allowing them to cooperate with public authorities, which would otherwise have been unable to counteract the management of content on private spaces worldwide, which lies outside of the traditional concept of national jurisdiction.[107]

These lines of action are also reflected in the Artificial Intelligence Act (AI Act, 2024),[108] which also attempts to reconcile the EU's fundamental values with the commercial relations between corporations and individuals. It represents a significant step towards regulation by providing harmonised rules that apply in areas such (i) the placing on the market, (ii) the service

104 Some Authors refer to a 'procedural fetishism': Monika Zalnieriute, 'Procedural Fetishism and Mass Surveillance under the ECHR' [2021] Verfassungsblog; Rachel Griffin, 'Procedural Fetishism in the Digital Services Act' (2025) 11 European Journal of Legal Studies.

105 Giovanni De Gregorio, 'The Digital Services Act: A Paradigmatic Example of European Digital Constitutionalism' [2021] Diritti Comparati <https://www.diritticomparati.it/the-digital-services-act-a-paradigmatic-example-of-european-digital-constitutionalism/?print-posts=pdf> accessed on 10 June 2025; Jennifer Urban and Martin Husovec, 'Will the DSA have the Brussels Effect?' [2021] Verfassungsblog <https://verfassungsblog.de/will-the-dsa-have-the-brussels-effect/> accessed on 10 June 2025: 'the most promising is the potential impact of the DSA content moderation rules on the industry standards for processes and tools, and potentially the data access regime'.

106 Pietro Ortolani, 'The Digital Services Act, Content Moderation and Dispute Resolution' (2022) 2 Giustizia Consensuale 533.

107 Uta Kohl, 'Jurisdiction in network society' in Nicholas Tsagourias and Russell Buchan (eds), *Research handbook on international law and cyberspace* (Edward Elgar 2021), 69-96.

108 Regulation (EU) 2024/1689 of the European Parliament and of the Council of 13 June 2024 laying down harmonised rules on artificial intelligence and amending Regulations (EC) No 300/2008, (EU) No 167/2013, (EU) No 168/2013, (EU) 2018/858, (EU) 2018/1139 and (EU) 2019/2144 and Directives 2014/90/EU, (EU) 2016/797 and (EU) 2020/1828 (Artificial Intelligence Act).

and use of artificial intelligence systems within the EU, (iii) the prohibition of certain AI practices, (iv) specific requirements for high-risk AI systems and obligations for their operators, (v) rules on market monitoring and supervision, and (vi) a European artificial intelligence governance system.

The unifying element of all recent legislative initiatives in this novel legal strategy is the fact that the EU is attempting to achieve a hybrid approach between hard law and self-regulation.[109] Even though such an approach could raise concerns due to the disrupting role of the aforementioned platforms, the EU's commendable intention is to strike a balance between the US model and the model proposed by authoritarian governments. This equilibrium is achieved by refraining from liberal positions that allow for the potential dominance of self-regulation, while at the same time avoiding extensive interventions in the market and in the pluralistic space that often occurs under illiberal regimes. In order to preserve market dynamics and to prevent the compression of the freedom of expression through the intervention of an authoritarian State and private power, it has been suggested to involve the private sector in a form of co-regulation through various systems, such as public-private partnerships or the regulation of public utilities, given that the increasing control over large parts of political, economic and social life leads online platforms to be critical and essential infrastructures.[110]

V. Concluding Remarks

This essay has demonstrated that the EU's regulatory turn represents a normative and strategic effort to reassert constitutional values in the digital sphere, offering a model of digital governance that balances fundamental rights, democratic oversight, and market regulation against the growing influence of private platforms; while not without limitations, it constitutes

---

109 As clarified in the White Paper 'On Artificial Intelligence – A European Approach to Excellence and Trust' (2020) 65 COM: 'it is also essential to make sure that the private sector is fully involved in setting the research and innovation agenda and provides the necessary level of co-investment. This requires setting up a broad-based public private partnership and securing the commitment of the top management of companies'.

110 K. Sabeel Rahman, 'The New Utilities: Private Power, Social Infrastructure, and the Revival of the Public Utility Concept' (2018) 39 Cardozo Law Review 1612; Nikolas Guggenberger, 'Essential Platforms' (2021) 24 Stanford Technology Law 237.

a solid starting point from which further legal and political developments can evolve.

The analysis of the position assumed by the EU in the international scenario reveals a desire to stand as a standard-setter at the regulatory level. This goal is evidenced by the EU's refusal to engage in a race to develop new technologies, given that leadership in the digital sphere is held at other continents. Besides, the EU's approach shows a noteworthy attempt to condition the regulatory framework of Big Tech companies, rather than an unconditional exploitation of their potential. The pursuit of an extraterritorial framework does not imply autocratic intentions, but rather aims at designing a comprehensive political and normative model to protect fundamental rights worldwide, given the inherent non-territorial, or better, *aterritorial* nature of the Internet and, consequently, of its dangers.

Within the domain of Internet governance, scholars have identified the primary objective to be the mitigation of self-regulation by platforms. However, self-regulation persists in the intrinsic dynamics of large online platforms and search engines, following the regulatory logic introduced by the Digital Services Act. It is therefore crucial to recognise the importance of preserving the constitutional identity of the EU by ensuring continuous involvement of public authorities in cyberspace, so to continue regulating the selection of value systems, including democratic principles, in the digital sphere. This is an essential step in preventing the private sphere from becoming a self-constitutionalising force that favours the logic of profit.[111]

While there is still a long way to go before reaching a complete and comprehensive approach to regulating platforms, significant progress has been made by the EU in the protection of the intertwined aspects of fundamental freedoms, economic rights and interests, and democratic values.[112] The EU has managed to move beyond a libertarian approach, building on the principles developed by case law, and is still currently attempting to manage the regulatory phenomenon by anticipating, and not merely reacting to, the challenges posed by digital technology within a renewed constitutionalism.

111 Giovanni De Gregorio, 'From constitutional freedoms to the power of the platforms: protecting fundamental rights online in the algorithmic society' (2018) 11 European Journal of Legal Studies 65.

112 Sophie Robin-Olivier, 'The "Digital Single Market" and Neoliberalism: Reflections on Net Neutrality' in Margot E Salomon and Bruno De Witte (eds), *Legal Trajectories of Neoliberalism: Critical Inquiries on Law in Europe* (2019) 43 EUI Working Paper RSCAS <https://papers.ssrn.com/sol3/papers.cfm?abstract_id=3425753> accessed 10 June 2025, 45.

The latter is based on traditional constitutional categories and seeks to adapt them constructively to the challenges of the digital realm. The European strategy aims to promote the long-term development of a sustainable and human-centred digital environment, leaving a legacy consistent with the democratic values on which the EU is rooted. Essentially, the EU is establishing itself as a significant global regulator, guided by the constitutional balance inherent in its nature as an entity 'founded on the values of respect for human dignity, freedom, democracy, equality, the rule of law and respect for human rights'.[113]

113 Consolidated version of the Treaty on European Union, 2012, Art. 2; De Gregorio (n 25) 284.

Climate Citizens' Assemblies: An Effective Tool to Protect the Interests of Future Generations?

Andrea Fiorentino[*]

The climate crisis poses a significant threat to the rights and freedoms of present and future generations. Countering it requires incorporating environmental protection into the legal and political horizon of public authority action. However, the temporal limitations of representative democracy, driven by short election cycles and permanent campaigning, make it challenging to prioritise future generations' interests over short-term demands. In this context, participatory and deliberative democracy offers a way to 'break the spell' of presentism, encouraging decision-makers to address the long-term needs of those most affected by climate change.

This study will address the recent flowering of the so-called climate citizens' assemblies, focusing on national cases in France, the United Kingdom, and Spain. The analysis aims to assess whether, and under what conditions, these bodies can effectively connect representative democracy with future generations' interests in the framework of the decision-making processes that shape climate and environmental policies.

I. The Climate and Environmental Crisis and Participatory Democracy Against the Backdrop of the Crisis of Representative Democracy

The climate crisis, unfolding its catastrophic effects in an increasingly widespread and frequent manner, is undoubtedly among the greatest challenges political communities are facing today. It threatens their very existence: in its scientifically proven and highly probable outcomes, it is in fact on a collision course with the preservation of the supreme good of

---

* Postdoctoral Researcher in Comparative Public Law, University of Rome *Unitelma-Sapienza.* This contribution is the result of a further development and a substantial reworking of the essay 'La democrazia partecipativa tra crisi della democrazia rappresentativa e crisi climatico-ambientale: alcune riflessioni sulla fioritura delle assemblee dei cittadini per il clima' (2023) 24 Federalismi.it 66.

life, which, in a *Hobbesian* perspective, constitutes the main legitimising reason for the social contract (*pactum societatis*) and the acceptance of the representative principle by the people (*pactum subiectionis*).[1]

Faced with this looming threat, in recent years constitutionalism, faithful to its essence as a legal-political doctrine aimed at the limitation of power and the pursuit of freedom, has made environmental protection an outpost of its missions to organise and transform societies.[2] In connection with the increased awareness of the issue, rising to the legal and symbolic-political dimension of the emergency,[3] the so-called 'environmental constitutionalism' is successfully expanding on a global scale,[4] committed to the establishment and the improvement of more or less advanced legal instruments

1 See Thomas Hobbes, *Leviathan* (first published 1651, Penguin 2017).

2 For an overview of transformative constitutionalism, see Gaurav Mukherjee, 'Transformative Constitutionalism', *Max Planck Encyclopedia of Comparative Constitutional Law* (2023).

3 This is demonstrated by the spread, in recent years, of environmental and climate 'state of emergency' declarations, adopted at local and national levels: e.g. the Opposition motion declaring an 'environment and climate emergency' passed by the House of Commons (House of Commons, Environment and Climate Change, Vol 659: debated on Wednesday 1 May 2019), the declaration of a 'climate and biodiversity emergency' by the Irish Lower House (*Dáil Éireann* debate – Thursday, 9 May 2019, Vol. 982 No 5), the Government's motion on National climate emergency approved by the Canadian House of Commons (House of Commons, Vote No 1366, 42nd Parliament, 1st session, Sitting No 435 – Monday, June 17, 2019), the legislative recognition of the 'urgence écologique et climatique' by the French Parliament (Loi n° 2019-1147 du 8 novembre 2019 relative à l'énergie et au climat), the European Parliament resolution of November 28, 2019, on the climate and environmental emergency (2019/2930(RSP)) (2021/C 232/06), the Italian Chamber of Deputies motion that committed the Government to recognise the state of climatic and environmental emergency (AC Mozione 1/00181, approvato il 11/12/2019), and finally the Spanish Government declaration of the 'emergencia climática y ambiental' (Gobierno de España, Acuerdo de Consejo de Ministros por el que se aprueba la Declaración del Gobierno ante la emergencia climática y ambiental, 21 de enero 2020). On this argument, see Matteo Nicolini, 'Law, the Humanities and Political Incertitude in a Time of Climate Change' (2021) 1 Legalities 100. See the list of the adopted declarations: http://climateemergencydeclaration.org/climate-emergency-declarations-cover-15-million-citizens/.

4 Domenico Amirante and Silvia Bagni (eds), *Environmental Constitutionalism in the Anthropocene: Values, Principles and Actions* (Routledge 2022); Domenico Amirante, *Costituzionalismo ambientale. Atlante giuridico per l'Antropocene* (Il Mulino 2022). See also Lorenzo Cuocolo, 'Modelli di costituzionalismo ambientale tra formante legislativo, giurisprudenziale e culturale' (2023) 58(Sp2) DPCE Online 79.

aimed at the constitutional protection of the environmental values.[5] In other words, we are witnessing a widespread political-institutional reaction to a growing awareness of an elementary fact: that all the individual and social projections of the human person, protected through the recognition and guarantee of inviolable rights, find their basic premise in the permanence of conditions favourable to life; with the consequence that the future exercise of those rights would be hampered, if not even impossible, if the protection of the '*natürlichen Lebensgrundlagen*' (meaning natural foundations of life, Art. 20a of the German Basic Law) did not fall within the teleological and intertemporal horizon of public authorities' action.[6]

The need to address this situation in a long-term perspective unveils a serious structural weakness of today's representative democracies: the brevity of election cycles and the permanent campaign climate that follows. These factors tend to push the political class into an 'eternal presentism', i.e. a situation in which, to maintain consensus and win re-election, satisfying short-term interests is all that matters. In such a context, elected representatives are encouraged to ignore or downplay long-term interests such as taking effective measures to reduce greenhouse emissions and mitigate the effects of climate change.

Actually, this is only one of the current problems of constitutional democracies, which have long been affected by rollbacks and regressions due, briefly, to two factors: the processes of globalisation and supranational integration, which tend to marginalise national political representation, and

5 Consider, for example, the Italian Constitutional Law No 1/2022, which included among the fundamental principles of the Constitution 'the protection of the environment, biodiversity and ecosystems, also in the interest of future generations'.

6 Section 20a was introduced into the German *Grundgesetz* by the Constitutional Amendment Act of 27 October 1994, which came into force on 15 November 1994. It was subsequently amended by the Revision Act of 26 July 2002, which extended constitutional protection to 'animals'. Art. 20a was used by the *Bundesverfassungsgericht* as a constitutionality parameter in the recent ruling on the case *Neubauer et al. v. Germany* of March 2021, in which the complaints of four young environmental activists concerning the Federal Law on Climate Protection were partially upheld, on the assumption that the federal legislature, having agreed to large amounts of emissions up to 2030 and not having prepared sufficient measures for the subsequent period, would have shifted more of the burden of emission reductions onto the latter, thus leading to an undue advance interference with the freedoms of 'future generations': see BVerfG, 1 BvR 2656/18.

the crisis of the political parties, ever more incapable of catching and recomposing the demands of an increasingly fragmented and volatile society.[7]

As a result of these difficulties, the push for a combination of representative democracy's pillars with forms of direct citizen involvement has been strengthened at both political and academic levels. Generally, the ideal objective of these claims is to pursue and achieve a 'continuous democracy'[8] or a further 'democratisation of democracy'[9] that would correct the perceived structural flaws of the representative system. This involves not only the traditional instruments of direct democracy (such as referenda and popular initiatives)[10] but also, above all, the practices and the institutions of participatory and deliberative democracy.[11] These constitute a broad family

7 See *ex multis* Mark A. Graber, Sanford Levinson and Mark Tushnet (eds), *Constitutional Democracy in crisis?* (OUP 2018); Larry Diamond and Marc F. Plattner, *Democracy in Decline?* (JHUP 2015).

8 For the proposal of a form of 'démocratie continue' see Dominique Rousseau, *Radicaliser la démocratie. Propositions pour une refondation* (Seuil 2015).

9 Umberto Allegretti, 'Democrazia partecipativa: un contributo alla democratizzazione della democrazia', in Umberto Allegretti (ed), *Democrazia partecipativa. Esperienze e prospettive in Italia e in Europa*, (Firenze UP 2010), 23; Umberto Allegretti, 'Democrazia partecipativa e processi di democratizzazione' (2008) 2 Democrazia e diritto 176.

10 For an in-depth comparative overview of the institutes of direct democracy, see Eloy Garcia, Elisabetta Palici Di Suni and Martin Rogoff, *Gli istituti di democrazia diretta nel diritto comparato* (Wolters Kluwer 2018).

11 On participatory democracy, *ex multis*, see Paola Piciacchia, 'Le "vie infinite" della democrazia partecipativa e il dilemma costituzionale della sua integrazione nei processi decisionali basati sulla rappresentanza. Quali modelli per gli ordinamenti del XXI secolo?' (2024) 22 Federalismi.it 216; Angela Di Gregorio, 'Strumenti ed esperienze di citizens' engagement" in ottica comparata: potenzialità e prospettive per il rinnovamento della democrazia rappresentativa e per la difesa dello stato di diritto' (2024) 3 Nomos. Le attualità nel diritto 1; Gabriele Pepe, *Il modello della democrazia partecipativa tra aspetti e profili applicativi. Un'analisi comparata* (Wolters Kluwer 2020); Martina Trettel, *La democrazia partecipativa negli ordinamenti composti: studio di diritto comparato sull'incidenza della tradizione giuridica nelle* democratic innovations (ESI 2020); Laurence Bherer, Pascale Dufour and Françoise Montambeault (eds), *The Participatory Democracy Turn* (Routledge 2019); Cristina Fraenkl-Haeberle et al. (eds), *Citizens Participation in Multi-Level Democracies* (Brill-Nijhoff 2015); Jean-Pierre Gaudin, *La démocratie participative* (Colin 2013); Umberto Allegretti, 'Democrazia partecipativa', *Enciclopedia del diritto* (Annali IV, Giuffrè 2011), 295. On deliberative democracy, *ex multis*, see James S. Fishkin, *Democracy When the People Are Thinking: Revitalizing Our Politics Through Public Deliberation* (OUP, 2018); James S. Fishkin, *Democracy and Deliberation: New Directions in Democratic Reform* (YUP 1991); Andre Bächtiger et al. (eds), *The Oxford handbook of deliberative democracy: An introduction* (OUP 2018); Antonio Floridia, *La democrazia deliberativa:*

of mechanisms through which people participate directly in decision-making processes established by institutional actors (political or bureaucratic). Within this framework, citizens - and sometimes even residents - can contribute, to varying degrees, to shaping decisions in interaction with institutions, through a structured process of information, discussion, and deliberation.

This leads to the point this study is the most interested in highlighting. Political institutions are increasingly resorting to participatory democracy, attempting both to reduce the distance between representatives and those they represent and obtain a genuine democratic input to break party-political deadlocks on issues perceived as divisive and polarising (e.g. same-sex marriage, abortion, assisted death, etc.). Among them are, obviously, climate change mitigation policies needed to achieve the emission reduction targets mainly set by the 2015 Paris Agreement, as they inherently involve measures aimed at significantly altering production systems, social protection models, and numerous aspects of citizens' daily lives. After all, it is no coincidence that, over the last three decades, environment-related decision-making processes have provided a privileged ground for the development and application of participatory tools, especially in the local and community dimensions[12]. These tools promise to 'break the spell' of the 'eternal presentism', making parliaments and governments more responsive

teorie, processi e sistemi (Carocci 2013); Jhon Dryzek, *Deliberative Democracy and Beyond. Liberals, Critics, Contestations* (OUP 2000); Jürgen Habermas, *Between Facts and Norms: Contributions to a Discourse Theory on Law and Theory* (MIT Press 1996); Jürgen Habermas, *The Theory of Communicative Action. Volume 1: Reason and the Rationalization of Society* (Beacon Press 1984). With respect to the relationship between participatory and deliberative democracy, it should be noted that although authentic participatory democratic procedures do incorporate deliberative elements, they also involve additional components that cannot be reduced to the deliberative dimension; see Umberto Allegretti, 'La democrazia partecipativa in Italia e in Europa' (2011) 1 Rivista AIC 3.

12 For the decisive role of international law and, in particular, the 1998 Aarhus Convention (implementing Principle 10 of the 1992 Rio Declaration on Environment and Development), which requires States Parties to recognise specific rights of information and participation, pillars of an 'environmental democracy', see Eva J. Lohse and Margherita Poto (eds), *Participatory Rights in the Environmental Decision-making Process and the Implementation of the Aarhus Convention: a Comparative Perspective* (Duncker & Humblot 2015); Jonas Ebbeson, 'Public participation', in Daniel Bodansky, Jutta Brunnée and Ellen Hey (eds), *The Oxford Handbook of International Environmental Law* (OUP 2007), 682.

to the demands for greater and urgent action to combat climate change and its impacts, in the interest of present and future generations.

This study will address the most popular instrument of environmental participatory democracy of the last five years: the so-called climate citizens' assembly. The analysis of selected cases of climate citizens' assemblies held at the national level will make it possible to assess whether and under which conditions these bodies can effectively connect representative democracy with future generations' interests in the framework of the decision-making processes that shape climate and environmental policies.

II. Climate Citizens' Assemblies: Three Case Studies

1. Introduction

A citizens' assembly (sometimes named citizens' 'convention' or 'council') is a body composed of citizens randomly selected using stratified sampling, convened upon the initiative of an institutional actor (at any level of government) to deliberate and adopt recommendations or proposals on a specific issue chosen by the latter.[13] Usually formed by more than one hundred members, it is the most numerous of the so-called 'deliberative mini-publics', which include smaller constituencies such as citizens' juries or consensus conferences. These are all people's forums characterised by both the deliberative method, aimed at enhancing the legitimacy of public policies through a dialogic and argumentative process of building consensus around them[14], and the random selection of participants as representative

13 Recently, on citizens' assemblies, see Min Reuchamps, Julien Vrydagh and Yanina Welp (eds), *De Gruyter Handbook of Citizens' Assemblies* (De Gruyter 2023); Giulia Mannarini, 'Citizens' Assemblies as Articulations of Democratic Participation between Criticalities and Perspectives' (2023) 4 DPCE 943; Marthe Fatin-Rouge Stefanini and Xavier Magnon (eds), *Les Assemblées Citoyennes. Nouvelle utopie démocratique?* (DICE 2022).

14 See Habermas, *The Theory of Communicative Action* (n 11). On the deliberative potential of mini-publics, see James S. Fishkin, *When the People Speak: Deliberative Democracy and Public Consultation* (OUP 2009); Kimmo Grönlund, Maija Setälä and Kaisa Herne, 'Deliberation and Civic Virtue: Lessons from a Citizen Deliberation Experiment' (2010) 2 European Political Science Review 95.

samples of the sociodemographic composition of the wider population[15], sometimes referred to as the '*minipopulus*'[16].

A citizens' assembly is not a new tool, nor has it been used only for deliberation on ecological transition. In the past, it has been repeatedly employed as part of a broader institutional reform processes. The world's first citizens' assembly took place in *British Columbia* in 2004, where participants deliberated on whether the Canadian province should adopt a new electoral system.[17] The electoral reform was also the topic of the citizens' assemblies convened in the Netherlands in 2004, and *Ontario* in 2006. This form of mini-public was further incorporated into the ultimately unsuccessful Icelandic constitution-making process (2010),[18] as well as in the framework of constitutional amendment procedures. The latter application is particularly exemplified – and indeed epitomised – by the Irish case, often described as a 'world leader in the use of citizens' assemblies in the constitutional and policy reform arenas'.[19] Ireland's experience includes the Convention on the Constitution (2012–2014), which led to two landmark referendums legalising same-sex marriage (2015) and abolishing the crime of blasphemy (2018), and the Citizen Assembly of 2016-2018, which resulted in a referendum that removed the constitutional ban on abortion (2018).[20]

---

15 This recruitment method will be specifically assessed in section III.

16 Robert A. Dahl, *Democracy and Its Critics* (YUP 1989), 340. On deliberative mini-publics, see Oliver Escobar and Stephen Elstub, 'Forms of Mini-Publics: An introduction to deliberative innovations in democratic practice' (*newDemocracy Research and Development Note*, 8 May 2017); Stephen Elstub and Gianfranco Pomatto, 'Mini-publics and Deliberative Constitutionalism', in Ron Levy et al. (eds), *The Cambridge Handbook of Deliberative Constitutionalism* (CUP 2018), 295.

17 On this experience, see Patrick Fournier et al., *When citizens decide. Lessons from Citizen Assemblies on Electoral Reform* (OUP 2011); Mark E. Warren and Hilary Pearse (eds), *Designing Deliberative Democracy: The British Columbia Citizens' Assembly* (CUP 2008).

18 The reference is to the *National Forum* convened in 2010 as part of the constitution-making process then underway, tasked with identifying the principles and values guiding the future constitution: see Hannah Filmore-Patrick, 'The Iceland Experiment (2009-2013): A Participatory Approach to Constitutional Reform' (2013) 2 DPC Policy Notes. On constituent processes that emphasised direct citizen participation, see Umberto Allegretti, Cecilia Corsi and Giovanni Allegretti, 'Constituent Process and Constituent Assembly: the making of Constitutions through the larger involvement of citizens' [2016] Forum Costituzionale.

19 Seána Glennon, 'The Role of Deliberative Minipublics in Enhancing Democracy in Canada' (*UK Constitutional Law Association Blog*, 22 May 2024).

20 On the Irish model, see Dimitri Courant, 'Citizens' Assemblies for Referendums and Constitutional Reforms: Is There an "Irish Model" for Deliberative Democracy?'

This inquiry will focus on the recent rise of citizens' assemblies dedicated to deliberating climate and environmental policies. It will specifically examine those convened by constitutional bodies at the state government level, where the primary legislative authority over these issues resides. In particular, it will analyse the first and most significant cases: the French *Convention Citoyenne pour le Climat* (2019-2020), the *Climate Assembly UK* (2020), and the Spanish *Asamblea Ciudadana para el Clima* (2021-2022). These national citizens' assemblies are assumed to be representative of those that have been flourishing across Europe in recent years, insofar as, having preceded them, they implicitly served as models for their design and development (e.g. climate citizens' assemblies held in Denmark,[21] Austria,[22] Luxemburg[23] and Ireland[24]).

Although beyond the scope of this inquiry, it is worth mentioning the growing popularity of climate citizens' assemblies at sub-national and local levels within nation-states, to give an idea of the extent of the phenomenon[25] (notably, in the former, we can mention the cases of Scotland[26]

(2020) 2 Frontiers in Political Sciences 1; David M. Farrell and Jane Suiter, *Reimagining Democracy: Lessons in Deliberative Democracy from the Irish Front Line* (Cornell UP 2019).

21 *Borgerting på klimaområdet* (2020–2021).

22 *Klimarat der Bürgerinnen und Bürger Gemeinsam fürs Klima* (2020).

23 *Klima-Biergerrot* (2022). For a comparative overview, see Fiorentino (n *) 75 ff.

24 Note that the Irish Citizens' Assembly has also addressed climate change, though only as part of a broader mandate. Its recommendations on the issue (see Citizens' Assembly, *Third Report and Recommendations of the Citizens' Assembly: How the State Can Make Ireland a Leader in Tackling Climate Change*, 18 April 2018), after being examined by the Joint Committee on Environment and Climate Action, subsequently inspired the 2019 declaration of a 'climate and biodiversity emergency' by the Irish Lower House (*Dáil Éireann* debate – Thursday, 9 May 2019, Vol. 982 No 5). Later, the Irish tradition of citizens' assemblies found a new expression in the Citizens' Assembly on Biodiversity Loss (2022–2023): see Ursula Quill, 'Ireland's Citizens' Assembly on Biodiversity Loss: Potential and Limitations for Deliberative Democracy' (*ConstitutionNet*, 31 January 2023).

25 For an overview, see https://knoca.eu/map-of-national-assemblies. See also the list of citizens' assemblies established in Germany at Länder and municipal level: http://www.buergerrat.de/. On the wave of citizens' assemblies convened at the local level in the UK, dedicated to climate issues, but not only, see Lauren Brown, 'Local citizens' assemblies in the UK: a second report card' (*The Constitution Unit*, 25 March 2022); Robert Liao, 'Local citizens' assemblies in the UK: an early report card' (*The Constitution Unit*, 8 January 2021).

26 Scotland's Climate Assembly (2020–2021; 2022). See 'Citizens' Assembly of Scotland: research report' (*Gov.scot*, 25 January 2022).

and Jersey[27]). Equally outside the scope of this analysis are the numerous experiences of climate citizens' assemblies that, although similar to those previously mentioned, cannot strictly be classified as institutes of participatory democracy. This is because they have been launched and self-governed from 'below' (e.g. by social movements, nonprofit associations, NGOs, etc.), without any initiative or direction from institutions.[28] Nonetheless, these practices of so-called 'spontaneous institutionalism'[29] are not unimportant, as they have proven to be capable of stimulating the establishment of 'official' citizens' assemblies.[30]

2. The French *Convention Citoyenne pour le Climat*

The first-ever citizens' assembly to be convened at the state level specifically to deliberate on carbon reduction policies was the French *Convention Citoyenne pour le Climat*. The context from which it derived highlights the antidotal value attached to the participatory instruments in times of difficulty. In recent years republican institutions have been undergoing a crisis of legitimacy, stemming from the overlapping of the general crisis of political representation and a harsh political, social and territorial conflict

27 *Citizens' Assembly on Climate Change* (2021). On these case studies, see Fiorentino (n *) 81-82.

28 These practices should be brought under the category of 'spontaneous institutionalism' (Feliciano Benvenuti, *Il nuovo cittadino. Tra libertà garantita e libertà attiva* (Marsilio 1994), 34 ff.), which includes 'those forms of basic autonomy that are on the side of society and its autonomy' and whose 'eventual influence on institutional action is registerable in fact but remains informal', so that 'the public action that is produced remains qualified only as such' (Umberto Allegretti (n 11) 305, translation by the author).

29 Allegretti (n 11) 305.

30 We can mention as examples the climate citizens' assemblies organised at the national level both in Germany (the *Bürgerrat Klima*, promoted by BürgerBegehren Klimaschutz and Scientists for Future, 2021) and Poland (the Assembly on Energy Poverty – *Narada Obywatelska or Energii* – 2022). In Germany, following the success of the *Bürgerrat Klima* and numerous other assemblies, whether spontaneous or convened by institutions, the *Bundestag* issued a call in 2022 for the implementation of three citizens' assemblies by the end of 2025, to be tasked with making recommendations on predetermined topics. The first citizens' assembly installed by the *Bundestag*, on 'Nutrition in Transition: Between Private Concerns and State Responsibilities', started its work in September 2023 and adopted its final recommendations in January 2024: see *Bürgerrat Ernährung des Deutschen Bundestages, Recommendations to the German Bundestag – Citizens' Assembly 'Nutrition in Transition'*, Berlin, 14 January 2024.

over the distribution of the costs and burdens of the ecological transition process.[31] In an attempt to address this crisis, in early 2019 President *Emmanuel Macron* launched a massive participatory forum called *Grand Débat National*.[32] In late 2019, following the success of that broad consultation – more in terms of participation than of impact on decision-making[33] – the executive launched the *Convention*.

The initiative was announced by the Head of State in April 2019, at the press conference closing the *Débat*. As a result of this political input, the *Convention* was established by the *Conseil économique, social et environnemental* (*CESE*) based on a *lettre de mission* signed by the Prime Minister *Édouard Philippe*. This letter gave the citizens' assembly the mandate to deliberate and report to the President and the Government 'structuring measures to reduce greenhouse gas emissions by at least 40 % by 2030 compared to 1990 levels, in a spirit of social justice', and defined its composition and structure.[34]

The assembly was composed of 150 citizens randomly selected with stratification sampling to ensure the representation of French social diversity by age, gender, level of education, geographic origin, urban or rural residence, and occupation. Accordingly, young people were represented in proportion to their share of the demographic pyramid of the population aged 16 and over (divided into six age groups for participant recruitment): those aged

31 See Paola Piciacchia, 'La ricerca dell'incerta sintesi tra democrazia rappresentativa e democrazia partecipativa. Riflessioni a margine del *Grand Débat National*' (2020) 3 DPCE Online 3193, 3195.

32 ibid. The author notes that the *Grand Débat National*, through a translation from administrative law to constitutional law and the elevation of the local territorial scale to the national level, was derived from the virtuous institution of participatory environmental democracy known as the *débat public*, which has existed in France for nearly thirty years. On the 2019 *Grand Débat National*, see also Fabrizio Politi, 'Democrazia rappresentativa versus democrazia diretta. Riflessioni preliminari su democrazia parlamentare, democrazia partecipativa e democrazia deliberativa' (2021) 1 Dirittifondamentali.it 526. On the *débat public*, consisting in the prior submission of projects with a major impact on the territory or the environment to an informed public discussion, see Martine Revel et al. (eds), *Le débat public: une expérience française de démocratie participative* (La Découverte 2007).

33 See Piciacchia (n 31) 3215 ff., according to whom 'the *Grand Débat National*, while it contributed to raising public awareness on certain major issues and to a renewed realization by French public authorities of the need to offer more spaces for bottom-up participation and listening, has nevertheless left open the issue of *suivi*, that is, the effective translation of what emerged from the debate at the national level into concrete reforms' (translation by the author).

34 Premier Ministre, *Lettre de mission*, Paris, 2 juil. 2019.

16–34 accounted for 29 % of the total, compared to less than 5 % of deputies under 35 in the National Assembly elected in 2017.

The *Convention* carried out its work from October 2019 to June 2020, under the direction of a *comité de gouvernance* (fifteen people, including representatives of the *Ministère de la transition écologique et solidaire*, experts in ecology and participatory democracy, economic and social actors, and two members of the Assembly drawn by lot at each session), the supervision of a *collèges de garants* charged with ensuring its independence (three members appointed by the President of *CESE* and the Presidents of the Houses of Parliament), and with the support of facilitating agencies and technical as well as legislative drafting consultants.[35] Citizens' assembly members were divided into five thematic groups (on housing, labour and production, transportation, food, and consumption), which held hearings with experts and stakeholders, engaged in debates, and developed policy proposals.[36] Finally, during the seventh and final session, held in plenary, the packages of measures introduced by the groups were submitted to a simple majority vote. The work resulted in a 460-page final report containing 149 proposals for carbon emission reduction.[37]

The impact of those proposals on the subsequent decision-making process, which was set to remain a monopoly of the constitutional bodies bound by the confidence relationship (Government and Parliament), was disappointing, especially in light of the President's original promise to submit citizens' proposals 'without filters'[38] to a parliamentary vote, a referendum, or direct regulatory application – giving the assembly a sort of 'quasi-legislative mandate'.[39] Indeed, most of the conventional proposals

35 On the *Convention*, extensively, see Christian Mosquera Arias, 'Le assemblee cittadine come meccanismo di democrazia partecipativa. Le esperienze delle assemblee per il clima in Francia e in Spagna' (2023) 2 DPCE Online 1930; Enrico Buono and Chiara Pizi, 'La democrazia climatica tra *climate change mitigation* e *climate change litigation*. Spunti comparati per l'elaborazione di strumenti partecipativi' (2023) 2 DPCE Online 1945.

36 For testimonies regarding the extensive work carried out by experts to inform and collaboratively develop proposals with citizens, see Louis-Gaëtan Giraudet et al., 'Deliberating on Climate Action: Insights from the French Citizens Convention for Climate' (*Institute Polytechnique de Paris*, 7 October 2021).

37 See Convention citoyenne pour le climat, *Les propositions de la Convention Citoyenne pour le Climat*, Version corrigée 29 janvier 2021.

38 *Conférence de presse à l'issue du Grand Débat national*. Publié le 25 avril 2019.

39 Leslie-Anne Duvic-Paoli, *Re-imagining the Making of Climate Law and Policy in Citizens' Assemblies* (2022) 11 Transnational Environmental Law 235, 254. In the *lettre*

were rejected, while the others found only a partial and/or watered-down acceptance withing the framework of two acts. On the one hand, the reform of the *CESE*, endowed with the power to initiate randomly selected citizens' public consultations on its initiative or demand of the Prime Minister or one of the Presidents of the Chambers.[40] On the other hand, the Act on climate and resilience,[41] whose draft was criticised by the Convention itself during a special session held in March 2021, in which its members lamented the failure to fulfil the promise of a '*sans filtre*' transposition of the proposed measures and pointed out that the bill – having diluted or ignored these measures and made them less systemic – was insufficient to address the challenges of climate change.[42] Some estimates suggest that only 10 % of proposals were accepted 'unfiltered', while 37 % were modified or watered-down and 53 % were rejected.[43]

---

de mission, the Prime Minister formally only committed on behalf of the government to respond to the recommendations and to publish a provisional timetable for their implementation.

40 *Loi organique n° 2021-27 du 15 janvier 2021 relative au Conseil économique, social et environnemental.* On the reform of the *CESE*, cf Julien Padovani, 'La réforme du Conseil économique, social et environnemental: une citoyenneté en question' (2022) 22 Revue des droits de l'homme; Denis Baranger, 'Démocratie participative: l'inopportune réforme du CESE' (*Jus Politicum blog*, 5 September 2020). In implementation of the reform, the *CESE*, mandated by a letter from Prime Minister Borne, organised the *Convention citoyenne sur la fin de vie*, which met between December 2022 and March 2023 (see Giuliaserena Stegher, 'La democrazia partecipativa a sostegno della democrazia rappresentativa: quale futuro per la legislazione sul "fine vita" in Francia?' (*Diritti comparati blog*, 1 March 2023).

41 V. *Loi n° 2021-1104 du 22 août 2021 portant lutte contre le dérèglement climatique et renforcement de la résilience face à ses effets.*

42 V. Convention Citoyenne pour le Climat, *Avis de la Convention Citoyenne pour le Climat sur les réponses apportées par le gouvernement à ses propositions*, Version corrigée le 2 mars 2021. Similarly, see also Conseil national de la transition écologique, *Avis du Conseil national de la transition écologique rendus en 2021. Délibération 2021-01: Avis du CNTE sur le projet de loi portant lutte contre le dérèglement climatique et renforcement de la résilience face à ses effets*, 2 ff.

43 See Gaspard d'Allens, Nicolas Boeuf and Léa Dang, 'Convention pour le climat: seules 10% des propositions ont été reprises par le gouvernement' (*Reporterre*, March 31, 2021). For a comprehensive analysis of the proposed measures, see Robin Denz, '"End of the world, end of the month, same struggle": On depoliticized transitions and emancipatory sustainability transformations. A case study of the French Citizens' convention on climate' [2021] LUP student papers.

3. The *Climate Assembly UK*

The second case study is that of the *Climate Assembly UK.* In June 2019, after the Parliament of the United Kingdom had amended the Climate Change Act 2008 to incorporate and implement the 2015 Paris Agreement commitment to reach net zero carbon emissions by 2050, six Select Committees of the House of Commons, following the French initiative,[44] called for the establishment of a citizens' assembly tasked with making recommendations on measures needed to achieve that goal.

The Assembly was composed of 110 citizens (of which 108 attended), selected using random stratified sampling to guarantee the representation of the wider population in terms of both demographics (age, gender, ethnicity, education, geographic origin, residence in urban or rural areas) and level of concern about climate change. Even in this case, young people (16–29 years old) were represented in proportion to their weight in the total population (23 %),[45] and still almost eight times more than in the House of Commons (in 2019, barely 3 % of the elected were 18–29 years old).

The Climate Assembly took place over six weekends between January and May 2020, under the joint governance of the parliamentary administration and the facilitation contractor, and with the assistance of expert leads charged with ensuring the information provided to the participants was balanced, accurate, and complete (supported by a panel of academics, which reviewed the written briefings created for assembly members, and an advisory panel of stakeholders chosen to be representative of a broad range of political and ideological perspectives). In the first session of work, members were briefed by experts on the scientific and ethical aspects of climate change and transition, alternative scenarios of a zero-emission future, and policy options for getting there, and on this basis developed some underpinning principles for the path to zero net emissions. Then, thematic meetings were held in subgroups and in plenary (on mobility, housing, consumption, land use, food and agriculture, energy sources, and response to the COVID-19 pandemic), in which policy options tabled by the experts were discussed and voted on, but to which participants were able to add further recommendations. A 556-page report was released in September

44 On the *Climate Assembly UK*, compared to the French *Convention*, see Claire Mellier and Rich Wilson, 'Getting Climate Citizens' Assemblies Right' (*Carnagie Europe*, 5 November 2020).

45 Climate Assembly UK, *The path to net zero*, 10 September 2020, 40.

2020,[46] containing an opening statement from the Assembly members and fifty recommendations approved by secret ballot (on ten areas: how we travel; what we eat and how we use land; what we buy; heat and energy use in the home; how we generate our electricity; and greenhouse gas removals), with the voting results and participants' views on advantages and disadvantages of each.

The impact of the Climate Assembly's recommendations on decision-making was quite modest. On the parliamentary side, they influenced the scrutiny agenda of the six Select Committees, some of which conducted inquiries into the proposals and asked the Government to adopt them as a basis for its policies.[47] Outside of Westminster, they were largely considered by the independent experts of the Committee on Climate Change in the drafting of *The Sixth Carbon Budget. The UK's path to Net Zero*,[48] which was incorporated into Government's *Carbon Budget Order 2021* in June 2021,[49] i.e., the act of secondary legislation that set the permitted greenhouse gas emissions for 2033–2037. In addition, the Government replied on its own initiative to the Assembly report,[50] and later stated that it had taken it into account when drafting of the *Net Zero Strategy* of October 2021,[51]

---

46 See ibid.

47 V. House of Commons, Business, Energy and Industrial Strategy Committee, *Climate Assembly UK: where are we now?*, Second Report of Session 2021–22, HC 546, 8 July 2021. See Stephen Elstub et al., *Evaluation of Climate Assembly UK* (Newcastle 2021), and Stephen Elstub, 'How has the UK Climate Assembly impacted parliament?' (*Wfd.org*, 25 November 2021), asserting that this experience ultimately constituted 'a valuable process that enabled a diverse group of UK citizens to engage in parliamentary scrutiny of government on climate policy in a meaningful manner' (at 104).

48 *The Carbon Budget Order 2021, UK Statutory Instruments 2021 No 750.*

49 See Robert Liao, 'The momentum behind climate assemblies' (*Constitution Unit Blog*, 4 August 2021).

50 See House of Commons, Business, Energy and Industrial Strategy Committee, *Written evidence submitted by the Department of Business, Energy and Industrial Strategy*, CAUK0014, August 2021.

51 House of Commons, Business, Energy and Industrial Strategy Committee, *Climate Assembly UK: where are we now?: Government Response to the Committee's Second Report of Session 2021–22*, Fifth Special Report of Session 2021–22, HC 680, 9 September 2021, 5: 'These recommendations are an important part of the evidence base that needs to be considered alongside other research to develop policies for reaching net zero that are feasible and equitable. This evidence base is being used in several ways, including to inform development of the Net Zero Strategy. For example, Government invited the Climate Assembly UK's expert leads to present the recommendations via seven briefings for officials from across government, covering all the policy areas discussed in the report and attended by over 400 HMG officials'.

which constitutes the policy document outlining policies and proposals for decarbonising the economy.

4. The Spanish *Asamblea Ciudadana para el Clima*

The third case study is the Spanish *Asamblea Ciudadana para el Clima*. In its January 2020 declaration on the climate and environmental emergency the *Pedro Sánchez*'s coalition Government committed to establishing a citizens' assembly on this issue.[52] In order to implement this promise, Art. 39(1) of the Climate Change and Energy Transition Act provided for the creation of a citizens' assembly composed according to the principle of gender equality and including young people, as a forum for structured citizen participation in climate change decision-making.[53] Under its terms, the Assembly was finally established by an Order of the Ministry of Ecological Transition in September 2021.[54] It represents a unique case in the national level comparative landscape insofar as it has been conceived as a reconstitutable body for citizens' participation. To date, it has only been convened once (November 2021–May 2022), with the mandate to respond to the question 'A safer and fairer Spain in the face of climate change, how do we do it?'. In the future, it may be summoned again by another ministerial Order, entrusted with new tasks, new members and renewed governance bodies.[55] This organisational structure, according to Art. 4 of the Order, is primarily comprised of an independent and multidisciplinary technical-logistical coordination panel run by civil society organisations, as well as an advisory group of independent and recognised experts in climate change-related fields, responsible for setting a work agenda and ensure a

52 See Gobierno de España (n 3) 5.

53 See Art. 39(1), *Ley 7/2021, de 20 de mayo, de cambio climático y transición energética*, BOE núm. 121, de 21 de mayo de 2021: '[...] el Gobierno [...] garantizará de forma estructurada la participación ciudadana en el proceso de toma de decisiones en materia de cambio climático a través del establecimiento de una Asamblea Ciudadana del Cambio Climático a nivel Nacional [...]. Su composición tendrá en cuenta el principio de representación equilibrada entre mujeres y hombres e incluirá la participación de jóvenes. La composición, organización y funcionamiento de la misma se desarrollará mediante Orden Ministerial'.

54 See *Orden TED/1086/2021, de 29 de septiembre, por la que se estayblece la composición, organización y funcionamiento de la Asamblea Ciudadana para el Clima*, BOE núm 241 08/10/2021.

55 See *Disposición adicional primera. Establecimiento de nuevos mandatos*, Orden TED/1086/2021.

broad, informed and accessible debate through the provision of accurate, balanced, and comprehensive information to the Assembly.[56] Administrative and technical support is provided by the competent governmental office (*Oficina Española de Cambio Climático* within the Ministry of Ecological Transition), while contractors are in charge of citizen recruitment and facilitating the participatory process.

This Assembly was composed of 100 citizens randomly selected using stratified sampling to represent the diversity of society by age, gender, level of education, geographical origin and area of residence. Young members (16–35 years old) made up 27 % of the Assembly – a high share compared to the 5 % of under-35s elected to the Congress of Deputies in 2019.

Assembly members, divided into five thematic groups (consumption; food systems and land use; labour; community, health and care; ecosystems), underwent a learning process with inputs from experts and then discussed and developed recommendations. Final plenary sessions were dedicated to the presentation and approval of these recommendations by simple majority votes, with the stipulation that if abstentions exceeded 30 %, approval would require 66 % of the votes in favour. As a result of a total of six sessions, the final report, containing 172 recommendations, was published in June 2022.[57] It was submitted to the Government, which was committed to examine the proposals with a view to their possible incorporation into its actions, as well as to the Congress of Deputies, with the aim – set in the ministerial Order – of 'facilitating debate and decision-making on climate change policies'.[58] It is worth noting that representatives of the *Asamblea* ran an information campaign across Spain to bring its recommendations to the attention of the Autonomous Communities, local authorities, third-sector entities, and social-economic actors.[59]

Nevertheless, citizens' proposals did not have a noticeable impact. Some scholars have dismissed the citizens' assembly as a case of 'simulated' or 'misleading' participation, as it was established downstream of the decision-

56 Under Art. 4(1)(b), the appointment of its twenty members must be 'based on the recommendations of the National Climate Commission, the Advisory Council on the Environment, and the Congressional and Senate Committees on the Ecological Transition'.

57 See Asamblea Ciudadana para el Clima, Una España más segura y justa ante el cambio climático, ¿Cómo lo hacemos? (*Informe final de recomendaciones*, Junio 2022).

58 Art. 3(3), Orden TED/1086/2021.

59 See https://asambleaciudadanadelcambioclimatico.es/novedades/. On this case, compared to the French one, see Mosquera Arias (n 35) 1937 ff.

making process, after the Climate Change Act had outlined the decarbonisation strategy up to 2050 and after the distribution of the NextGeneration EU's green appropriations.[60] The Government did not even respond to the report, later stating that it had taken certain, unidentified recommendations into account in updating the Integrated National Energy and Climate Plan 2021–2030 (June 2023).[61]

III. The Features of Citizens' Assemblies and Future Generations' Interests

Out of this brief comparative analysis, a citizens' assembly, in its recent climate-related version, appears as a highly standardised institution, characterised by well-defined features resulting from an intensive process of circulation between legal systems.

Its most peculiar feature undoubtedly lies in the method for member recruitment: a selection by lot aimed at achieving the egalitarianism of the *Hellenic* ideal of democracy,[62] the randomness of which is mitigated through stratification sampling to ensure that the assembly reflects the broader social reality.[63] This recruitment method is intended to realise the ideal of the representation as 'resemblance', also known as the sociological, descriptive or statistical representation of the people[64]. From its perspective, stratified sampling effectively enhances the legitimacy of the participatory process and its outcomes by fostering the identification of

---

60 See Rafael Jiménez Aybar and Agnès Delage Amat, 'Preguntas incómodas al finalizar la primera Asamblea para el Clima en España' (*La Vanguardia*, 4 June 2022).

61 See *Plan Nacional Integrado de Energía y Clima* (PNIEC 2023-2030), June 2023, 19-20.

62 Aristotele, *Politics* (OUP, 1995), 1294b. On the lottery as a method for the allocation of public offices, see, *ex multis*, Bernard Manin, *Principes du gouvernement représentatif* (Calmann-Lévy 1995), 19 ff.; Fulco Lanchester, 'Il sorteggio in campo politico come strumento integrativo dell'attività delle assemblee parlamentari' (2016) 2 Nomos. Le attualità nel diritto; Yves Sintomer, 'Sorteggio e democrazia deliberativa. Una proposta per rinnovare la politica del XXI secolo' (2016) 2 Nomos. Le attualità nel diritto; Astrid Zei, 'L'arbitrato del caso: applicazioni del metodo del sorteggio nel diritto pubblico' (2017) 1 Nomos. Le attualità nel diritto; Astrid Zei, *Il diritto e il caso. Una riflessione sull'uso del sorteggio nel diritto pubblico* (Jovene 2023).

63 See Oliver Dowlen, *The Political Potential of Sortition: A Study of the Random Selection of Citizens for Public Office* (Imprint Academic 2008), 23; Jane Mansbridge, 'Should Blacks Represent Blacks and Women Represent Women? A Contingent "Yes"' (1999) 61 Journal of Politics 631.

64 See Hanna Fenichel Pitkin, *The Concept of Representation* (UCP 1967), 60 ff.

the non-participating majority of the *demos* with the participating minority that 'looks like them'. As political scientist *Robert Dahl* argued, the output of the *minipopulus* expresses the views that the *demos* would express, had it the opportunity to access the best information and knowledge and to engage in a deliberative process.[65]

One might doubt the actual correspondence of the starting views and stances of the selected sample to those of the wider population it is drawn from: an assembly that almost perfectly reflects the socio-demographic composition of the people may not also reflect its internal distribution of political and ideological standpoints, either general or on the subject matter under deliberation. This point was addressed only by the designers of *Climate Assembly UK*, who included attitudes toward climate change among the sample stratification criteria: an element that may, to some extent, favour the representation of a broad range of political preferences regarding the agenda and approach to the issue.[66]

The chosen recruitment method can be considered functional to achieving the counter-majoritarian objective of giving a voice to interests typically marginalised in political representation – above all, those of young generations in influencing decisions affecting their ability to enjoy fundamental freedoms and minimum conditions of existence. As observed, it allowed for the participation of young people in proportions roughly reflective of their actual size in society: a minority share compared to other demographic groups, but still greater than their representation in elected assemblies.

Young people are the demographic group that, on a global scale, expresses the greatest concern about the effects of climate change.[67] Therefore, one may assume that giving them a greater voice could potentially introduce stronger instances of environmental protection into the deliberative process. While this conclusion has a grain of truth, it should not be overstated. Young generations do not constitute a monolithic and homogeneous political group that carries *en bloc* the social interest in more transformative environmental policies. As with other sociodemographic groups, it holds true that 'not all identity groups are interest groups, and group identity

65 Dahl (n 16).

66 See also the cases of Scotland's *Climate Assembly*, Luxembourg's *Klima-Biergerrot* and the *Citizens' Assembly on Climate Change* of Jersey, whose members were also selected to represent the spectrum of possible views on climate change.

67 See Caroline Hickman et al., 'Climate anxiety in children and young people and their beliefs about government responses to climate change: a global survey' (2021) 12 Lancet Planetary Health e863.

often exists prior to and conflicts with any sense of shared interest'.[68] Furthermore, the interests of young generations do not necessarily and entirely align with those of future generations merely for reasons of 'age proximity'. Indeed, the interests of future generations, since their bearers are not yet in existence, are ontologically distinct from those of the legal subjects living in the present as well as impossible to predict. Rather, the concept of 'future generations' is part of the concept of 'the people' as holders of sovereignty, as considered in its historical dimension. Therefore, the acknowledgment of 'future generations' implies that they are holders of a sovereign power they cannot exercise, but which must nevertheless be exercised in their 'interests' by the people of the present.[69] In other words, this sovereign power needs to be 'imperfectly' objectified in the principle of intergenerational equity,[70] which requires meeting the needs of the present without compromising the ability of future humanity, as we can currently perceive it, to meet its own.

In conclusion, the proportional representation of young people within climate citizens' assemblies, while certainly enhancing the input legitimacy of the participatory process, does not necessarily, *per se*, steer its outcomes toward greater protection of future generations. After all, even if the young members of an assembly uniformly bore the strongest demands for environmental protection, they would still fall far short of the majority needed to approve recommendations.

In any case, there is another key feature of climate citizens' assemblies that may favour the development of proposals consistent with the presumed interests of future generations in the sustainability of current political choices. This is the deliberative component of these mini-publics, which endows participation with transformative power – namely, the ability to shift citizens' initial opinions and positions by enabling them to engage in a structured and informed discussion, and dialectically converge around the 'constraint-free force of the better argument' on the policies to be

68 See Mark B. Brown, 'Citizen Panels and the Concept of Representation' (2006) 2 Journal of Political Philosophy 218.

69 See Cristina D'Orazi, 'Le generazioni future e il loro interesse: oggetti sconosciuti di rilievo costituzionale. Osservazioni a prima lettura della l. cost. n. 1/2022' (2022) 2 Biolaw Journal 93, 99. See also Giacomo Palombino, *Il Principio di equità generazionale. La tutela costituzionale del futuro* (Le Monnier 2022).

70 See *ex multis* Daniel Bertram, '"For You Will (Still) Be Here Tomorrow": The Many Lives of Intergenerational Equity' (2023) 12 Transnational Environmental Law 121; Edith Brown Weiss, 'Intergenerational Equity', *Max Planck Encyclopedias of International Law* (2021).

pursued.[71] At the organisational level, a well-designed network of coordinating, guaranteeing, and supporting bodies can significantly empower citizens' assembly members and facilitate the drafting of proposals that are both qualitatively sound and effective in addressing the high complexity and technicality of the issues at stake. This is precisely what occurred in the cases examined, where the organisational set-ups, similar though not entirely overlapping, appeared to successfully fulfil the fundamental requirements of a transformative deliberative process. First, they provided accurate, complete, and balanced information to members, thereby creating the conditions for accessible and informed debate on climate policies. Second, they safeguarded the independence of the deliberative process from interference by both political actors and opposing stakeholders, while also promoting inclusiveness, transparency, and a fluid, orderly progression of the process itself – thanks to the decisive contribution of experts in participatory processes, such as facilitators.

The reference to these professional figures highlights another common feature of the three case studies, that is the 'outsourcing' of the organisation of the process. The necessarily experimental nature of the national citizens' assemblies examined posed information, organisational and logistical challenges beyond the perimeter of the bureaucratic and technical competences of the convening institutions.[72] This implied the entrusting of some core functions – such as designing, coordination, management, and logistical and technical support – either wholly or partially to external professionals from consulting firms or non-profit organisations. While this was a pragmatic solution, if the use of these instruments were to be normalised, a shift (at least partial) from contract management to the establishment of new dedicated public departments that provide better guarantees of independence and impartiality might be necessary.

The functioning of the three assemblies showed a common articulation of the work in three phases of the deliberative process: 'first to know, then to discuss, then to deliberate',[73] where the third is understood as the development and adoption, by a simple majority, of proposals more or less

71 Habermas, *The Theory of Communicative Action* (n 11) 24.

72 On the need for participatory instruments to conform to the 'principle of the appropriateness of methods', which 'creates the need for the use (and training) of appropriate professionalism' (translation by the author), see Umberto Allegretti (n 11) 328–329.

73 Luigi Einaudi, *Prediche inutili. Dispensa prima* (Einaudi 1956), 6 (translation by the author).

in principle or detail, finally included in a public report to be transmitted to the convening institutional actors. A further, albeit optional, phase should be added to enhance the assemblies' ability to influence public decisions: the phase in which institutions provide feedback in response to the assemblies. This step was absent in the Spanish case due to vague regulatory references regarding follow-up, but was fulfilled in France, where it was established in the summoning document, and in the United Kingdom, where it resulted from political commitments by the Select Committees and the Government. Such feedback, by implying a more or less detailed and reasoned political stance on each proposed climate measure, can facilitate the opening of a dialogue channel between, on one side, the political institutions within the representative circuit and, on the other, the citizens' assemblies and the broader *demos* they sociologically represent. However, both the feedback and the dialogue are insufficient to ensure the effective translation of proposed measures into final public decisions. In the French case, a partial and watered-down legislative reception was observed, while in the United Kingdom, citizens' inputs informed parliamentary scrutiny of the Government and were partially taken into account in the drafting of programmatic documents and regulations.

IV. The Perspective of the Institutionalisation of Climate Citizens' Assemblies

The complete lack of an institutional response and/or an incomplete, diluted, and filtered transposition of assemblies' proposals may generate a sense of frustration among their members,[74] as well as undermine the pursuit of future generations' interests to a healthy environment, if the short-termism of representative politics disproportionately prevails. The actual risk is to devalue and miss the opportunities offered by the newest instruments of environmental democratic participation, and to widen further the gulf separating the governors and the governed, and the former from the interests of future humanity.

Yet, it is neither desirable to vest climate citizens' assemblies (and citizens' assemblies in general) with direct and unilateral decision-making

74 On the frustration of the members of the French Assembly, see Adrián Galván Labrador and Christos Zografo, 'Empowerment and disempowerment in climate assemblies: The French citizens' convention on climate' (2024) 4 Environmental Policy and Governance 337.

power, nor to attribute binding value to their proposals. Such solutions could result in a harmful confusion of roles, and, at worst, in destructive competition between elected parliamentary assemblies and randomly selected citizens' assemblies. In the current conditions of growing complexity in mass societies, political decision-making must remain vested in elected representatives, who are directly legitimised by the electorate to represent the general interests of society: this means staging the confrontation and conflict, and seeking a synthesis, among the multiple and fragmented demands and interests that bubble up within political communities.

The future of constitutional democracy cannot rest on inverting the hierarchy between parliamentary institutions and mini-publics. Rather, it could benefit from better integrating deliberative processes into the system of representative democracy to compensate for its limitations.[75] Climate citizens' assemblies succeeded in mobilising a plurality of social, political, and cultural voices that are decentralised from the traditional decision-making processes based on political representation. When properly designed, these assemblies can support parliamentary bodies and government departments by capturing demands that would otherwise remain marginal or unheard. In this sense, citizens' assemblies (not only climate-related ones) have the potential to offer an innovative form of 'outsourced' legislative inquiry, qualitatively enhanced compared to classical methods (such as calls for evidence, committee hearings, etc.), as they are more independent, inclusive, and grounded in the virtues of public deliberation.

In any case, the pre-eminence of the democratic-representative circuit cannot be invoked *ad libitum* to unreasonably water down or even ignore citizens' proposals. Despite the infeasibility of legal sanctions, institutional actors who are minimally or not at all receptive could still be held politically accountable. This could be achieved through the establishment and sustained operation of the channels of dialogue mentioned above, either by the assembly members themselves (by reconvening to take a position on the implementation, as in France, or by running information campaigns on their activities' outcomes, as in Spain), or by opposition parties, stakeholders, and civil society actors (such as associations, NGOs, social movements, etc.), who might find it useful to leverage the results of direct citizen participation to advance their respective goals.

75 Regarding the 'constitutional dilemma' of integrating participatory democracy into decision-making processes based on representation, see Piciacchia (n 31) 216 ff.

For institutions to be effectively held accountable, three conditions should be met. Firstly, citizens must be enabled to draft qualitatively appreciable proposals by allocating sufficient time for the deliberation process, providing informative and technical support to participants, and offering financial remuneration for their commitment (thus far, this is the only condition that has been fulfilled). Secondly, an 'osmosis' between assemblies and public opinion must be established, which requires not only the inclusiveness and transparency of the assemblies (already achieved), but also proactive public measures to ensure media visibility for their work and outcomes (a condition not yet fully met). Thirdly, assemblies must be institutionalised, meaning they need a legal framework that channels participation into predefined procedures, allowing for their regular establishment (even through a bottom-up dynamic),[76] and setting the stage for continuous, structured dialogue between citizens and political institutions (e.g., requiring institutions to justify their decision not to comply with a given proposal). At the national level, this last requirement can only be seen in embryonic form in the legislative regulations of the Spanish climate citizens' assembly. However, should there be political willingness in the future, the design of improved climate citizens' assemblies could benefit from emulating some general models that have emerged at both the sub-state and national levels. For example, recently a leading scholar on the subject identified the *Ostbelgien Model*,[77] the 'mixed deliberative commissions' of certain Belgian local legislatures, and the French experience of the reformed *CESE* as examples of successful institutionalisation of participatory procedures from which it would be useful to draw, insofar as they have

76 In this sense, see Allegretti, *Democrazia partecipativa* (n 11) 306, according to whom the 'strongest' forms of participatory democracy are not episodic, but 'provided regularly and with precisely constructed rhythms in terms of time, continuity and content'.

77 The reference is to the system adopted by the Parliament of the German-speaking Community of Belgium (see Parlament der Deutschsprachigen Gemeinschaft, 25. Februar 2019 – *Dekret zur Einführung eines permanenten Bürgerdialogs in der Deutschsprachigen Gemeinschaft*). It provides, on the one hand, for a permanent *Bürgerrat* with the task of determining the agenda of the citizens' assemblies and organising and monitoring them, and, on the other hand, for temporary *Bürgerversammlungen* with the task of drawing up recommendations to which parliament and government are obliged to respond. On this model, see Christoph Niessen and Min Reuchamps, 'Designing a Permanent Deliberative Citizens' Assembly. The Ostbelgien Modell in Belgium' (Centre for Deliberative Democracy & Global Governance, Working Paper Series No 2019/6).

proven capable of creating a 'closer connection' between citizens and the involved institutions (whether parliamentary, governmental, or advisory) 'to achieve the ultimate goal of integrating citizens into decision-making'.[78]

A proper institutionalisation of citizens' assemblies is crucial not only to foster more genuine and substantial citizen participation in climate and environmental decision-making but also to prevent a looming risk: where not adequately regulated, deliberative instruments – although less divisive than the inherently polarising mechanisms of direct democracy[79] – can be instrumentalised as tools for populist or authoritarian 'appeals to the people'. Such appeals may seek to establish plebiscitary disintermediation[80] and/or offer only superficial and symbolic gratification to pressing social demands that elected political actors find inconvenient to address.

The future of the most promising participatory instrument, including the climate citizens' assembly, will be decided on the terrain of their institutionalisation. Embracing the challenge of integrating citizen participation into a legal framework and doing so in the most appropriate way to best serve the functioning of the representative system will be decisive in addressing the most critical challenges of our time: saving future generations from the anthropogenic destruction of the planet while preserving a healthy democracy for them.

78 See Piciacchia (n 31) 257 (translated by the author).

79 See Yves Meny, 'Populismo: dalla protesta al consolidamento giuridico', in Giacomo Delledonne et al. (eds), *Populismo e Costituzione. Una prospettiva giuridica* (Mondadori 2022); Angela Di Gregorio, 'Democrazia partecipativa e integrazione dei gruppi deboli. Una premessa' (2023) 2 DPCE Online 1837, 1844.

80 With regard to the French context, see Paola Piciacchia, '*Conseil National de la Refondation* e *Permanences citoyennes*: nel contesto di un difficile rapporto tra Parlamento e Governo e di un sistema partitico frammentato e polarizzato, la legittimazione in Francia passa (ancora una volta) per l'appello alla democrazia partecipativa' (2022) 3 Nomos. Le attualità nel diritto.

Deliberative Practices in Western Democracies and 'Authoritarian Deliberation' in China: Opposing Trends and Ambiguities of Deliberative Methods

*Giulia Mannarini**

The crisis in the legitimacy of stabilised democracies has been a well-known fact for some time now: scholars from a variety of disciplines have embarked on various strands of reflection, first and foremost, on whether democracy was in crisis, and then on why it was going through a pathological phase that was now systemic in nature. In this context, since the second half of the 20th century, new theorisations on the concepts of democracy and reflections on deliberative politics began to mature. And the 2000s saw the gradual spread of new practices and articulations of deliberative democracy: citizens' assemblies. However, deliberative instruments have not only developed within democratic contexts. As a matter of fact, 'controlled' forms of political participation and deliberation have long since found application in some authoritarian regimes in Asia, South America, and Africa. Among these, the Chinese experiences are particularly significant. The paper aims to propose some reflections in a comparative perspective about the concept of 'authoritarian deliberation' and the deliberative practices in Western democratic regimes. Subsequently, an attempt will be made to analyse the reasons why such tools may be functional to authoritarian patterns and dynamics: the comparison will be played on the ground of the deliberative instrument within different political contexts.

I. A Necessary Premise

The aim of this contribution is to highlight a number of considerations concerning so-called deliberative democracy. This model has increasingly come to represent one of the key tools for addressing emerging issues in public law, such as environmental protection, the rights of future generations,

* PhD Candidate in International, European and Public Law, School of Law, University of Milano-Bicocca.

and ethically sensitive questions, including end-of-life decisions. As such, it belongs fully within the broader debate on future-proofing in public law.

This paper seeks to critically reconstruct – through the lens of comparative law and with the support of the relevant scholarly literature – the role of deliberative discourse within consolidated democracies and its development in non-democratic contexts. The central objective is to critically assess whether deliberative democracy can serve as a truly effective instrument in contemporary Western democracies. From this perspective, the comparison with experiences arising in authoritarian regimes proves particularly fruitful, offering valuable insights into both the potential and the limitations of this paradigm.

Among such experiences, the Chinese case stands out as the most structured and thought-provoking, not only because the hybrid dynamics caused by the use of instruments typically attributable to democracies in an authoritarian system is highly complex, but because the comparison provides an opportunity to reflect on deliberative practices within the democratic form of state as well.

Indeed, there are lively debates on how to place the tools of deliberative democracy within the mechanisms of representative government. Therefore, it is an extremely delicate subject in itself. And it becomes even more so when applied to an authoritarian context. However, paradoxically, and perhaps apparently, there the complexities of the application of deliberative instruments seem to vanish: so far, in comparison to the West, China has had many more applications of participatory forums in the last 20 to 30 years, and the process is continuously growing and stabilising.

However, the reflections of scholars who deal with 'authoritarian deliberation' move, in comparison to Western theorists, from the level of the functioning of the form of government to that of the form of state. The question that arises is whether deliberative instruments, born inherent to theories of democracy, can be key to a democratic evolution of a country that is not yet perceived to be democratic. Or one might ask whether the starting point might be wrong: that is, to believe *a priori* that deliberative instruments are necessarily inherent to democratic dynamics.

II. Deliberative Practices in the West

The need to create political communities and to enable them to fulfill the political functions assigned to them, and to do so in the most optimal way possible, has always determined the need to question and reflect continuously on the modes of legal and political organisation.[1] From *Xenophon* to *Herodotus*, from *Polybius* to *Thucydides*, via *Aristotle* and his fundamental Ἀθηναίων πολιτεία[2], the ancients were already questioning the best possible form of government, introducing - and then practising - the idea of a diffuse exercise of political power, entrusted to the *demos*.[3]

Today, in the precipitate aftermath of first the medieval and then the modern age, where the theory and history of constitutionalism has become the conceptual and historical essence and thread, the need for the preservation of the best arrangements of government and political organisation has certainly not waned, quite the contrary. While it is the democratic form that is most successful in the Western world today, it cannot but coexist with severe limitations: for it is not and has never been an achieved state, but rather an ever-changing and evolving process, the vicissitudes of which must be carefully followed. Therefore, the search for ever better refinement and adaptation to the concrete needs of reality was born with democracy and accompanies it every step of the way.

If 'the idea of deliberative democracy and its practical implementation are as old as democracy itself',[4] in times closer to us, it is the maturing of certain transformations that began a few decades ago that have given rise to many reflections on how to 'refine' our democracies:[5] especially numerous are those that fall under the large and heterogeneous umbrella of deliberative democracy,[6] the most recent theorisations of which stem from

1 For the most significant passages from the works of these authors, see Gustavo Zagrebelsky, *Imparare democrazia* (Einaudi 2007).

2 Aristotele, 'Costituzione Degli Ateniesi', in Pietro Boitani (ed), *La Democrazia in Grecia* (Mondadori 2016).

3 In Aristotle's political theory, 'democracy' was not seen as a virtuous form of political power of the masses, but as a non-ideal form; instead, '*politeia*' would be the virtuous form of government of the masses.

4 Jon Elster, *La democracia deliberativa* (Gedisa Editorial 2001) 13, translation by author.

5 Salvatore Taranto, 'Dilemmi intrinseci, irrisolvibili della democrazia deliberativa' [2013] Sociologia del diritto 29, 30.

6 The deliberative literature is indeed vast. *Ex multis*, see Fabrizio Cattaneo, 'Democrazia deliberativa: l'idea (nuova?) e i modelli di realizzazione' (2009) 15 Teoria politica 107, where the author carries out a reconstructive and comparative reflection for the

'communicative theory', the public sphere and reflections on deliberative method and politics, to which *Jürgen Habermas* is attributed the primogeniture; and for this reason, it is the German philosopher who is certainly to be singled out among the indispensable classics of deliberative literature.[7]

---

purpose of identifying a conceptual model of deliberative democracy, resorting to the thought of *Hans Kelsen*, *Norberto Bobbio* and *Jürgen Habermas,* with attention also paid to that of *Josef Schumpeter* and realist theories of democracy. See also the recent work by Min Reuchamps, Julien Vrydagh and Yanina Welp (eds), *De Gruyter Handbook of Citizens' Assemblies* (DeGruyter 2023).

It is worth noting, however, that the earliest reflections, in general, on the inclusion of groups in public policy-making processes are those of *Alexis de Tocqueville*, who, observing the US experience, argued the need for free association among citizens as an essential condition for the development of democracy, for two reasons: *Tocqueville* identified associations as the context in which '*i sentimenti e le idee sono rinnovate, il cuore allargato e la comprensione sviluppata*' (Alexis de Tocqueville, *La democrazia in America* [first published 1835, Einaudi 1931] 36). Thus, the author looked at associations as the privileged space of sociability in which individuals could approach politics, learning to limit the pursuit of individual interest. Moreover, associations potentially contained the capacity to reduce the danger of excessive centralisation of power in the legislative body. *Tocqueville's* reflections were a source of inspiration for those scholars of political theory who dealt with the subject during the 20th century, such as *Arthur Bentley* (Arthur K. Bentley, *The process of government: a study of social pressures* [Harvard University Press 1908]) introducing the pluralistic polity scheme, on which see Mauritio Cotta, Donatella Della Porta and Leonardo Morlino, *Fondamenti di scienza politica* (il Mulino 2001).

7 Jürgen Habermas, *Storia e critica dell'opinione pubblica* (Laterza 1971); ibid, *Teoria dell'agire comunicativo* (il Mulino 1986); ibid, *Fatti e norme. Contributi a una teoria discorsiva del diritto e della democrazia* (Guerini e associati 1996); ibid, *Storia e critica dell'opinione pubblica* (Roma-Bari 2000). The philosopher recently returned to the subject in ibid, *Nuovo mutamento della sfera pubblica e politica deliberativa* (Raffaello Cortina Editore 2023). The public sphere is understood as the sphere in which ideas and values are formed and reproduced and, above all, in which 'the decisive battle is being fought for the formation of consensus, which supports the system of power embodied in the State', Simone Chambers and Will Kymlicka (eds), *Alternative Conceptions of Civil Society* (Princeton University Press 2002).

According to *Habermas*, the space in which subjects' convictions are formed and different positions are compared constitutes one of the crucial nodes of social life, at the basis of which we find precisely the human capacity to speak and communicate, aimed at understanding and through which human beings continuously recreate the social world. The arena of public discourse is, therefore, that in which social subjects, through the instrument of communication, seek to forge collective criteria of judgement as to what is to be considered worthy of value. This phenomenon, in the German philosopher's opinion, is all the more relevant in a post-traditional context such as the current one, in which the only way to build the foundations of social solidarity is to develop a set of values and norms of behaviour that are, even provisionally, shared.

In this context, the studies classifiable within the theory of participatory democracy should not be forgotten either.[8]

Indeed, consensus can no longer be based on inherited conventions but must become reflexive and be based on open communication processes.

8 Copious is the literature, legal but not only, on the distinction, the overlap and the intersection between deliberative democracy and participatory democracy (and direct democracy). In fact, a firm point on the univocity of a definition and a distinction does not appear to have been reached in doctrine, as recalled by Viviana Molaschi, *Le arene deliberative. Contributo allo studio delle nuove forme di partecipazione nei processi di decisione pubblica* (Editoriale Scientifica 2018); on this point, see Luigi Bobbio, 'Dilemmi della democrazia partecipativa' [2006] Democrazia e diritto 11; Raffaele Bifulco, 'Democrazia deliberativa, partecipativa e rappresentativa' in Umberto Allegretti (ed), *Democrazia partecipativa. Esperienze e prospettive in Italia e in Europa* (Firenze University Press 2010); according to Umberto Allegretti, 'Democrazia partecipativa: un contributo alla democratizzazione della democrazia', in ibid 17: '*la democrazia partecipativa trova nel momento deliberativo un suo elemento essenziale, e d'altronde la democrazia deliberativa ha il suo luogo privilegiato proprio nelle procedure partecipative. Tuttavia rimangono tra le due correnti di idee importanti differenze [...] nella democrazia partecipativa la componente deliberativa è soltanto elemento di un fenomeno più complesso e matrici che non si limitano all'interesse per il valore e le tecniche dell'argomentazione razionale, che rappresenta invece la preoccupazione assorbente della democrazia deliberativa*'. It is, therefore, possible to say that deliberative democracy places the emphasis on the deliberative method and process (for what is meant by 'deliberation', see below), an aspect that not all participatory instruments necessarily possess. Evidence of this is the observation that many Citizens' Assemblies and many other deliberative processes discussed below, such as the Citizens' Initiative Review (CIR), are not constructed in such a way that the outcome is a 'decision'. They are and remain deliberative processes, but without decision-making effects not only because they have no binding effects, but because they are equally devoid of the very qualification of 'decision': such assemblies often do not aim to decide anything, but rather to inform, as in the case of the CIR. In any case, a fundamental contribution to such reflections is certainly the thought of *Karl Marx*, who in the elaboration of a model of direct democracy applicable with the advent of communism and in overturning *Hegel's* theoretical construction of the relationship between the public and private sphere, between civil society and the state (Karl Marx, *La guerra civile in Francia* (first published 1850, Savona International 1973); ibid, *Per la critica dell'economia politica* (first published 1859, Editori riuniti 1974) contributed to the theoretical developments of participatory democracy that flourished in the 1970s, which were followed by experiments with participatory budgets. On participatory democracy, see also Carol Pateman, *Participation and Democratic Theory* (Cambridge University Press 1970); ibid, *The problem of political obligation: a critique of liberal theory* (Cambridge University Press 1985); Nicos Poulantzas, *Il potere nella società contemporanea* (Editori riuniti 1979); Crowford MacPherson, *La vita e i tempi della democrazia liberale* (Il Saggiatore 1980).

Beyond, however, the conceptual and definitional questions, the 'dissemination' – to borrow the terminology used by *Umberto Allegretti* – and the stratification of all these practices, which some can synthetically call 'deliberative arenas', or those that

In particular, these studies and reflections, precipitated by a strong critique of traditional models, revolve around the polemic against (only) political representation and the conviction that it is possible to erect more solid and effective ways of reaching public decisions,[9] not so much through the methods of elected assemblies and negotiation with the social partners, but through discussion and confrontation between preferences, so as to arrive at changing 'progressively [one's] positions, agreeing to limit one's initial demands and making concessions to others, until an agreement is reached that, at least in part, satisfies everyone'.[10] Deliberation means that 'citizens exchange views on public policy issues, and discuss the reasons behind them',[11] with the additional effect of involving citizens to participate actively and consciously in political life. And it is in the etymological meaning of the term 'deliberation', well maintained in the English language, that the epistemic value of the deliberative process is preserved: 'deliberation' is the procedure, the dialogical and discussion method by which the final decision is reached rather than its result.[12] Thus, communicative

---

involve participation and deliberation together since they are 'spazi sociali nei quali tutti i diretti interessati prendono parte, in modo strutturato, a un processo collettivo di decisione fondato sull'uso di argomenti [...]', Luigi Bobbio, 'Le arene deliberative' [2002] Rivista Italiana di Politiche Pubbliche 4, is growing.

9 For producing a greater balance between the need to respect the democratic ideal and the need to protect individual rights, see Taranto (n 5) 32; Jon Elster, *Argomentare e negoziare* (Mondadori 1993); Paolo Comanducci, 'Argomentare e negoziare: un confronto' (1994) 2 Ragion pratica 215; Aldo Schiavello, 'Diritti umani e pluralismo tra argomentazione e negoziazione' (2010) 34 Ragion pratica 129.

10 Taranto (n 5) 32, translation by author. In other words, initial preferences are transformed, refined and limited to take into account the point of view of others (David Miller, 'Deliberative Democracy and Social Choice' (1992) 40 Political Studies 54), since 'the route to the decision is via arguments offered *by* and *to* the participants based on values of rationality and impartiality', Elster (n 4) 8.

11 Jon Rawls, *Il diritto dei popoli* (Einaudi 2001) 283.

12 Luigi Pellizzoni, 'Cosa significa deliberare? Promesse e problemi della democrazia deliberativa', in ibid (ed), *La deliberazione pubblica* (Meltemi 2005) 7; Andrea Pintore, *Democrazia e diritti. Sette studi analitici,* (Edizioni ETS 2010) 49. In literature there is also talk of the 'transformative power' of deliberation, see John S. Dryzek and Valerie Braithwaite, 'On the Prospects for Democratic Deliberation: values Analysis Applied to Australian Politics' (2000) 21 Political Psychology 241. On this topic, see also James Bohman and William Rehg, *Deliberative Democracy: Essays on Reason and Politics* (The MIT Press 1997); Raffaele Bifulco, 'Democrazia deliberativa' in *Enciclopedia del diritto* (Annali, IV, Giuffrè 2011) 271–294. On the ways in which citizens interact, and on the discussion that generates the reasons for making decisions, see Amy Gutmann and Dennis F. Thompson, *Why Deliberative Democracy?* (Princeton University Press 2004) 7.

forms of exchange and information, based on rational arguments, become essential. In other words, it is the phase of collective decision-making that is central, becoming an instrument of legitimisation and justification of political choices, having the merit of not incurring, for example, certain paradoxes detected by studies on the theories of games and collective choices.[13] Going beyond a particularistic vision, 'through deliberation, a kind of communicative rationality would be realised, expressing a form of collective reasoning that is deemed superior to individual reasoning. In this way, a conscious and impartial transformation of individual positions would take place until a unanimous decision is reached, the best'.[14]

And in the variety of theories and experiments,[15] there are in fact two unavoidable keystones of deliberative democracy processes: information and discussion. The first, which is varied and plural, allows an issue to be dealt with and assessed from several points of view in order to create a context that is as rational as possible; the second allows free expression of one's own opinion and at the same time stimulating the listening of others.[16]

Hence the possible purposes of deliberation, as identified by the doctrine, are: to stimulate citizens' interest in the public sphere,[17] even if many

On the issue of the legitimacy of deliberative mini-publics see Kristinn Màr and John Gastil, 'Do Voters Trust Deliberative Minipublics? Examining the Origins and Impact of Legitimacy Perceptions for the Citizens' Initiative Review' [2023] XLV Political Behavior 975.

13 On this topic see Carlos S. Nino, *La constitución de la democracia deliberativa* (Gedisa editorial 1997) 178, 189; Shmuel N. Eisenstadt, *Paradossi della democrazia: verso democrazie illiberali?* (il Mulino 2002); Douglas G. Baird, *Game Theory and the Law* (Cambridge University Press 1994).

14 Taranto (n 5) 42, translation by author.

15 Among the forerunners of this innovative democratic process is undoubtedly the United Kingdom, where in 1998 the two visionaries *Anthony Barnett* and *Peter Carty* launched the idea of transforming the House of Lords into a chamber of 600 citizens drawn by lot. Since then, whether at city, state, supranational or even global level, civic assemblies have increasingly become a tool for collective thinking that can better guide legislators.

16 Stefania Ravazzi, 'Una chiave per la democrazia deliberativa' [2007] Meridiana 21, 22.

17 Micheal Neblo, 'Thinking about democracy' (2005) 40 Acta Politica 169. This objective seems to have been achieved by many participatory budgets, see Gianpaolo Baiocchi, 'Participation, Activism and Politics: the Porto Alegre Experiment', in Archon Fung and Erik O. Wright (eds), *Deepening Democracy. Institutional Innovations in Empowered Participatory Governance* (Verso 2003); Jane Mansbridge, 'On the Idea that Participation Makes Better Citizens' in Stephen L. Elkin and Karol Edward Soltan (eds), *Citizen Competence and Democratic Institutions* (Penn State

authors relegate it as a secondary effect, certainly desirable, but not a priority,[18] to know conscious opinions on a public issue, and thus, tend to produce better and mutually acceptable decisions[19] in the presence of value implications;[20] to formulate public policies with the direct contribution of citizens;[21] to obtain a decrease in social conflict and an increase in the legitimacy of decisions and, possibly, of the authorities that decide to resort to this type of process;[22] to produce positive influences and feedback on the responsiveness and effectiveness of administrative apparatuses.[23]

The second objective, which is well embodied in deliberative polling,[24] determines a lower degree of planning, which is instead decisive in the case of collective decision-making on matters of public interest. From the organisational point of view, too, as the purpose changes – development of social capital, knowledge of citizens' opinions or 'policy-making' –, a number of variables change, albeit in the knowledge that it is not easy to speculate in the abstract on the optimal modalities and dimensions of a deliberative body.[25] First of all, the method of selection can be different: a total openness of the arenas or a random but reasoned selection by virtue of the need to create a representative microcosm from a socio-demographic

University Press 1999) 291. Building on *Tocqueville's* considerations on town meetings and citizen juries in America, *John Stuart Mill* emphasised how they could function as 'schools of public spirit', see ibid, *Considerazioni sul governo rappresentativo* (first published 1861, Editori riuniti 2000).

18 Thus, for example, Jon Elster. See ibid, 'La democrazia deliberativa' (2009) 36 La società degli individui 40.

19 Jan Gastil, *By popular demand: Revitalizing Representative Democracy Through Deliberative Elections* (University of California Press 2000).

20 Luigi Pellizzoni, 'Uncertainty and Participatory Democracy' (2003) 12 Environmental Values 195.

21 Elster (n 4) 24; Luigi Pellizzoni, 'Opinione o indagine pubblica?' [2007] Rivista italiana di politiche pubbliche 101.

22 Luigi Bobbio, 'La democrazia deliberativa nella pratica' [2005] Stato e Mercato 67.

23 Archon Fung, *Empowered participation. Reinventing urban democracy* (Princeton University Press 2004).

24 James S. Fishkin, *Deliberative Polling: Executive Summary* (Center for Deliberative Democracy at Stanford University 1988); James S. Fishkin, Robert C. Luskin and Roger Jowell, 'Deliberative polling and public consultation' (2000) 53 Parliamentary Affairs 657. An outline of this practice can be found at https://participedia.net/method/147, which describes the activities of *James Fishkin* at the Center for Deliberative Democracy at Stanford University.

25 See what *Jon Elster* points out in Elster (n 4) 47–48.

point of view to avoid possible under-representation;[26] the way of articulating the topic can change, to govern the problem of the inevitable manipulation of information and opinions. Hence the intervention of professional figures such as experts and facilitators or the exclusive use of documentary information material, or the introduction of interactive moments with professionals can be regulated.[27]

To all this one could add another purpose of deliberation, partly assimilable to the first mentioned above (to stimulate citizens' interest in the public sphere), namely that of stimulating greater public affection for public affairs. This is embodied in the Citizens' Initiative Review procedures, or the Oregon model – named after the US state that first adopted this practice –, designed to allow a restricted group of citizens to inform themselves and discuss the issues that will be the subject of the referendum, so as to provide real information leaflets to the citizens for a more informed choice at the time of the vote. The Citizens' Initiative Review is the interconnection and interpenetration between referendum and deliberative instruments, the subject of fruitful experimentation in the United States, where it originated, but also in European countries, particularly Finland and Switzerland.[28]

In the extreme variety of deliberative practices and new articulations of participation as well as in their long process of emergence and difficult classification, citizens' assemblies can be found: they are a hybrid form

26 Identifying the typology of subjects targeted by involvement is a central element in the analysis of deliberative practices, because it often has significant consequences for the functioning and results achieved by the processes. Who participates is functional to the success and results of these practices.

27 Ravazzi (n 16) 35 et seq. On the importance of facilitators in deliberative practices, see also Greg Myers, 'Enabling talk: how the facilitator shapes a focus group' [2007] Text & Talk – An Interdisciplinary Journal of Language Discourse & Communication Studies 79.

28 John Gastil and Robert Richards, 'Making direct democracy deliberative through random assemblies' (2013) 41 Politics & Society 253; Simon Niemeyer and Julia Jennstal, 'Scaling up Deliberative Effects: Applying Lessons of Mini Publics', in Andre Bachtinger et al. (eds), *The Oxford Handbook of Deliberative Democracy* (Oxford University Press 2018); Nenad Stojanović, 'Democrazia diretta e populismo' in Enrico Biale and Corrado Fumagalli (eds), *Innovazioni democratiche* (Fondazione Feltrinelli 2019); Marthe Fatin-Rouge Stefanini, 'Assemblée citoyenne et référendum: quelques exemples étrangers à méditer' (2020) 175 Pouvoirs – Revue française d'études constitutionnelles et politiques 77; Maia Setälä et al., 'Beyond polarization and selective trust: A Citizens' Jury as a trusted source of information' (2023) 43(4) Politics 472. For each individual US experience see https://healthydemocracy.org/programs/citizens-initiative-review/; for the experiences in Switzerland see https://demoscan.ch/it/uber-uns/.

at the crossroads of the old and the new. Inspired by the mechanisms of government that flourished in ancient Greece between the 5th and 4th centuries B.C.,[29] they differ from other deliberative practices by the larger number of participants, all selected by the method of drawing lots, by the longer and more intense duration of the work and by the elaboration of detailed recommendations, which tend to be non-binding, concerning the topic on which the assembly is convened.[30]

Since their very first experimentation in the Canadian state of British Columbia in the early 2000s, many other countries have seen an implementation, in some cases structural while sometimes more sporadic and disorganised, of these participatory arrangements. Particularly in the last decade, CAs have begun to find their own revitalisation in many large European democracies – Ireland, Belgium, the United Kingdom, France and Germany.[31] And they have found it in relation to certain, specific

29 However, they are characterised by a radically different conception of power compared to ancient Athenian democracy. For a reflection on the different *ratio* of the drawing of lots in Athenian democracy and in contemporary Citizens' Assemblies, let it be permitted to refer to Giulia Mannarini, 'Citizens' Assemblies as Articulations of Democratic Participation between Criticalities and Perspectives' in (2023) 4 Diritto Pubblico Comparato ed Europeo, 943, 949 ff.

30 Oliver Escobar and Stephen Elstub, 'Forms of mini-publics. Research and development' (2017) newDemocracy <https://newdemocracy.com.au/wpcontent/uploads/2017/05/docs_researchnotes_2017_May_nDF_RN_20170508_FormsOfMiniPublics.pdf> accessed 28 July 2024; OECD, 'Innovative Citizen Participation and New Democratic Institutions: Catching the Deliberative Wave' (2020) OECD Publishing, Paris <https://doi.org/10.1787/339306da-en> accessed 28 July 2024.
It is worth remembering that, in general, deliberative practices have not yet found widespread institutionalisation, except at the local level in Belgium, Austria and Germany. For the Belgium experience in the German-speaking Province of *Ostbelgien,* see Cristoph Niessen and Min Reuchamps, 'Institutionalising Citizen Deliberation in Parliament: The Permanent Citizens' Dialogue in the German-speaking Community of Belgium' (2022) 75(1) Parliamentary Affairs <https://www.g1000.org/sites/default/files/2022-10/Niessen-Reuchamps_2020_Institutionalising Citizen deliberation_Ostbelgien.pdf> accessed 20 July 2024. In Austria, institutionalisation took place in the *Vorarlberg* region, while in Germany in the city of *Aachen*. For the structure of these CAs and their competences, see the dedicated web portals for each of these bodies: https://www.oidp.net/en/practice.php?id=1292 and https://www.buergerrat.de/en/news/permanent-citizens-assembly-in-aachen/. Finally, in Oregon the CIR model, which combines CA and referendum, has been institutionalised.

31 There are also experiences in Poland, Finland, Denmark, Luxembourg, Sweden. An overview of deliberative experiences in the world can be found at the following link https://www.sortitionfoundation.org/where and https://participedia.net/search?selectedCategory=case.

issues. Whereas the first case of CA, the one in Canada, concerned the state's electoral law as its topic, for some years now these assemblies have tended to be installed because of the need for a public discussion around today's sensitive and divisive issues, such as egalitarian marriage, gender issues, abortion[32], the end of life, or the environment[33]. Anyway, even in British Columbia, at that given historical moment, the topic of the British Columbia's citizens' assembly was very controversial; the character of divisiveness, after all, changes over time and historical epochs. It is this latter character that makes it possible to identify, perhaps, a minimum common denominator to the phenomenon of citizens' assemblies, which tended to

---

Furthermore, the Centre for Deliberative Democracy and Global Governance at the University of Canberra in Australia, together with an international network of researchers, is organising the first global citizens' assembly on genome editing from 2020.

32 On this topic, the Irish experience is a milestone: see Antonia Baraggia, *Stati Uniti e Irlanda. La regolamentazione dell'aborto in due esperienze paradigmatiche* (Giappichelli 2022) 178 ff.

33 On the topic of CAs in environmental matters, see *ex multis* Andreas Møller Mulvad and Benjamin Ask Popp-Madsen, 'Sortition-infused democracy: Empowering citizens in the age of climate emergency' (2021) 167(1) Thesis Eleven 77; Andrea Fiorentino, 'La democrazia partecipativa tra crisi della democrazia rappresentativa e crisi climatico-ambientale: alcune riflessioni sulla fioritura delle assemblee dei cittadini per il clima' (2023) 24 <https://www.federalismi.it/nv14/articolo-documento.cfm?Artid=49422&content=&content_author=> accessed 4 July 2024.

At the EU level, random democracy has been used by calling citizens of all member states to discuss food waste and student learning mobility. In Austria, democracy, transport, and climate change were discussed. The latter theme, which is among the most recurrent, was also discussed in France, Finland, Denmark, Spain, Germany, the United Kingdom, and Luxembourg. In Belgium, living wills, reimbursement of medical care, social security, distribution of wealth, and financing of political parties were also discussed; in Bosnia and Herzegovina, electoral reform. The French discussed assisted suicide, as well as social cohesion, agricultural policies, demography, and health. The Germans discussed artificial intelligence, nutrition in transition, Germany's role in the world, and the future of Europe in as many assemblies. In Ireland, they discussed drug use, gender equality, and biodiversity. In Montenegro, the topic was corruption. In Poland, the first civic assembly was in 2016, when citizens of *Gdansk* discussed how to prepare the city for extreme rainfall. They talked about sustainable food consumption in Sweden and Switzerland, while in Macedonia, measures to control pandemics were discussed. Outside Europe: the Chilean confrontation on the possible pension and healthcare system, the assemblies in Canada to discuss hate, discrimination and fake news on the internet. And Singapore continues to show great interest in technology and health: the topics are war on diabetes and data sharing with private industry in precision medicine.

be very diverse.[34] In fact, what they are convened for today are issues that, being themselves controversial and a potential source of great polarisation in the area of civil rights, constitute a terrain from which authorities often shy away. It, indeed, is them who give impetus to these experiences, delegating the role of mediation and discussion to bodies drawn by lot. Suffice it to think, for example, of euthanasia and assisted suicide: excluding those European countries that have already legislated on the subject for some time, such as the Netherlands, Belgium, Switzerland, Spain and Portugal, in France it was a citizens' assembly that expressed itself in favour of active assistance in dying, a body that followed in the footsteps of the previous (and failed) climate convention.[35] In the United Kingdom the Labour Party announced a few months ago that it would hold a CA on assisted dying laws if it obtained a majority in the next general elections,[36] although there was no trace of this in its Electoral Manifesto. In Italy too, euthanasia associations have been pushing for some time for deliberative mechanisms on assisted dying – after having obtained the decriminalisation of assisted suicide by case law in 2019 –, often emphasising, on the one hand, the inability of the Italian Parliament to legislate on these matters, and on the other hand, the need to oppose random democracy to the invisibility of legislative assemblies and the verticalisation of power for the revitalisation of democratic institutions. Such arguments are even stronger, where today events as the pandemic, recent wars close to Western Europe, inflation, and immigration have shifted priorities, and issues such as the environment or the end of life pass through deliberative practices, proof that these articulations give space to the needs of the minority part of society, especially the young.

---

34 The first common denominator is precisely their extreme diversity: there are many recipes with which CAs are celebrated, from the impulse from which the formation of a CA comes, to the number of participants, to the organisation of the work, to the effects of the deliberative discussion.

35 The *Convention citoyenne pour le climat* began its work in September 2019 and finished it in July 2020, presenting a dossier of 149 proposals and recommendations, which the French institutions have, however, subsequently followed up on very little.

36 *Susan Gray, Keir Starmer's* Chief of Staff, had announced it in February 2024, see Hannah Camilleri, 'A future Labour government would be right to use Citizens' Assemblies' *Electoral Reform Society* (19th February 2024) <https://electoral-reform.org.uk/a-future-labour-government-would-be-right-to-use-citizens-assemblies/>; Henry Zeffman and Jennifer McKiernan, 'Citizens' Assemblies could propose assisted dying laws, says Labour' *BBC News* (19 February 2024) <https://www.bbc.com/news/uk-politics-68338042>.

All this represents the impetus that comes as a precipitate of the crisis of the vote, incapable of summing up democracy. In short, there is a contemporary disenchantment with politics: the latter is no longer a place for exercising the will, or rather a will that is anaemic due to the powerful acceleration of the rhythms imposed by the world of our time.[37] All these elements are linked to another essential transformation, namely the dissolution of a society 'composed of coherent social worlds' where 'it was sufficient to delegate to represent these social worlds that had their own internal coherence, their own meaning. Today what is at issue is the legibility of society, that is, being able to narrate society. We have moved from a world in which processes of representation and delegation were at work to one in which processes of narrative representation are expected, i.e. a representation capable of making society readable for those who make it up and which makes it possible to make the realities experienced in society itself present and visible in public debate, realities that are not simply static in character, but which concern the stories of individuals and their trajectories. All this produces collective identities that are simultaneously more fragmented and at the same time more historical, more tied to events. Societies are communities of evidence, communities of events and not simply communities of position',[38] and thus change and are constructed by the force of history. These changes, which bring with them polarising and populist dynamics, constitute the humus in which the tendencies of verticalisation and caesarism come to maturity in a twofold direction. On the one hand, one finds the need to count by relying on individual personalities in a delegation operation that is, however, simplistic: this reflects the need for leadership; on the other hand, the complexity of following up and introjecting that social fragmentation by traditional representative bodies leads to bypassing them, effectively entrusting the reins of decision-making to the executives.

A democratic regime, however, finds its essence in the 'the antithesis of the concentration of power, the opposite of the idea that social complexity and heterogeneity can be annulled in the figure of a leader, the opposite

37 Pierre Rosanvallon, 'Sulla crisi della democrazia' (2020) 20 il Mulino 692, 693.

38 ibid, translation by author. These are reflections that recall and connect to the considerations conducted by authors such as *Durkheim*, *Mead* and *Weber* on the concept of modernity and modernisation as well as on *Gehlen's* concept of crystallisation. For a more in-depth analysis on the topic, see Jürgen Habermas, *Il discorso filosofico della modernità* (Laterza 1997) 2 ff.

of the cult of personality'.[39] And so, in an attempt to remedy this, in some sectors of society and in the academic world, people are betting on a new and additional subject to whom they can delegate those instances of representation, often belonging to the youngest segment of the electorate, that fail to be introjected by the rulers. Society changes, but parties and parliaments struggle to keep up.

That new subject becomes the assembly where citizens drawn by lot on a sample basis meet precisely because, as deliberation theorists have argued, something more than the mere aggregation of individual preferences is required for a living and vibrant democracy: the quality of decisions comes from the degree of quality of the public debate that precedes the voting stage. In other words, the quality of decisions depends on extensive argumentation about political choices, even before voting on them. But CAs are nothing more than (another) body of delegation: different, but still a body of delegation, a different expression of the desire of citizens to participate in political life. All in all, this leads paradoxically to combine 'mobilisation and passivisation of the will of the people [...] releasing at once participation and indifference, dynamism and inertia'.[40] Today, deliberative practices are the participatory piece that is increasingly trying to find its own space within these dynamics, which today confront us with the need to ask ourselves whether, perhaps, once again we are in a moment in which 'our age is

39 Luigi Zanotti, *La sana democrazia* (Giappichelli 2005) 106.

40 Alfonso Di Giovine, 'Un modello di democrazia in linea con i tempi' in Alfonso Di Giovine and Anna Mastromarino (eds), *La presidenzializzazione degli esecutivi nelle democrazie contemporanee* (Giappichelli 2007) 7, translation by author. The author speaks of it with reference, in particular, to the phenomena of 'verticalisation': it is appropriate to add that the push towards the direct inclusion of citizens, paradoxically cohabiting with passivisation, are embodied by the increasingly frequent implementation of participatory and deliberative practices: an implementation, often, as mentioned above, played on the terrain of the most uncomfortable matters for the rulers, precipitated by that vicious circle that the drastic decline in the quality of representation and responsiveness cause; hence, the fear of the ruling class to expose itself on divisive issues that could determine a loss of consensus in a complex and extremely volatile society. It is interesting to note how these dynamics also occur in systems in which a good quality of electoral culture is quite rooted: that is, where electoral legislation is strong, and does not change with the change of political colour of the rulers, and often tends to be based on majoritarian mechanisms: proof of this is, for example, is France.

an age of gestation and transition to a new era'.[41] From all this, it seems important to avoid the risk of reviving and reducing long-standing theories and practices on the wave of a populist and potentially destructive polemic against the representative circuit.

In short, it could be said that all that glitters is not gold and pragmatically, many scholars over time have highlighted some of the critical aspects of deliberative practices, some emphasising the inability of ordinary citizens to deal with complex issues,[42] others stating that these deliberations would in any case be distorted by class and gender inequalities,[43] and still others fearing the polarisations that these methods would not, in any case, eliminate.[44] Moreover, if on the one hand deliberative practices have a transformative, awareness-raising power – thus becoming a sort of wake-up call, proof of the malfunctioning of democracies –, on the other hand their coexistence with the dynamics of representative democracy brings with it the risk of a boomerang effect: that is, implementing frustration where governments, legitimately, do not follow up on the work of these assemblies. And if they do follow up, the results are often disappointing – see, i.e., the French case on aid to die[45] – because the path followed is

41 Habermas (n 38), *Il discorso filosofico della modernità* 6–7, where the Author mentions Georg H.W. Hegel, *Fenomenologia dello spirito* (first published 1807, La Nuova Italia 1963) 8 ff.

42 See Richard A. Posner, *Law, Pragmatism and Democracy* (Cambridge University Press 2004) 163.

43 See Lynn M. Sanders, 'Against Deliberation' (1997) 25 Political Theory 347; Iris M. Young, *Inclusion and Democracy* (Oxford University Press 2000) ch. 2.

44 See Cass R. Sunstein, 'Deliberative Trouble? Why Groups Go to Extremes' (2000) 110 Yale LJ 71; ibid, 'The Law of Group Polarization' in James Fishkin and Peter Laslett (eds), *Debating Deliberative Democracy* (Oxford University Press 2000).

45 The *Convention Citoyenne sur la fin de vie*, was announced in September 2022 by President *Macron*. Its task was to assess whether and how *'le cadre d'accompagnement de la fin de vie est-il adapté aux différentes situations rencontrées ou d'éventuels changements devraient-ils être introduits'*. The organisational structure closely mirrored that of the previous Climate Convention, with the sole difference being that the CESE appointed a Governance Committee composed of members of the CESE itself, members of the National Consultative Ethics Committee, a health ethics specialist, an expert from the National Centre for Palliative and End-of-Life Care, several experts in citizen participation, and, finally, some citizens who had taken part in the Climate Convention.

A total of 184 citizens participated in the assembly, selected according to the same criteria used in the previous one.

The final report of the assembly's work was presented to the President of the Republic on April 3, 2023. Seventy-five percent of its members expressed support for assisted always just to please all political forces, without ever really taking a decision on divisive issues.

Thus, perhaps, the implementation of democratic participation must once again be pursued through what democracies already have: the representative circuit and parliaments within the inalienable framework that is liberal-democratic constitutionalism.

III. The Curious Case of 'Authoritarian Deliberation': the Chinese Experience

Since the 1990s, a deliberative wave has curiously also involved some authoritarian regimes in Asia, Africa and the Americas.[46]

Among the most interesting experiments is the Chinese one in particular,[47] where the hybrid formula created by the combination of authoritarianism and participatory elements is very numerous, variegated and strong-

dying, deeming the existing legal framework largely inadequate. However, one-quarter of the participants opposed the introduction of assisted dying, highlighting *'les risques de dérives que l'ouverture de l'aide active à mourir pourrait faire peser sur les personnes vulnérables [...] ainsi que les risques de déstabilisation de notre système de santé, face aux réticences fortes d'une partie des professionnels de santé'*.
The French government subsequently committed to drafting a bill on end-of-life care that would incorporate many of the proposals emerging from the deliberative process.
The bill was eventually — and with considerable difficulty — submitted to the National Assembly in April 2024, a full year after the conclusion of the assembly's work. It regulated the matter in accordance with the majority position that had emerged within the Convention, defining and legislating for *'aide à mourir'* from Article 5 onwards.
However, due to President Macron's political decision to dissolve the National Assembly in light of the results of the June 2024 European elections, the bill subsequently lapsed. This represents further proof that the fate of such measures inevitably remains subject to the contingencies of political and institutional developments.

46 For a comparative analysis of these countries on deliberative methods see Baogang He, 'Citizens' assemblies in authoritarian regimes: China, Cuba, and Libya' in Reuchamps, Vrydagh, Welp (eds) (n 6).

47 *Ex multis*, see Suzanne Ogden, *Inklings of Democracy in China* (Cambridge University Press 2002); Baogang He, 'Participatory and Deliberative Institutions in China' in Ethan Leib and Baogang He (eds), *The Search for Deliberative Democracy in China*, (Palgrave MacMillan 2006); Baogang He and Stig Thøgersen, 'Giving the people a voice? Experiments with consultative authoritarian institutions in China' (2010) 19 Journal of Contemporary China 675; Baogang He and Mark E. Warren, 'Authoritarian Deliberation: The Deliberative Turn in Chinese Political' in (2011) 9(2)

ly desired by the governing party, especially at the local level, which, it is possible to peacefully affirm, has no interest in the so-called regime-level democratisation. And yet, in China 'authoritarian deliberation is conceptually possible, empirically existent, and functionally motivated'.[48] Here the interest of scholars was, therefore, focused precisely on the curious circumstance whereby articulations of participation such as those that were born and theorised as participatory and deliberative democracy in the West are also applied in non-democratic regimes. This could prove that deliberation is an autonomous method and not necessarily linked to the democratic form of state. As a method it can bend to the needs of the context in which it is applied. What the doctrine that has dealt with the subject has questioned and is still questioning is the type of deliberation, whether and to what degree the deliberative methods that have flourished in those regimes have a democratic nature or not, and whether or not they can and will contribute to a democratic naturalisation of the countries that apply them. Proof of this can be found in the very transposition of 'deliberative democracy' in the Chinese language: *xie shang min zhu*, a term first used as a translation in the early 2000s by Chinese doctrine, combines *xie* (doing things together, cooperation, harmonisation) with *shang* (dialogue, consultation, discussion). Thus, democracy (*min zhu*) is modified by *xie shang*: i.e., discussing issues in a communal and collaborative spirit.[49] However, by some Chinese scholars, it has been considered rather erroneous, as *xie shang min zhu* often refers to consultative democracy, while among academics, it is used as a genuine synonym for deliberative democracy.[50] The problem, however, rather seems to lie upstream, i.e. in the inherent ambiguity as to whether or not the deliberative arenas practised in the country are democratic in nature, and thus, whether they are a genuine expression of practices comparable to deliberative ones or closer to forms of mere consultation.

Perspectives on Politics 269. Besides China, participatory experiences in authoritarian countries have taken place in Cuba, Vietnam, and Singapore.

48 He and Warren (n 47).

49 Baogang He and Mark E. Warren, 'Authoritarian Deliberation in China' (2017) 146(3) Daedalus 155, 157 <https://www.amacad.org/sites/default/files/publication/downloads/14_he_warren.pdf> accessed 26 June 2024.

50 Deyong Ma and Szu-chien Hsu, 'The Political Consequences of Deliberative Democracy and Electoral Democracy in China: An Empirical Comparative Analysis from Four Counties' (2018) 18(2) The China Review, fn 20 <https://www.jstor.org/stable/26435646> accessed 27 June 2024.

For this reason, many scholars have referred to these practices with a number of neologisms, all very expressive of the ambiguity of these experiences:[51] 'deliberative dictatorship'[52], 'consultative Leninism'[53], 'consultative authoritarianism'[54], 'networked authoritarianism'[55] or 'authoritarian deliberation', as defined by academics such as *Baogang He* and *Mark Warren*, who were among the first to deal with the subject:[56] This opened up a strand of reflection that became a real challenge for Western jurists, constitutionalists and political scientists, if not a rather uncomfortable presence in the deliberative literature.[57] Indeed, 'the clear and robust connection between democracy and deliberation has led democratic theorists to ignore the difficult problem of identifying deliberative influence under authoritarian circumstances'.[58] And in fact, 'authoritarian regimes are, on average, unfriendly to deliberative approaches to conflict. Decision-making is closed and strict limits are placed on spaces of public discourse, such as the press, publishing houses, the Internet, advocacy groups, and universities. Authoritarian rulers typically command; they do not invite the people to deliberate'.[59] Yet, the Chinese regime still uses deliberative methods.

But how did deliberative practices originate in China? About thirty years ago, in the late 1980s, the Chinese communist regime introduced village-

51 For an empirical summary study of the subject of deliberation in China see Dezhi Tong and Baogang He, 'How democratic are Chinese grassroots deliberations? An empirical study of 393 deliberation experiments in China' (2018) 19 Japanese Journal of Political Science 630 <https://www.researchgate.net/publication/328999635_How_democratic_are_Chinese_grassroots_deliberations_An_empirical_study_of_393_deliberation_experiments_in_China> accessed 27 June 2024.

52 Mark Leonard, *What Does China Think?* (William Collins 2008).

53 Steve Tsang, 'Consultative Leninism: China's new political framework' (2009) 18 Journal of Contemporary China 865.

54 He and Thøgersen (n 47).

55 Rebecca MacKinnon, 'China's networked authoritarianism' (2011) 32 Journal of Democracy 32.

56 The term first appeared in Baogang He, 'Western theories of deliberative democracy and the Chinese practice of complex deliberative governance', in Leib and He (eds) (n 47), 133–148. Later, in He and Warren (n 47), the authors develop the concept and carry out a theoretical reflection on the possibility of speaking of something qualifying as authoritarian deliberation, and they do it starting from the split between the concept of deliberation and democracy, which in almost all Western studies on deliberative theories and practices cannot be traced.

57 Baogang He, 'Deliberative culture and politics: the persistence of authoritarian deliberation in China' (2014) 42 Political Theory 58, 60.

58 He and Warren (n 47) 159.

59 ibid.

level elections and other participatory practices. Subsequently, 'other innovations have followed, including approval and recall voting at the local level, public hearings, deliberative polls, citizen rights to sue the state, initiatives to make government information public, an increasing use of Peoples' Congresses to discuss policy, and acceptance of some kinds of autonomous civil society organisations'.[60] In short, forms of inclusion and participation of citizens in public policy-making processes were gradually introduced, due to the need for rulers to obtain cooperation and greater legitimacy in policy-making operations.[61] This objective made them interested in inaugurating the application of deliberative instruments in the absence of democratic empowerment. Indeed, 'this local deliberative democracy with Chinese characteristics can be seen as an uneasy and unstable marriage of democratic (participation, deliberation, and limited empowerment) and authoritarian (heavy handed top-down rule, despotism, disempowerment of dissident groups, and erosion of human rights) elements. This marriage is situated firmly within policy processes that incorporate mechanisms and procedures to reduce and control social conflicts against the background of economic, political, and social developments and complex governing issues in China.[62] Thus, in the discussion concerning the democratic nature of these instruments, many authors have pointed out that they are in fact closer to mere public consultations and manipulations. In fact, even where it is possible to trace, in some experiences, characteristics of deliberation, it would not be democratic at all. And where it is possible to extrapolate positive effects, such as fairness, citizen representation, citizen empowerment and the establishment of a genuine collective will among peoples, these would rather be mere expressions of a 'phantom democracy'[63] and a 'participation without democracy'[64], because, in the end, it would have nothing to do with the substantial dynamics of a democratic form of state.

---

60 He and Warren (n 47) 269; Baogang He, *Rural Democracy in China. The Role of Village Elections*, (Palgrave MacMillan 2007) ch. 6.

61 By the way, it is worth mentioning how the neo-Confucian culture of post-Maoist China imposes non-trivial moral responsibilities on elites, see He and Warren (n 47) 162.

62 Baogang He and Hendrik Wagenaar, 'Authoritarian Deliberation Revisited' (2018) 19 Japanese Journal of Political Science 622–29 <http://dx.doi.org/10.1017/S1468109918000257> accessed 28 June 2024.

63 John Keane, *When Trees Fall, Monkeys Scatter: Rethinking Democracy In China* (World Scientific Publishing Europe Ltd 2017).

64 Garry Rodan, *Participation Without Democracy: Containing Conflict in Southeast Asia* (Cornell University Press 2018).

In fact, the use of these instruments would be fully in line with the state's need to address problems of governance, the ever-increasing complexity of society and the presence of multi-actor contexts, where a high degree of expertise and information is required of the ruling classes to overcome the challenges of post-contemporaneity, in which China, like the West, is also placed.[65] And the difficulty of doing so without a dialogue with people pushes to rely on instruments of inclusion and deliberation, as has been already experienced in the Western world and has become nothing more than a means of forming preferences and policies, of creating consensus, and of doing so in the absence of a democratic power distribution structure[66] and indeed, of reinforcing its authoritarian basis, in a full and functional preservation of the regime.

Investigating the reasons why these instruments have been able to take root in the country, it is worth pointing out that in Chinese political culture, the characteristics of deliberative dynamics – i.e. discussion, mutual listening and rational argumentation – do indeed have ancient roots[67] by virtue of the tradition in this sense implemented by Confucianism and its practices of common discussion and consultation[68], so much so that 'like the Maoist mass line, the current system remains justified by the Confucian notion of *minben* (people-centric) rule. According to this ideal, elites express the voice of and serve the people. No doubt these inheritances help to explain why deliberative democracy is now a common topic in academic and policy circles within China, indeed, so much so that the CCP (Chinese Communist Party) has developed a system of rewards for party officials who develop new deliberative processes'.[69] It is particularly significant that today many deliberative forums are called *kentan* (heart-to-heart talks) there.[70]

---

65 In particular, moreover, bearing in mind that the Chinese economy is based on a capitalist-type system, carefully guided and strongly conditioned by the state, i.e. by the role played by the Communist Party.

66 ibid 271–272.

67 ibid 276; Shawn Rosenberg, 'Human Nature, Communication and Culture: Rethinking Democratic Deliberation in China and the West', in Leib and He (eds) (n 47).

68 Daniel Bell and Hahm Chaibong (eds), *Confucianism for the Modern World* (Cambridge University Press 2003); Baogang He, 'Four Models of Relationship between Confucianism and Democracy' (2020) 37(1) Journal of Chinese Philosophy 18 <https://www.researchgate.net/publication/349565746_Four_Models_of_the_Relationship_Between_Confucianism_and_Democracy> accessed 27 June 2024.

69 He and Warren (n 47).

70 ibid.

In 1987, Party General Secretary *Zhao Ziyang* stated that a system of social consultation dialogue would be one of the major innovations of the 30th Party Congress, to be followed by a reform that would increase the use of public consultation formulas throughout the country. All of this came to an abrupt halt following the events of Tiananmen Square in 1989, which was followed by a period of severe repression. And yet, at the same time, the flame of deliberation remained alive, because the Chinese ruling classes were aware of the opportunity that these practices could bring in terms of channeling and managing dissent and the increasing complexity of the society.

These deliberative practices spread progressively over time as a method applicable within the Party organisation itself as well as outside; and in the municipality *Wenling*, between 1996 and 2000, more than 1,190 deliberative practices were tested at the municipal level, 190 at the township level, and 150 in government organisations and schools.[71] Also in *Wenling* city, and particularly in *Zeguo* city, a deliberative polling was conducted for the first time in 2005, a first experience that, according to some authors, was characterised by having many features of a true democratic deliberation.[72] These included composition by drawing lots: a circumstance that, in cases of deliberative practices in China, is rather rare,[73] because most participants are selected by the promoters of the arenas mostly managed by the central state. This is one of the features that makes these practices most different from those in the West. As is well known, deliberative arenas have the peculiar characteristic of drawing lots. It is this detail that contributes to act as a litmus test and make visible the Chinese twist used on democrat-

71 *Democratic Sincerely Talk: The Innovation from Wenling*, Department of Propaganda (Wenling 2003) 98.

72 See the analysis of the *Zeguo* experiment, with all related data, conducted by James Fishkin et al., 'Deliberative Democracy in an Unlikely Place: Deliberative Polling in China' (2010) 40(2) British Journal of Political Science 435. See also Philip Hsu, 'In Search of Public Accountability: the 'Wenling Model' in China' (2010) 68(1) Australian Journal of Public Administration 40; Joseph Fewsmith, *The Logic and Limits of Political Reform in China* (Cambridge University Press 2013). And the deliberative polling theorised by *James Fishkin* could become the solution that could reconcile the dilemma between deliberation and representation in authoritarian states, see Baogang He, 'Reconciling Deliberation and Representation: Chinese Challenges to Deliberative Democracy' (2015) 51(1) Representation <https://www.tandfonline.com/doi/abs/10.1080/00344893.2015.1026209> accessed 30 June 2024.

73 Tong and He (n 51).

ic deliberative practices to adapt them and make them functional in an authoritarian-type context.

Some authors, as mentioned earlier, then focus on the distinction between deliberation and consultation, considering Chinese participatory practices more as an expression of the latter than of the former. In fact, consultation turns out to be a means of communication used by the government to obtain information. Deliberative practices, on the other hand, contain more, because in addition to gathering information, an environment of confrontation and discussion is encouraged, with the possibility for those who participate to have an impact on decisions. And often, when participatory forums are held in China, in most cases, there is a reluctance to create a properly deliberative space.[74] Indeed, it is often more about improving governance than building deliberative democracy as an intrinsic value of political dynamics. Moreover, it has been pointed out that discussions do not undermine legitimacy *vis-à-vis* the regime as they are largely related to specific local issues, having nothing to do with the general social politics of the country.[75] If anything, as some scholars who have reflected on a case of participatory practice in China concerning the health care system have argued, the deliberative process is far from producing a democratic transition; it rather leads to a mere improvement in governance,[76] after all, a goal perhaps largely sought by the CCP.

According to other authors, the trend towards a democratic evolution is clear: members of communities could, on those occasions, practise democracy, confronting concrete problems, acquiring information about them and discussing how to solve them.[77] For others, still, an eventual evolutionary process can only take place if, through deliberative practices, a gradual development of a more consolidated public sphere, a much more effective government accountability, and a greater implementation of participation

74 Yoel Kornreich, Ilan Vertinsky and Pitman B. Potter, 'Consultation and deliberation in China: the making of China's health-care reform' (2012) 68 The China Journal 176.

75 Beibei Tang, 'The discursive turn: deliberative governance in China's urbanized villages' (2015) 24 Journal of Contemporary China <https://www.tandfonline.com/doi/abs/10.1080/10670564.2014.918414> accessed 30 June 2024.

76 Kornreich, Vertinsky and Potter (n 74).

77 Jonathan Unger, Anita Chan and Him Chung, 'Deliberative democracy at China's grassroots: case studies of a hidden phenomenon' (2014) 42 Politics & Society <https://www.researchgate.net/publication/275515517_Deliberative_Democracy_at_China's_Grassroots_Case_Studies_of_a_Hidden_Phenomenon> accessed 29 June 2024.

are put in place.[78] In this sense, there is no shortage of Chinese scholars expressing positive views on the likely prospects of a consolidation process of a genuine deliberative democracy.[79]

And yet, another aspect needs to be considered in this regard. As mentioned above, since the 1990s, so-called electoral democracy began to emerge, which can be refer to as those reforms introducing direct elections to select the governor or party secretary at the local level, specifically at the township level.[80] Between 2000 and 2012, after the very first experiment in *Sichuan* province, this method became the main method for selecting and appointing local secretaries. These 'elections', however, were entirely party-controlled and party-driven, the candidates were all members of the CCP and there were no independents or those belonging to other political forces. This is why they were referred to in doctrine as semi-competitive elections.[81] As an effect, such mechanisms led to an improvement in legitimacy and support for local governments as well as efficiency of governance and, thus, to real support for the regime.[82]

However, it is worth noting that the experiments in township-level elections were discontinued as of 2013, a fact that might reveal how there was a widespread fear in the party that electoral democracy at the local level

78 Tang (n 75).

79 See Shangli Lin, 'Citizen deliberation and the development of grassroots democracy in China' (2007) 39 Academic Monthly 13; X. Bao, 'On the construction of institution and value of deliberative democracy in practice' (2013) 46 Journal of Tianjin CPC School 3.

80 In Chinese it is called 'public appointment and direct election' (公推直選 *gongtui zhixuan*), Ma and Hsu (n 50).

81 Harong Lai, 'Semi-competitive Elections at Township Level in Sichuan Province' (2004) 51 China Perspectives 13. Between the late 1990s and 2012, more than a thousand townships used this type of election, see Zhengxu Wang and Deyong Ma, 'Participation and Competition: Innovations in Cadre Election and Selection in China's Townships' (2015) 24 Journal of Contemporary China 298 <https://www.tandfonline.com/doi/full/10.1080/10670564.2014.932164> accessed 28 June 2024.

82 Deyong Ma and Zhengxu Wang, 'Governance Innovations and Citizens' Trust in Local Government: Electoral Impacts in China's Townships' (2014) 15(3) Japanese Journal of Political Science 373 <https://www.cambridge.org/core/journals/japanese-journal-of-political-science/article/abs/governance-innovations-and-citizens-trust-in-local-government-electoral-impacts-in-chinas-townships/E15EC15079ABDC96A626C490E6887C3B> accessed 28 June 2024; Wen-Hsuan Tsai and Peng-Hsiang Kao, 'Public Nomination and Direct Election in China: An Adaptive Mechanism for Party Recruitment and Regime Perpetuation' (2012) 52(3) Asian Survey 484.

would in the long run become a potential enemy to the maintenance of authoritarian rule.[83]

Shortly afterwards, in November 2013, the third plenum of the party's 18th National Congress was held, in which instead strong encouragement was given to the development of deliberative democracy – officially, 'socialist consultative democracy'. This declaration of intent was, on the one hand, confirmed by a document of the party's Central Commission of 9 February 2015, which announced the strengthening of 'socialist consultative democracy' (the document was entitled *Opinions on Strengthening Socialist Consultative Democracy*); on the other hand, on 25th June 2015, the role of the Chinese People's Political Consultative Meeting in further deliberative practices was emphasised, thus demonstrating the regime's preference for this method.

In any case, the debate among scholars remains lively, particularly among those who emphasise the impossibility of the development of an electoral democracy in the country,[84] since it would be difficult to apply, while others advocate the full development of both, since deliberation would not exist without electoral democracy.[85] The doctrine seems to be fairly unanimous regarding the observation that both are means that could potentially lead to two opposite effects: helping the authoritarian regime or progressively breaking it down through a gradual and widespread democratisation. The question that those who have dealt with the issue have asked themselves is, therefore, what effects deliberative practices could have in the context of a non-democratic form of state and which of the two (electoral or deliberative democracy) is best applicable in a country like China. What is certain is that both were desired by the governing bodies in order to

---

83 'A professor of Peking University told the author in private that in 2012 President *Xi Jinping* rejected a political reform plan on the selection of party cadres designed by Vice *President Li Yuanchao*. The plan was intended to expand the range of the electoral democracy experiment implemented under *Hu-Wen*. The alleged reason for *Xi* rejecting this plan was that electoral democracy would threaten the CCP's control at the grassroots level', cf Ma and Hsu (n 50).

84 'To summarize the positions of these scholars, three points stand out for arguing why 'deliberative democracy' is more suitable in China than 'electoral democracy': first, 'deliberative democracy' by nature is superior to 'electoral democracy'; second, China's cultural traditions and existing institutions are more suitable for developing 'deliberative democracy' than 'electoral democracy'; and third, 'deliberative democracy' will face fewer obstacles in China and thus is more suitable for the Chinese', Ma and Hsu (n 50) 7.

85 ibid 3–4.

improve the quality of public governance and their relationship with the masses. Furthermore, the fear of a loss of control over electoral democracy paved the way for the government to deviate to the deliberative method.

Thus, the *raison d'être* of these instruments seems to stem from the desire to preserve and maintain authoritarian rule. The only experience closer to Western deliberative dynamics has been *Zeguo* city and, so far, there have been no other comparable experiments in deliberative polling, except at a local level.[86] As of today, particularly after the abandonment of direct village elections and the rise of *Xi Jinping*, it is very difficult to imagine an evolution towards a so-called 'deliberation-led democratisation'. The feeling is rather that of a construction of a 'deliberative authoritarianism',[87] whereby 'authoritarianism 2.0 may be about indefinitely extending authoritarianism rather than gradually paving the way for some kind of transition to more democratic ways of governing',[88] since the party is not showing, so far, any willingness to implement truly and genuinely democratic methods and reforms: and in themselves the deliberative instruments do not seem to have the strength to overturn such an established regime by themselves. So, the question to ask is not so much whether and in what way electoral democracy or deliberation can lead to potential democratisation, but why – as well as how – these instruments, born and conceived within an authoritarian context and functional in relation to it, cannot and will never have any democratic-led germs where there is still a monopoly of power. And indeed, despite the fact that the 'experiments with public deliberation in China appear to be increasingly genuine, substantive, inclusive, and often impressive',[89] the CCP still retains control.

The reflection to be conducted, if anything, is another with respect to deliberative methods. And that is the observation as to which instruments that today are standard-bearers for a modernisation of democracy in the Western world, often with salvific overtones, may at the same time have been borrowed from non-democratic regimes, and with what long-term

86 ibid 25. The authors also point out how 'in contrast to *He's* findings from a survey of *Zeguo* in 2005, we did not find strong evidence verifying the causal mechanism between deliberation reform and political legitimacy, nor did we observe a link between deliberation reform and aspirations for democracy'.

87 He and Warren (n 49) 156.

88 Suisheng Zhao, 'Xi Jinping's Maoist Revival' (2016) 27(3) Journal of Democracy 83 <https://www.journalofdemocracy.org/articles/xi-jinpings-maoist-revival/> accessed 5 July 2024.

89 He and Warren (n 49) 159.

effects. This proves that in constitutional law there is not only room for norms. The terrain of politics and the actors applying the law are fundamental elements in the functioning of institutions: everything is relative, not absolute, and the instruments of public law owe their functionality to a large extent to the legal, political and historical context in which they are placed.

The impression is that in China it is not so much a phantom democracy or even a democratisation process that is achieved, but rather a staggered democracy, an evolved authoritarianism concealed in the guise of quasi-democratic methods, a pure game of mirrors by using instruments that were thought to be intrinsically and exclusively linked to democratic dynamics, but that have not escaped the twist aimed at limiting them and shaping them according to the needs and requirements of those who hold the monopoly of power.

IV. Concluding Remarks

From the comparison I have conducted – seeking to move beyond mere institutional forms – a classic dualism re-emerges, which is far from outdated. On the one hand, there is the Western tradition continuously striving, despite numerous errors and considerable idealism, to identify new and alternative forms to articulate the governance of democratic societies, particularly with a view to advancing newly emerging and hermeneutically complex rights related to the environment and future generations. On the other hand, there are authoritarian regimes – undeniably sophisticated and strategically intelligent – perceiving the need to reinforce legitimacy through mechanisms of popular involvement, which, however, are far from subversive or threatening to established power.

In essence, and beyond appearances, the comparison is between the pluralism of liberal-democratic constitutionalism versus authoritarian conceptions of power grounded in the denial of plurality.

Indeed, Western democracies have begun employing deliberative instruments in an attempt to mend the widening gap between governors and the governed. The increased involvement of citizens – especially through so-called 'deliberative participation', where they come together to discuss a specific issue – is seen as a means to revitalise democratic processes. Conversely, there are systems deploying the same instruments within contexts that are manifestly undemocratic. This might suggest a remarkable adaptability of deliberative practices, but I do not believe this to be the case.

Several issues arise, of both theoretical and practical nature. There is no guarantee that the application of the deliberative method within Western democracies will lead to a revitalisation of the representative system. The underlying reason is simple: the deliberative method is premised on consensus, whereas democracy is fundamentally based on conflict. Democracy, in fact, has always thrived on compromise and on institutional systems – especially parliamentary and representative – that make compromise possible. It is, therefore, legitimate to question whether deliberation, as theorised and implemented in certain practical experiences, genuinely strengthens representation. I think that it risks, in other words, to become a mere illusion. Evidence of this can be found in the Chinese experience: there, in a non-democratic system where conflict is institutionally suppressed, deliberative methods appear to function quite effectively.

This leads to a crucial question: is deliberation, fundamentally structured around the pursuit of consensus, truly suited to democracy, which, by its very nature, is grounded in conflict? And thus, is it genuinely capable of addressing the challenges of democratic crisis and responding to new legal demands? The comparison with the Chinese system certainly highlights the opposition between authoritarianism and democracy, as well as the former's capacity to strategically repurpose legal tools to its own advantage. But is this truly a distortion of such tools? Or does it rather suggest that the deliberative essence itself may be better suited to a political and social context that, by definition, cannot exist within democratic frameworks?

As always, when dealing with institutions and constitutional law, utmost caution is required. In this specific case, excessive enthusiasm might obscure the greatest risk posed by deliberative democracy: namely, that it becomes a mere and hollow simulacrum of participation – since more participation does not necessarily equate to more democracy.

This does not preclude, however, the possibility for deliberative democracy to play a meaningful role within representative democracies. When conceived as a tool to enhance the quality of public debate and improve citizens' access to information – particularly in the context of referenda, as exemplified by the Citizens' Initiative Review model – it holds significant potential. In such cases, deliberative democracy may function as a supportive instrument of democratic logic, rendering it fully compatible with representative democratic systems.

How to Ensure the Future-proofing of EU Decision-making: The Case for Supranational Deliberative Democracy

Jan Philipp Huth[*]

The claim that the EU legal order is shaped by an inherent democratic deficit is a longstanding truism. However, despite intensive academic engagement with the challenge of how to enhance the democratic quality of EU decision-making, progress has remained limited. While not finally resolving the gordian knot of transboundary democracy, the present contribution suggests to mobilise deliberative democratic theory as a theoretical underpinning to a reform of supranational decision-making. Based on the assumption of a fundamental, yet underexplored deliberative rationale of the Lisbon Treaty, with the value-based 'society' of Article 2 TEU as its most meaningful expression, it argues in favour of implementing a permanent European Citizens' Assembly to sustainably enhance the democratic legitimacy and deliberative quality of supranational legislative procedures, and their outcomes.

I. Introduction

Over the past two and a half decades, the European integration process faced a particularly demanding culmination of highly heterogenous challenges. They resulted both from inner tensions and disunity about the future path of the integration project, and from outward pressure due to increased geopolitical competition. Yet, against all gloomy predictions, none of those crises, from the financial and Eurozone crisis over considerable migratory movements, Brexit, and rule of law backsliding in several Member States to the Covid-19 pandemic and the still ongoing Russian war against Ukraine, have led to a decay of the European integration project.

Quite the contrary is the case. After all it seems that tackling (and partly overcoming) these challenges as part of the European *Schicksalsgemeinschaft* rather contributed to overall internal cohesion. The current (relative)

* Doctoral Candidate at European University Viadrina Frankfurt (Oder), Germany, and Research Assistant at BLOMSTEIN, Berlin, Germany.

stability can, however, hardly conceal the ever more visible limits of the existing procedural set-up of supranational decision-making. Still to a considerable degree characterised by the international law origins of the Union, the need to adapt decision-making structures to keep up with the complex nature of the numerous transboundary challenges ahead and thus making the integration project more resilient and future-proof is beyond doubt.

Countless reform proposals have been issued over the past decades. However, besides allowing the Union to efficiently address the challenges it faces, they also have to (and for the most part do) address the widely assumed *democratic deficit*[1] of supranational decision-making structures. The reason for why the debate on how to alleviate the EU's comparatively weak democratic legitimacy is still highly controversial arguably lies in the legal nature of the EU itself. How to enhance the democratic quality of a non-state entity's decisions endowed with considerable public authority, without compromising the very same value of democracy within its sovereign sub-entities? This unresolved enigma behind any discourse on the EU's democratic deficit is well-known. But while it is conceivable that there is space for an equally valid, distinctively *supranational* understanding of democratic legitimacy, a fully convincing conceptualisation has not yet been achieved. Is transboundary democracy thus condemned to remain the 'Achilles' heel of democratic theory'[2]? Such a prospect would be highly worrying since, as *Weiler* has put it, '[d]emocracy is not about states', but 'about the exercise of public power – and the Union exercises a huge amount of public power'[3].

While it would go beyond the confinements of this contribution to sketch-out fully-fledged answers to this perennial conundrum, it will be argued that the Treaties themselves already provide for promising approaches to enhance the democratic quality of supranational decision-making. The analysis will proceed in a three-pronged approach. The first part elaborates on the theoretical groundwork (II.), outlining the status quo of citizens' in-

1 The literature on whether or not such a deficit exists at all, where exactly it is to be located in the legal structure of the Union, and how it might be alleviated is virtually boundless. For a general overview on the issue, see Erik Oddvar Eriksen, 'An Emerging European Public Sphere' (2005) 8 European Journal of Social Theory 341, 343.

2 Erik Oddvar Eriksen, *The Normativity of European Union* (Palgrave Macmillan 2014) 11.

3 Joseph H. H. Weiler, 'Van Gend en Loos: The Individual as Subject and Object and the Dilemma of European Legitimacy' (2014) 12 International Journal of Constitutional Law 94, 100.

volvement in EU decision-making beyond elections (1.) and the basic tenets of deliberative democratic theory (2.). It further aims at shedding light at the notion of 'society' in Article 2 TEU as the cornerstone and focal point of the Lisbon Treaty's underlying deliberative rationale (3.). The ensuing part of the contribution turns towards past and present examples of deliberative democracy in practice (III.), both on the Member State (1.) and EU level (2.). On this basis, the third chapter draws on the concept of a permanent *European Citizens' Assembly* (ECA), outlining a set of fundamental design challenges such a deliberative set-up would face (IV.). The final section concludes (V.).

II. Supranational Deliberative Democracy in Theory: Mapping the Discursive Rationale of the Lisbon Treaty

Over the past decades, a plethora of proposals outlining possible remedies to the EU's democratic deficit has been issued. Leaving aside for the time being those voices arguing in favour of rolling back integrational steps (at least allegedly) in favour of (Member State) democracy, more integrationist proposals are for a large part following two strands. First and foremost, the request to endow the European Parliament with greater weight in the legislative procedure, in particular by a direct right of legislative initiative, and thus strengthening its institutional positioning within the Treaty architecture is no less than an 'evergreen' of the debate on supranational democracy. The claim will most likely remain central to the discourse on the democratic deficit, and rightly so, since there is no principal doubt that a strong parliamentary representation is vital for any (nation-based or transboundary) democratic system. At the same time, it constitutes a fairly traditional approach, borrowing from a state-centred idea of democracy,[4]

4 There has been (and still is) an intense debate on the complex questions arising from an (assumed or de facto) transfer of state-centred concepts to the supranational level, which cannot be reiterated here in full detail. While there is little doubt that the proposal to enhance the role of the EP rather borrows from a state-based idea of democracy, other aspects (such as, to name but one, the degree of centralisation of decision-making) are much more difficult to categorise as *state-centred*; '(...) the state tradition', as Walker notes, 'is not singular and monolithic but diverse and contested', Neil Walker, 'The European Public Good and European Public Goods' in Jan Komárek (ed), *European Constitutional Imaginaries: Between Ideology and Utopia* (OUP 2023) 214. Thus, the questions of whether or not current characteristics of the EU legal order or proposed amendments are 'shaped by the touch of stateness', Jo Shaw and Antje

which sooner or later comes to certain limits on the supranational level as long as the state quality of its sovereign sub-divisions remains as a final integrational barrier.[5] A more recent strand in the literature is emphasising the necessity to strengthen the participatory side and *deliberative quality* of supranational decision-making. The nascent debate on supranational deliberative democracy is part of the larger field of *deliberative democratic theory*, which is itself deeply embedded in more abstract theoretical concepts of social communication such as discourse theory in a *Habermasian* and *Alexian* sense. While theoretical elaborations on supranational deliberative democracy, however, for the most part lack a convincing account on their practical implementation, those commentators engaging with the latter aspect often do so without anchoring their assumptions in a convincing theoretical framework. In the remainder, this contribution attempts to bring both together.

1. The Status Quo of Citizens' Participation in EU Decision-Making

The idea of addressing the EU's democratic deficit by bringing the Union and its citizens closer together dates back (at least) to the aftermath of the Maastricht Treaty.[6] It was, however, only in the run-up to the Lisbon Treaty

Wiener, 'The Paradox of the "European Polity"' in Maria Green Cowles and Michael Smith (eds), *The State of the European Union. Risks, Reform, Resistance and Revival. Volume 5* (OUP 2000) 65, and if so, which effect this has on the integration process, requires meticulous case-by-case analysis.

5 The dilemma has been aptly summarised by *von Bogdandy*, albeit in the context of international law more generally, highlighting the 'common understanding that operative parliamentarian institutions are very difficult to achieve on a global scale, while the question of democratic legitimation of public authority exercised by transnational actors demands a response', Armin von Bogdandy, 'The European Lesson for International Democracy. The Significance of Articles 9 to 12 EU Treaty for International Organizations' (2011) Jean Monnet Working Paper 2/2011, 21 https://jeanmonnetprogram.org/wp-content/uploads/2014/12/110201.pdf accessed 30 June 2025.

6 Irena Fiket, 'Citizens' assemblies at supranational level: Addressing the EU and global democratic deficit' in Min Reuchamps et al. (eds), *De Gruyter Handbook of Citizens' Assemblies* (De Gruyter 2023) 200; Thomas Hieber, *Die Europäische Bürgerinitiative nach dem Vertrag von Lissabon. Rechtsdogmatische Analyse eines neuen politischen Rechts der Unionsbürger* (Mohr Siebeck 2014) 3. The process of calibrating the relation between the Union and its citizens (which are at the same time rooted in the respective Member States' societies) dates further back, however. Its origins are seen by some already in the Court's acknowledgement of direct effect of certain Treaty provisions in the Court's seminal judgment in *Van Gend en Loos*. *Halberstam* interprets the

(which largely borrowed from the 2004 *Draft Treaty establishing a Constitution for Europe*[7]), that the significance of strengthening the participatory side of EU decision-making for the legitimacy of supranational governance was more widely debated.

Indeed, at least on a rhetorical level, the Lisbon Treaty concedes EU citizens a more central role in decision-making on the European level in several respects. Firstly, while the European Parliament was composed of 'the peoples of the States brought together in the Community' under the EC Treaty,[8] the Lisbon Treaty refers to the 'Union's citizens'[9]. This rhetorical shift was accompanied by a non-negligible transfer of powers in favour of the Parliament, such as the right to elect the president of the Commission as well as an increased weight in the legislative procedure. Increased emphasis in favour of a closer connection between the Union and its citizens can be discerned from other fundamental Treaty provisions as well. Article 10 para. 3 TEU confers the right to every EU citizen to *participate in the democratic life of the Union* and the obligation of the latter to take decisions *as openly and as closely as possible to the citizen*. In a similar vein, Article 9 TEU enshrines the duty of the Union's institutions to pay *equal attention* to all EU citizens. Finally, Article 11 para. 2 TEU obliges the very same to *maintain an open, transparent and regular dialogue with representative associations and civil society*,[10] displaying the fundamental

---

Court's reasoning therein as implying that '[t]he individual is both legally freed from the constitutional confines of her Member State and endowed with (...) immediate "jurisgenerative" capacity at the supranational level of governance', Daniel Halberstam, 'Pluralism in *Marbury* and *Van Gend*' in Miguel Poiares Maduro and Loïc Azoulai (eds), *The Past and Future of EU Law. The Classics of EU Law Revisited on the 50th Anniversary of the Rome Treaty* (Hart Publishing 2010) 29 et seq. Similarly, *Münch* speaks of the 'dialectic of constructing a European society and deconstructing nations' as being furthered by the Court's jurisdiction, Richard Münch, 'Constructing a European Society by Jurisdiction' (2008) 14 European Law Journal 519, 537.

7 Hereinafter '2004 Draft Constitution'.

8 Article 189 EC Treaty.

9 Article 14 para. 2 TEU.

10 However, Weber notes that most likely it was not European citizens' councils that the drafters of the Treaty had in mind here, see Ferdinand Weber, 'Auf der Welle der Deliberative(n). Bürgerräte und repräsentative Demokratie' (2023) 71 Jahrbuch des öffentlichen Rechts der Gegenwart 259, 277.

belief 'that such participation of interested and affected parties might be a further avenue to realizing the democratic principle'[11].

A combined reading of these provisions may be seen as pointing towards an interlinkage between the legitimacy of supranational decision-making and (deliberative) citizens' involvement in this process.[12] However, such a reading faces two challenges. First, the substance of such mellow 'constitutional' rhetoric may be contested, and indeed a majority of scholarly commentators denies that these Treaty provisions endow individual citizens with enforceable legal positions.[13] In addition, the Treaties remain for the most part silent on how this rapprochement of the Union and its citizens might play out in practice. The right for a *European Citizens' Initiative* (ECI) in Article 11 para. 4 TEU is an exception, yet an ambiguous one. The ECI was already included in the 2004 Draft Constitution, displaying an early attempt to tackle the EU's lack of 'responsiveness to the preferences

11 von Bogdandy (n 5) 21. According to von Bogdandy, in a more general sense, Article 11 TEU 'reflect[s] that [d]emocracy needs representation, but goes beyond it (...)', ibid 19.

12 Alberto Alemanno, 'Europe's Democracy Challenge: Citizen Participation in and beyond Elections' (2020) 21 German Law Journal 35, 36; Maaike Geuens, 'The Conference on the Future of Europe. Bringing the EU Closer to its Citizens?' in Davor Jančić (ed), *The Changing Role of Citizens in EU Democratic Governance* (Hart Publishing 2023) 149.

13 See Sebastian Heselhaus, 'EUV Art. 10: Demokratische Grundsätze' in Matthias Pechstein et al. (eds), *Frankfurter Kommentar zu EUV, GRC und AEUV* (Mohr Siebeck 2023) para. 32; Ricardo García Macho, 'Article 11: Participatory Democracy' in Hermann-Josef Blanke et al. (eds), *The Treaty on European Union. A Commentary* (Springer 2013) para. 20. For a different reading of Article 10 TEU as enshrining a subjective legal position cf Marcel Haag, 'EUV Art. 10: Demokratische Grundsätze' in Hans von der Groeben et al. (eds), *Europäisches Unionsrecht* (Nomos 2015) para. 12. Going even further, Borgmann-Prebil and Ross emphasise assumed similarities between the obligation to pay 'equal attention' in Article 9 TEU and the *Dworkinian* notion of 'equal concern and respect', see Yuri Borgmann-Prebil and Malcolm Ross, 'Article 9: The Principle of Equality and Citizenship of the Union' in Hermann-Josef Blanke et al. (eds), *The Treaty on European Union. A Commentary* (Springer 2013) para 5 with reference to Ronald Dworkin, *Taking Rights Seriously* (Duckworth 1977) 180: 'We might say that individuals have a right to equal concern and respect in the design and administration of the political institutions that govern them'. Kochenov and Lock point towards an interlinkage between Articles 9 and 11 TEU in that the notion of *equal attention* 'shows that the principle of equality entails a positive duty to act in particular when it comes to the realization of Article 11 TEU' (Dimitry Kochenov and Tobias Lock, 'Article 9 TEU' in Manuel Kellerbauer et al. (eds), *The EU Treaties and the Charter of Fundamental Rights: A Commentary* (OUP 2019) para. 3).

of its citizens'[14]. It received particularly broad attention in the run-up to the Lisbon Treaty, being hailed by commentators as an 'important symbol of genuine, bottom-up democracy (...) apt to overcome the citizens' feeling of powerlessness *vis-à-vis* a gigantic European bureaucracy',[15] entailing a potential 'fundamental impact on the essence of the EU itself'[16]. It is, however, due to high admissibility thresholds that it never lived up to these expectations and remained of only limited practical significance.[17]

2. In Brief: On the Concept of Deliberative Democracy

Various approaches to deliberative democratic theory have been developed over the past decades. Interestingly, for the most part they are not put forward as fully-fledged alternatives to existing models of *representative* or *aggregative* democracy, but rather as an enhancement of (and addition to) the latter.[18]

At the intersection of legal and political theory, *Habermasian* (in particular in his groundbreaking work *Between Facts and Norms*) and *Alexyan* discourse theory has been an important driving force in the development of

14 Gráinne de Búrca, 'An EU Citizens' Assembly on Refugee Law and Policy' (2020) 21 German Law Journal 23.

15 Anne Peters, 'European Democracy after the 2003 Convention' (2004) 41 Common Market Law Review 37, 45.

16 Alex Warleigh-Lack, 'On the path to legitimacy? A critical deliberativist perspective on the right to the citizens' initiative' in Carlo Ruzza and Vincent Della Sala (eds), *Governance and civil society in the European Union, volume 1: Normative perspectives* (Manchester University Press 2007) 65.

17 A requirement that turned out to be a particularly intricate barrier in practice is that an ECI can (for obvious reasons) only be initiated within the (fragmented) sphere of Union competences, see further on this point Thomas Hieber and Carsten Berg, 'Mitreden in der EU – die Europäische Bürgerinitiative in Theorie und Praxis' in Thomas Hauser and Daniela Winkler (eds), *Gehört werden: neue Wege der Bürgerbeteiligung* (Kohlhammer 2022) 141.

18 *Young* argues that the most common delimitation is the one between *deliberative* and (what she calls) *interest-based* democratic models, Iris Marion Young, 'Communication and the Other: Beyond Deliberative Democracy' in Seyla Benhabib (ed), *Democracy and Difference. Contesting the Boundaries of the Political* (Princeton University Press 1996) 120. This may however be confusing at some point since *deliberative* democratic models can well be understood as entailing 'process[es] of expressing one's preferences and demands', a trait *Young* reserves for *interest-based* democracy. It is beyond doubt that deliberative democracy has the potential to enable 'processes (...) oriented around discussing th[e] common good rather than competing for the private good of each' (ibid 121) but whether or not this aim is realised depends on the specific problem at stake as well as the overall setting.

concepts of deliberative democracy. However, while *Alexyan* discourse theory is primarily legal theoretical, *Habermas* puts greater weight on political scientific and sociological aspects.

In a nutshell, for *Habermas*, deliberative democratic thinking turns out as a (practical) consequence of his overarching communication theoretical considerations. Both *Habermas* and *Alexy* share the basic assumption that, based on the nature of discourse theory as a 'procedural theory of practical correctness',[19] 'the correctness of a norm or the truth of a proposition depends upon whether or not the norm or proposition is or can be the result of a certain procedure'[20]. A great deal of discourse theorical writings engage with the rules discourses have to follow in order to increase the legitimacy of their results, and to allow for the 'peculiarly constraint-free force of the better argument',[21] as well as the exceptionally intricate question of final justification of these rules. According to *Habermas* and *Alexy*, discursive deliberation has a crucial, and by times even existential significance for democratic societies, with *Alexy* accordingly holding it to be 'the basic theory of the institutions of a democratic constitution that incorporate the idea of discussion'[22]. In a similar vein, *Sajó* highlights the interdependency of (legal) discourses and the existence of a public sphere due to its 'potential to contribute to (...) and to act as a safeguard for continued social discourse'[23].

Deliberative democratic approaches seek to grasp the insight of the legitimising potential of *discursive* deliberation and develop institutional structures which enable and promote forms of *rational discourse*. This should not hide the fact that there is no such thing as *the* concept of deliberative democracy, but countless variations. For the present purposes, however, it suffices to keep in mind that most approaches share the assumption that political systems shall be 'organised around communicative principles in which policy decisions are taken as a result of an open communication

19 'Die Diskurstheorie ist eine prozedurale Theorie der praktischen Richtigkeit' (Robert Alexy, 'Diskurstheorie und Menschenrechte' in Robert Alexy (ed), *Recht, Vernunft, Diskurs. Studien zur Rechtsphilosophie* (Suhrkamp Verlag 1995) 129, my translation).

20 Robert Alexy, 'Problems of Discourse Theory', in Robert Alexy (ed), *Law's Ideal Dimension* (Oxford University Press 2021) 275.

21 Jürgen Habermas, *The Theory of Communicative Action. Volume 1: Reason and the Rationalization of Society* (Beacon Press 1984) 24.

22 Alexy (n 32) 287 with reference to Martin Kriele, *Recht und praktische Vernunft* (Vandenhoeck & Ruprecht 1979) 30 et seq.

23 András Sajó, 'Constitutional Adjudication in Light of Discourse Theory' in Michel Rosenfeld and Andrew Arato (eds), *Habermas on Law and Democracy. Critical Exchanges* (University of California Press 1998) 368.

process'[24] to allow for the 'rule of considered public opinion'[25]. In a nutshell, conducting deliberation while respecting certain upstream principles (which are themselves not subject to contestation) endows the result of such deliberation with legitimacy.[26]

When elaborating on ideas of deliberative democracy, *Habermas* distinguishes between three different levels of political communication: institutionalised discourse, everyday communication, and the public sphere. In democratic systems, the latter has an existential significance, as it serves as an 'intermediate system'[27] between the former two and 'contributes to legitimation by producing political communication, by keeping it active, by steering – and *filtering* – it'[28]. This is first and foremost thanks to its capacity to '[mobilise] the relevant issues and controversial answers, requisite information and appropriate arguments for and against [...]'[29]. These considerations have, however, been developed before the background paradigm of the nation-state, and thus presupposes a certain stability as to the social reference point of any such communication (i.e. the *people*). The respective prerequisites are much more precarious when it comes to the *European* level.

3. The European 'Society/ies' of Article 2 TEU

The existence of a *public sphere* in the meaning of a 'sphere of "discursive power"'[30] is widely contested.[31] Such doubts seem reasonable, given alone the near-total absence of European mass media[32] which may serve as a cata-

24 Firat Cengiz, 'Bringing the Citizen Back into EU Democracy. What Can Deliberative Democracy Offer?' in Alberto Alemanno and James Organ (eds), *Citizen Participation in Democratic Europe. What Next for the EU?* (ECPR Press 2021) 119.

25 Cristina Lafont, *Democracy without Shortcuts. A Participatory Conception of Deliberative Democracy* (Oxford University Press 2020) 102.

26 Lafont (n 37) 103; Geuens (n 12) 150.

27 Habermas (n 37) 159.

28 ibid 159 (emphasis added).

29 ibid 162.

30 Hauke Brunkhorst, 'The European dual state. The double structural transformation of the public sphere and the need for repoliticization' in Jiří Přibáň (ed), *Self-Constitution of European Society. Beyond EU politics, law and governance* (Routledge 2016) 240.

31 See Eriksen (n 1) 343.

32 Reiner Grundmann, 'The European public sphere and the deficit of democracy' in Dennis Smith and Sue Wright (eds), *Whose Europe? The turn towards democracy*

lyst. A truly *European* media landscape would further ways of reasoning on shared challenges from another than the domestic perspective.[33]

The fact that the supranational level lacks the strong identity-shaping forces of the Westphalian nation state has already been the subject of the famous controversy between *Grimm* and *Habermas* in the aftermath of the *Maastricht* decision of the German Federal Constitutional Court.[34] Even if one agrees with *Habermas* in that the emergence of a *European public sphere* requires an impetus by institutional reform (an admittedly very brief synopsis of his argument),[35] the question remains whether and in how far such an impetus may already be enshrined in the Treaties. It has already been noted that, at least at the rhetorical level, the Lisbon Treaty entails traces of an underlying deliberative rationale.[36] At the same time, it has become clear that these traces alone are way too faint to mobilise the idea of *deliberative democracy* as a basic theory of the legitimacy of supranational decision-making. This may change once the 'society' of Article 2 TEU is brought to the forefront of considerations.

It is fair to say that, since it has been enshrined in the Treaties, the 'society' of Article 2 TEU has for the most time led a rather shadowy existence. The, until recently, low degree of attention stands in stark contrast

(Blackwell Publishers 1999) 136; Alberto Alemanno, 'Das EU-Projekt auf der langen Bank? Eine selbstverschuldete Situation durch mangelnden politischen Integrationswillen' (*Verfassungsblog*, 7 June 2024) accessible via <https://verfassungsblog.de/das-eu-projekt-auf-der-langen-bank/> accessed 1 July 2025, 3.

33 It is important here to differentiate between opinion formation and will formation, since another reading would neglect the degree to which the 'modern public sphere is institutionalized in opposition to government', Eriksen (n 1) 344. The latter undoubtedly takes places in *Europeanised* forms through the EU organs, but is still preceded by a process of opinion formation which takes place mainly from domestic perspectives.

34 See Dieter Grimm, 'Does Europe Need a Constitution?' (1995) 1 European Law Journal 282 and the reply by Jürgen Habermas, 'Remarks on Dieter Grimm's "Does Europe Need a Constitution?"' (1995) 1 European Law Journal 303.

35 In a very similar vein to the Habermasian perspective, Eriksen submits that 'the modern collective identity should not be conceived of as stemming from a primordial identification, but from the practice of identifying commonality revolving on a collective self-understanding. It has to be made rather than merely discovered', Eriksen (n 1) 344.

36 The given examples for a deliberative rationale of the Lisbon Treaty are not exhaustive. Apart from citizens' participation, a fundamental deliberative orientation of the EU legal order can also be deduced from the Comitology system (see Eriksen [n 2] 35 et seq) as well as from the intense judicial dialogue resulting from the preliminary reference procedure.

to the overwhelming attention paid to Article 2 in general by academics and practitioners alike.[37] If dealt with, the notion has remarkably often been interpreted in a very restrictive manner, understanding 'society' as being primarily composed of the Member States themselves,[38] or as a collective term for the Member States' domestic societies[39] (potentially conflicting with the wording of the provision speaking of *a* [single] society). Barely less restrictive and nation-state oriented seems to be the attempt of declaring the mere transferral of a national understanding of 'society' to the European level as sufficient.[40] Only rarely has there been substantial engagement with *society* in the context of Article 2 TEU as a compound of *individual citizens*. Some commentators tried to make a virtue out of necessity and suggested to define the 'European society' by its very elusiveness, pointing to its 'structured diversity, disunity, polymorphy, poly-identity'[41].

The deliberative rationale of the Lisbon Treaty may be more of a rhetorical promise vested in somewhat ceremonious constitutional language than an actual virtue of the Treaties. However, this does not mean that it is without any meaning. In particular, it may inform and guide the interpretation of other related Treaty provisions, such as Article 2 TEU. It is by bringing together a rigid textual analysis of Article 2 TEU, and its 'society' in particular, and a teleological reasoning informed by this very deliberative rationale that the transformative potential of the 'society' of Article 2 TEU becomes more visible.

---

37 The issue has recently been put to the forefront of legal debate by the comprehensive account submitted by Armin von Bogdandy, *The Emergence of European Society through Public Law. A Hegelian and Anti-Schmittian Approach* (Oxford University Press 2024).

38 Marcus Klamert and Dimitry Kochenov, 'Article 2 TEU' in Manuel Kellerbauer et al. (eds), *The EU Treaties and the Charter of Fundamental Rights: A Commentary* (OUP 2019) para. 5.

39 Christoph Möllers and Linda Schneider, *Demokratiesicherung in der Europäischen Union. Studie zu einem Dilemma* (Bundeszentrale für politische Bildung 2020) 126; Christian Calliess, 'EU-Vertrag (Lissabon) Art. 2: Die Werte der Union' in Christian Calliess and Matthias Ruffert (eds), *EUV/AEUV: Das Verfassungsrecht der Europäischen Union mit Europäischer Grundrechtecharta, Kommentar* (C. H. Beck 2022) para. 31.

40 Hans-Peter Müller, 'Auf dem Weg in eine europäische Gesellschaft? Begriffsproblematik und theoretische Perspektiven' (2007) 17 Berliner Journal für Soziologie 7, 8.

41 Stefan Immerfall and Göran Therborn, 'Conclusion: European Integration and the Elusive European Dream' in Stefan Immerfall and Göran Therborn (eds), *Handbook of European Societies. Social Transformations in the 21st Century* (Springer, 2010) 668.

On the textual level, it should firstly be kept in mind that the values enlisted in the first recital of Article 2 TEU – such as respect for human dignity, democracy, the rule of law, and human rights – are 'common to the Member States in a society in which pluralism, non-discrimination, tolerance, justice, solidarity and equality between women and men prevail'. At the same time, it is these very values the 'Union is founded on'[42]. Attributing the values enlisted in the first recital of Article 2 TEU is thus, at least *prima facie*, a straightforward exercise – they simply characterise the Member States and the Union. Such an attribution is considerably more intricate when it comes to the characteristics – values? – enlisted in the second recital of Article 2 TEU. According to the wording of the provision, 'pluralism, non-discrimination, tolerance, justice, solidarity and equality between women and men prevail in a society'. It is safe to say that it has not been the intention here to characterise the Union *as an organisation*. However, anything going beyond this truism requires a viable understanding of the notion of 'society' itself. An entry point to a more sustainable understanding of the 'society' of Article 2 TEU can be found in a closer examination of the two sets of values and characteristics respectively. While the *foundational values common to the Member States* are strongly linked to essential (protective) functions of state-like entities, the attainment of, e.g., *tolerance* or *solidarity* laid down in the second recital of Article 2 TEU cannot be achieved but by mobilising the individual (rational) citizen. This points towards an underlying fundamental difference between these distinct enumerations in the sense that the first recital entails *obligations to protect*, which is clearly not the case for the second recital (the function of which will become clearer further below). A sustainable understanding of 'society' in the realm of supranational law needs to reflect this structural difference. This requirement is clearly not met by an overly restrictive and nation state-centred understanding of the notion, neither as an expression for a compound of sovereign nation states (i.e. a term synonymous to the 'Union'), nor as a collective term encompassing the distinct Member State societies *as such*. While there are often good reasons to object to

42 Article 2 TEU reiterates the wording of Article I-2 of the 2004 Draft Constitution. Before the background of the latter provision, Monjal noted that its wording, 'poussé à son extrême, suggérait presque que ce sont les valeurs de l'Union qui fondent, ou pour le moins qui inspirent, celles des Etats' (Pierre-Yves Monjal, 'Le projet de traité établissant une Constitution pour l'Europe : quels fondements théoriques pour le droit constitutionnel de l'Union européenne ?' [2004] Revue trimestrielle de droit européen, 443, 454).

transferrals of nation state structures and paradigms to the supranational level without thinking twice (or even more), here such a recourse to an established understanding of the term seems more than adequate: to understand the 'society' of Article 2 TEU, as has always been the case for national societies, as a compound of individuals, providing a 'unitary context in which European citizens expressly mentioned in the democratic principles may recognize themselves'[43].

It has remained open for the time being how the nature of the characteristics enlisted in the second recital can be captured more adequately beyond the assessment that they are in a diffuse way *structurally different* from those in the first recital. Starting with a seemingly trivial consideration once again, it is undeniable that societies of any kind require *communicative spaces*, which themselves rest on certain 'basic sociocultural characteristics'[44]. If this is already evident for the nation-state, the necessity of the emergence of such *communicative spaces* is all the more blatant when it comes to the supranational sphere, still characterised by a manifest '[lack of] responsiveness to the preferences of its citizens'[45] and thus in particular need of a place 'where civil society is linked to the power structure of the state'[46].

A merely superficial reading of Article 2 TEU may lead to the conclusion that the problem is already solved: as the said characteristics, according to Article 2 TEU, 'prevail' in 'a society', does not this mean that – by ratifying the Lisbon Treaty – the society of Article 2 TEU has simply become reality?[47] This seemingly elegant escape, however, turns a blind eye on the lacking preconditions of a 'European society', and is thus unsustainable. All the more, the wording and structure of Article 2 TEU actually point into a different direction.

Pursuant to the wording of the provision, the values of the first recital are 'common to the Member States in a society' in which the characteristics laid down in the second recital prevail. As it has already become clear that the

43 Stelio Mangiameli, 'Article 2: The Homogeneity Clause' in Hermann-Josef Blanke et al. (eds), *The Treaty on European Union. A Commentary* (Springer 2013) para. 38.

44 Eriksen (n 1) 342.

45 de Búrca (n 14) 23. According to de Búrca, this lack of responsiveness is 'at the core of the EU's democratic deficit' (ibid.).

46 Eriksen (n 1) 342.

47 von Bogdandy speaks of the 'factual statement in Article 2 TEU (...) that there is a European society (...)' (von Bogdandy [n 70] 5), promotion of which shall nevertheless be up to the Union and its Member States.

term 'Member States in a society' is not equivalent to a 'society consisting of Member States as principal actors', the interlinkage between these two parts of the provision must possess a different meaning. In the light of the foregoing, it is in no way far-fetched to assume a certain conditionality between the promotion of a European society and the very fulfilment of the values attributed by Article 2 TEU to the Union and its Member States. Put differently, compliance with the common values by the Member States includes the promotion of the characteristics of the second recital. Here, the reasoning on the structural difference between the enumeration of values in the first and the enlisting of characteristics in the second recital commenced above comes to full circle. The *promotion* of a '(European) society' shaped by the characteristics of the second recital and adherence to the values of the first recital are conditionally intertwined.

In contrast to its Member States, the Union does not rest on a given societal structure predefined by national borders, or common cultural traditions of a density that the existence of reliable and resilient societal structures may appear as self-evident. Furthering transboundary democracy thus necessitates to actively promote the emergence of, first and foremost, a public sphere. In recognition of the boundaries of extending representative democracy beyond the nation-state without giving up on the sovereign quality of the latter, participatory deliberative elements have an even greater significance on the supranational level (compared to the national sphere) for the democratic quality of its decision-making processes.[48]

48 With respect to the contested delimitation of *participative* and *deliberative* democracy, the present paper rests on the assumption that the structural difference between both lies in their explanatory aim. While *participatory* democracy rather characterises democratic systems which systematically take into account citizens' voices beyond elections, but does not further define the procedure, *deliberative* democracy emphasises the procedural aspect of rational will-formation without elaborating on the way it finds its way into the political decision-making process. While both approaches can thus be clearly separated from each other, they are not mutually exclusive, but can well appear in parallel. The various deliberative set-ups presented in the remainder are clear examples of such a participatory-deliberative approach.

III. Deliberative Democracy in Practice: Political Participation through 'Citizens' Assemblies'

Deliberative democracy as 'grounded in an ideal in which people come together, on the basis of equal status and mutual respect, to discuss the political issues they face'[49] may be theoretically persuasive as a functional supplement to its aggregative counterpart. This does, however, not automatically imply its practical applicability. As regards the latter, a comprehensive body of literature has evolved over the past decade, arguing in favour of realising deliberative democracy in practice by implementing so-called *Deliberative Mini-Publics* (DMPs) or 'mini-populi'[50] to inform democratic decision-making and enhance its legitimacy.

The range of proposals in literature on the design of such DMPs and their ideal place in the democratic constitutional state is extremely wide, and transferring such concepts to the non-state supranational level poses an additional challenge. This has to be critically taken into account when wide public support is cited in scholarly writing as an argument in favour of setting up DMPs without precisely outlining the design of the deliberative set-up at stake.[51] In addition, it is also crucial to clearly distinguish between mere *participatory* elements, which can take rather simple forms (such as polls and surveys), and *deliberative* involvement, requiring considerably more effort and sense of responsibility on the side of the participants.

1. Previous Implementation of Citizens' Assemblies at the Domestic Level

Following a surge in academic engagement with the potential of participatory and deliberative democracy, past years have seen the sprouting of a number of (often experimental) innovative deliberative bodies. Their roots are often seen in the widespread perception of an increasing complexity of today's societal debates, requiring more sophisticated elements of immediate participation of the wider citizenry than mere regular parliamentary elections. There is, however, considerable divergence as regards their re-

49 André Bächtiger et al., 'Deliberative Democracy: An Introduction' in André Bächtiger et al. (eds), *The Oxford Handbook of Deliberative Democracy* (Oxford University Press 2018) 2.

50 Robert A. Dahl, *Democracy and its Critics* (Yale University Press 1989) 340.

51 Nicole Curato et al., *Deliberative Mini-Publics. Core Design Features* (Bristol University Press 2021) 108.

spective point of departure – as either top-down or bottom-up approaches – as well as their specific design (which predetermines their respective potential political leverage). Among the ever-growing number of attempts to create 'more perfect public spheres',[52] the relatively prominent, more recent examples from Ireland, France and Belgium showcase exemplarily the potential and pitfalls of such formats.

a) Pioneering the Evolution: The Irish Convention on the Constitution and Citizens' Assembly

Among the EU Member States, Ireland spearheaded this evolution.[53] Not only did it run a first large-scale experimentation of a DMP as early as 2012, but it continued this practice over the following years, entrusting the different deliberative bodies without exemption with deliberating on highly contentious questions of constitutional significance.

In 2012, the *Irish Convention on the Constitution* was asked to deliberate on the question of legal recognition of same-sex marriage, which was then introduced in 2015. A remarkable design feature of this Convention was the selection of a 'one-to-one-shadow' per each selected participant to maintain the representativeness of the assembly in case of regular participants dropping out.[54] Only a year later, the *Dáil* (the Irish lower chamber) launched the *Irish Citizens' Assembly* and entrusted it with, inter alia, discussing the 'major, difficult, and divisive'[55] issues of abortion and how to make Ireland a leading power in the fight against climate change. The swift follow-up on the *Convention on the Constitution* was widely seen as remarkable, with some commentators hailing Ireland as 'a world leader in the linking of deliberative (...) and direct democracy'.[56] Finally, in 2020, another citizens' assembly started working on questions of gender equality, with the recommendations being, however, rejected in two referenda.

52 Archon Fung, 'Survey Article: Recipes for Public Spheres. Eight Institutional Design Choices and Their Consequences' (2003) 11 Journal of Political Philosophy 338, 338.

53 Curato et al. (n 84) 9.

54 Daniela Winkler and Marc Zeccola, 'Bürgerräte im europäischen Vergleich' in Thomas Hauser and Daniela Winkler (eds), *Gehört werden: neue Wege der Bürgerbeteiligung* (Kohlhammer 2022) 108.

55 de Búrca (n 14) 24.

56 David M. Farrell et al., 'Systematizing' constitutional deliberation: the 2016–18 citizens' assembly in Ireland' (2019) 34 Irish Political Studies 113, 119.

The Irish deliberative experiments have been criticised for several design flaws, such as the procedure of selecting participants and 'inadequate time for deliberation'.[57] In addition, the hesitant reaction by the Irish government to deal with some of the recommendations resulting from the 2016 *Irish Citizens' Assembly* despite an initially unambiguous commitment to duly take them into account[58] demonstrates the indispensable requirement of clearly defining the possible ways of implementation and enforcement in advance, as leaving this entirely to political discretion is prone to subsequent 'cherry-picking'. At the same time, there is little doubt that the continuity of participatory deliberation (or even 'systemization'[59]) in Ireland, as well as the significance of the debated questions, considerably contributed to the surging number of comparable formats in other Member States over the past decade.

b) The French *Convention citoyenne pour le climat*

At first sight, deliberative citizen participation through mini-publics seems to be rather at odds with a highly centralised political system characterised by a considerable accumulation of immediate power at the top, as it exists in France. However, the 2018–19 *gilets jaunes* manifestations reinforced the impression that a veritable rapprochement of the political class and the wider citizenry would require more than just regular elections.[60] After a rather experimental phase with different participatory formats – the *grand débat national* – the government launched the *Convention citoyenne pour le climat* ('Citizens' Convention on Climate/CCC'). Its mandate was to elaborate proposals for a 40 % reduction in greenhouse gas emissions until 2030 without a negative impact on social equality. The government committed itself to either hold a referendum or a parliamentary vote on the proposals,

57 de Búrca (n 14) 24 who, in addition, casts some doubt on the transferability to the EU level.

58 Farrell et al. (n 89) 119.

59 ibid 114.

60 On the link between the *gilet jaunes* protests and the CCC see Laurence Eymard, 'From the French Citizens' Convention on Climate to the Conference on the Future of Europe: A Participatory Science and Democracy Perspective' (2020) 26 European Law Journal 136; Diarmuid Torney, 'Deliberative Mini-Publics and the European Green Deal in Turbulent Times: The Irish and French Climate Assemblies' (2021) 9 Politics and Governance 380, 385.

or to implement them directly. Even though being a strongly top-down approach, including the definition of the mandate, this was perceived as promising when the CCC commenced to operate. The exact scope of the governmental commitment was, however, left rather nebulous,[61] which turned out as a decisive weakness in the aftermath. The draft bill, initially intended to reflect the work of the CCC, was considerably watered down in the course of the legislative process, and eventually widely perceived as not implementing appropriately the recommendations issued by the CCC.[62] However, despite the reticence of the legislative branch in translating the proposals into law, the deliberative process within the Council (after all on a highly controversial issue) was not only described as exceptionally constructive by the participants,[63] but it even led to the request to continue this form of deliberative participation in the future.[64]

c) The *Ostbelgien* Model

The *Permanenter Bürgerdialog* ('Permanent Citizens Dialogue') introduced in a federal sub-division of Belgium in 2019 is another remarkable example for the recent surge in innovative participatory mechanisms across Europe. Even though it is geographically limited to the *Ostbelgien* ('Eastern Belgium') region, it differs from comparable initiatives in that it has, from the very beginning, been an institutionalised body with clearly defined leverage on the legislative process. This made its design globally unique at the time it was launched.[65] It mainly consists of two entities, a *Citizens' Council* which is allowed to initiate *Citizens' Assemblies.*[66] Following deliberations in the Assembly, the recommendations are subject to debate between the Assembly and governmental as well as parliamentary representatives. If the recommendations are to be rejected, such a move needs specific justification. The *Bürgerdialog* was, however, not created out of nothing, but preceded by a long history of experimentation with different forms of (deliberative)

61 Torney (n 93) 386.
62 Critical with regard to the disappointment of expectations previously raised by the French government Weber (n 10) 274.
63 Eymard (n 93) 138.
64 ibid 140.
65 Geuens (n 12) 151.
66 The third body, the 'Permanent Secretary', is primarily endowed with administrative tasks and not involved in the deliberative process.

citizen participation in Belgium, as well as intense academic engagement with the results of the previous experimental set-ups[67] and the 'particular political dynamics'[68] leading to the implementation of the *Bürgerdialog*.

While the competence of the Council to decide independently on the issues which shall be debated by the Assembly reduces the risk of political instrumentalisation, it constitutes at the same time a potential risk for the task of the deliberating body to be fulfilled efficiently and effectively. In the specific case of the *Ostbelgien* model, issues were collected by a public call, and ranked accordingly to an online poll. Such a set-up is, however, prone to exclude those with no or weak digital literacy, and arguably to be captured by organised campaigns in favour of particular interests.[69] This process of 'public brainstorming' preceding the very first *Bürgerdialog* resulted in the question of 'how the conditions of employees and patients in the health care sector can be improved',[70] an undoubtedly important, but potentially boundless question. The focus on broader societal questions, rather than issues which would typically be regarded as regional or local concerns, was continued in the following years, with the Assembly deliberating on, inter alia, *inclusive education*, *housing*, and *digital skills*.[71] In the specific case of the *Bürgerdialog*, it, however, has to be taken into account that the Ostbelgien regional parliament possesses considerable legislative competencies in all these areas.[72]

2. Previous Attempts to Enhance Deliberative Citizens' Involvement on the Supranational Level

Experimentation with various instruments of citizen participation and deliberation has by no means been limited to the domestic sphere. Quite the

67 Christoph Niessen and Min Reuchamps, 'Institutionalising Citizen Deliberation in Parliament: The Permanent Citizens' Dialogue in the German-speaking Community of Belgium' (2022) 75 *Parliamentary Affairs* 135, 137 et seq.

68 Hadrien Macq and Vincent Jacquet, 'Institutionalising participatory and deliberative procedures: The origins of the first permanent citizens' assembly' (2023) 62 European Journal of Political Research 156, 157.

69 For an assessment of this risk in the context of the European Citizens' Initiative see Deven Burks and Raphaël Kies, 'A Gradualist Path Toward Sortition' in John Gastil and Erik Olin Wright (eds), *Legislature by Lot. Transformative Designs for Deliberative Governance* (Verso 2019) 272.

70 Niessen/Reuchamps (n 67) 150.

71 Geuens (n 12) 156.

72 Macq/Jacquet (n 68) 161.

contrary, the past two decades have seen a plethora of participatory set-ups advanced on the supranational level, carried out mainly under Commission leadership. That this process gained speed about two decades ago was no coincidence. After the definitive failure of the 2004 Draft Constitution due to negative referenda in France and the Netherlands and low overall approval rates of the EU, a 'new communication strategy (...) to react to its [the Union's] legitimacy crisis'[73] was sorely needed. The 2007 and 2009 *European Citizens Consultations*, the 2007 *Tomorrow's Europe* poll and the 2009 *Europolis* survey can be seen as the most immediate reactions, followed by a multitude of comparable (more or less ambitious) deliberative experimentation on the supranational level. They all shared, however, the fate of having remained exactly that – short-term experiments with their existence and respective impact depending on political goodwill. It does not come as a surprise that their actual leverage on the outcome of political decision-making processes, as well as their potential to mobilise citizens, is widely regarded as rather limited.[74]

A quite recent, and arguably one of the most notable attempts to date to (more or less) directly involve EU citizens in supranational decision-making has been the *Conference on the Future of Europe* (CoFoE). In her 2019 Political Agenda, European Commission President *von der Leyen* had announced to aim for 'giving Europeans a stronger role in decision-making'[75]. In order to enable 'Europeans to build the future of our Union'[76], she announced to set up the CoFoE, which – after pandemic-related delays – finally started in April 2021. The panels were assembled by blending random selection and stratification, and deliberation was carried out in a hybrid manner. The results of the panels' deliberations, published in the *Final Report* of the Conference,[77] demonstrated that there may be more willingness

73 Mundo Yang, 'Europe's New Communication Policy and the Introduction of Transnational Deliberative Citizens' Involvement Projects' in Raphaël Kies and Patrizia Nanz (eds), *Is Europe Listening to Us? Successes and Failures of EU Citizen Consultations* (Ashgate 2013) 17.

74 Burks/Kies (n 69) 270 et seq; Alemanno (n 12) 37.

75 Ursula von der Leyen, 'A Union that strives for more. My agenda for Europe, Political Guidelines for the Next European Commission 2019-2024' (9 October 2019) <https://op.europa.eu/en/publication-detail/-/publication/43a17056-ebf1-11e9-9c4e-01aa75ed71a1> accessed 1 July 2025, 19 et seq.

76 ibid 19.

77 'Conference on the Future of Europe, Report on the Final Outcome' (9 May 2022) <https://www.europarl.europa.eu/resources/library/media/20220509RES29121/20220509RES29121.pdf> accessed 1 July 2025 (hereinafter 'CoFoE Report').

among EU citizens for courageous steps towards closer integration than one might assume with regard to national political landscapes. In the end, nearly fifty proposals were made, including the abolishment of unanimity requirements for voting in the Council,[78] a shared competence of the Union for health issues[79] and transnational lists for European elections[80]. As the CoFoE had only the competence to make recommendations, there was (and is), however, no means of legal or political enforcement. Pursuant to Article 23 of the Conference Rules of Procedure, it was up to the European Parliament, the Council, and the Commission to 'examine swiftly how to follow up effectively' on the Final Report. Since the CoFoE sub-institutions were not designed as permanent bodies, but only existed for the time of the Conference, there was no possibility foreseen for them to check whether or not there would be diligent follow-up on its proposals.

IV. Core Design Challenges for a Future *European Citizens' Assembly*

It would go beyond the confinements of this contribution to provide an exhaustive outline of the numerous challenges DMPs pose in both theoretical and practical terms. On a more modest scale, it can however be argued that flowing from the foregoing is a set of particularly important design challenges which need to be considered when enhancing deliberative democracy on the supranational level.

1. Institutionalisation

First and foremost, there is virtual consensus on the necessity of institutionalising mini-publics instead of leaving the decision when and how to set up such bodies to executive discretion. This widespread assumption is closely linked to the delicate (and disputed) task to strike an appropriate balance between parliamentary and participatory elements within a system of democratic governance. Notwithstanding the potential merits of deliber-

78 ibid 83.

79 ibid 153.

80 ibid 81. For a more comprehensive overview on the proposals and an evaluation of the CoFoE see 'From Conference to Convention? Ideas and prospects for reform of the EU Treaties (Editorial Comments) (2022) 59 Common Market Law Review 1583, 1584 et seq.

ative political participation of the wider citizenry, there are some possible threats coming along with the integration of DMPs in democratic decision-making processes which are comparable to those of more common forms of direct democracy such as (binding and non-binding) referenda. In particular, there is an inherent risk of an arbitrary use of DMPs to 'legitimize existing political priorities and policy approaches'[81] and to circumvent a principled public parliamentary debate on potentially contentious political projects[82]. This danger seems even more acute in those cases where the parliamentary means to control executive action are relatively weak, as it is the case on the supranational level. This does in no way mean that a DMP might be an equally or even more suitable setting for contentious and potentially divisive questions gridlocked in the parliamentary process,[83] but unfolding the deliberative 'constraint-free force of the better argument' necessitates that the scope of the mandate and the procedure of referring issues to the DMP are precisely determined in advance.

When looking at the existing practice of the Commission in the field of deliberative citizen participation, such concerns do not seem to be in any way far-fetched.[84] Even though the Commission has carried out countless formats of citizens' involvement over the past two and a half decades, accompanied by the powerful rhetoric of a 'citizen-owned'[85] Union, there was at the same time a remarkable reluctance when it came to implementing such concepts into the architecture of supranational governance.[86] The (possibly intentional[87]) lack of substantial impact on the final legislative outcome is widely seen as a core weakness of EU participatory fora,[88] which

---

81 Alemanno (n 12) 37.

82 Robert E. Goodin and John S. Dryzek, 'Deliberative Impacts: The Macro-Political Uptake of Mini-Publics' (2006) 34 Politics & Society 219, 225.

83 de Búrca even assumes that 'this may be exactly the point at [which] a citizens' assembly can become most useful', de Búrca (n 14) 26.

84 For such concerns with regard to the EU see Alemanno (n 12) 37.

85 Luc van den Brande, 'Reaching out to EU citizens. A new opportunity. "About us, with us, for us"' (Publications Office of the European Union 2017) 10.

86 Alemanno (n 12) 37. The perception of a gap between the participatory commitments of the Lisbon Treaty and their effect in practice is shared by de Búrca (n 14) 27.

87 Alemanno (n 12) 37.

88 James Organ, 'EU Participatory Democracy. Citizens' Assemblies and the Conference on the Future of Europe', in Davor Jančić (ed), *The Changing Role of Citizens in EU Democratic Governance* (Hart Publishing 2023) 173.

have consequentially been characterised as 'participative governance rather than participative democracy'[89].

2. Participatory vs. Parliamentary Democracy?

While there is a near-consensus on the necessity of institutionalisation as such, a number of sub-questions are fiercely contested. This concerns in particular the relation between participatory and parliamentary bodies. Proposals in this regard are oscillating in the wide spectrum between deliberative democracy as a 'post-parliamentary approach'[90] and DMPs as purely advisory bodies.[91]

To make sense of this, it seems helpful to look again at the core reasons for which the broader concept of deliberative political participation enjoys widespread approval in many societies. This is often the case due to a phenomenon which has over time been coined the 'democratic mirror function'[92] of DMPs, evoking a '"like me" perception'[93].

Obviously, defending the establishment of DMPs with the 'mirror' argument entails some dangerous pitfalls. The mere fact that there is evidence of a 'perceived similarity of mini-public participants to non-participants'[94] does not say anything about the respective degree of legitimacy of non-parliamentary deliberative set-ups. With respect to overall political stability, it is insofar dangerous as it tends to root the legitimacy of DMPs in the already widespread alienation between the wider citizenry and elected representatives. A similarly dangerous path might take the reasoning issued by de Búrca, who sees the 'growth of issue-based activism'[95] as being part of a 'positive dimension to the growing distrust of conventional political

89 ibid footnote 35.

90 Jared Sonnicksen, 'Deliberative Democracy as a Model for the EU. Normative Implications of Adapting Democracy to Governance' in Erik Amnå (ed), *New Forms of Citizen Participation. Normative Implications* (Nomos 2010) 85.

91 John Parkinson, *Deliberating in the Real World: Problems of Legitimacy in Deliberative Democracy* (Oxford University Press 2006) 33.

92 See Curato et al. (n 84) 108, who are citing this phenomenon when countering *Lafonts* critique regarding the legitimacy of DMPs.

93 James Pow et al., 'It's Not Just the Taking Part that Counts: 'Like Me' Perceptions Connect the Wider Public to Minipuablics' (2020) 16 Journal of Deliberative Democracy 43.

94 ibid 44.

95 de Búrca (n 14) 24.

institutions and parties'[96]. Issue-based activism, even though evidently in no way illegitimate, does, however, not present in any way an alternative to the often lengthy, but indispensable weighing up of different interests prevalent in a given society. This process of weighing is at the core of the mandate of political (parliamentary) bodies.

This is not to say that the 'mirror' argument should be dismissed completely, but it should be acknowledged that such a mirror function is to a considerable degree contingent on a strong parliamentary counterpart. The other way around, parliamentary democracy can be disburdened to a certain degree by the parallel existence of DMPs with which identification may be subject to a lower threshold. If one departs from an understanding of democratic decision-making as 'a form of decision-making which we can own and identify with',[97] the coexistence of *parliamentary* and *deliberative-participatory* bodies should actually be the norm rather than the exception: while identification may be more straightforward with a deliberative body assembled by stratified sortition, to squeeze out parliamentary elements would come at the expense of *owning* the process and eventually amount to a 'loss of democratic control'[98]. Participatory deliberative elements should be seen as a meaningful addition and 'countervailing power',[99] rather than an alternative model, to representative democracy.[100]

3. Enforceability and Agenda-Setting

Adequately designing the intricate interplay between elected parliamentary and randomly assembled (but nonetheless, if this is done by stratified sortition, somewhat representative) deliberative bodies has to take into account the degree of enforceability of recommendations and decisions issued by deliberative bodies such as a future *European Citizens' Assembly* (ECA). If one goes on the abovementioned basic assumption regarding the relation between participatory deliberative and parliamentary democratic

96 ibid.

97 Philip Pettit, *Republicanism. A Theory of Freedom and Government* (Oxford University Press 2003), 184.

98 Pow et al. (n 93) 44.

99 Yves Sintomer et al., *Les budgets participatifs en Europe. Des services publics au service du public* (La Découverte 2008) 295; Yannis Papadopoulos, *Democracy in Crisis? Politics, Governance and Policy* (Palgrave Macmillan 2013) 147.

100 Cengiz (n 36) 121.

elements, this is particularly delicate on the supranational level, which is characterised by a long-standing and much-debated weakness of the European Parliament. This excludes an immediate and autonomous right of initiative of an ECA. It would, however, not sideline the EP if an ECA would be endowed with the right to launch a *Citizens' Initiative* and thus with an *indirect* right of initiative in the ordinary legislative procedure. This would constitute a considerable revaluation of the ECI, without running into the danger of being taken over by organised private campaigns, a phenomenon witnessed in the context of referenda.[101] If the agenda of the ECA was settled in advance in accordance with the EP, and backed by a consultative function of the Commission in competence questions, such a design would considerably enhance the democratic legitimacy of supranational legislative decision-making by interlinking its representative and participatory dimension.[102] Furthermore, as a side-effect, it would raise the prospects of success of ECIs, which today often fail due to an incorrect assessment of the Union's legislative competences. It would, however, be crucial to strictly limit the role of the Commission to such a consultative function, since taking the possibility of setting the agenda completely out of the hands of the ECA would dramatically weaken its potential to enhance the EU's democratic legitimacy.[103]

4. Publicity of Deliberation

Whether, and if so to which degree, deliberations of mini-publics should be subject to public scrutiny – e.g. by allowing an (on-site or virtual) audience to follow deliberations – is one of the most controversial and intricate design challenges such deliberative bodies are facing. On the one hand, it has been outlined that DMPs have to be provided with a sufficient degree of leverage in political decision-making processes, not only to raise interest in participation, but first and foremost to avoid an abuse of such bodies

101 This concern has inter alia been issued by *Organ* for the case that the scope of the ECI is widened to initiatives for Treaty change (James Organ, 'Direct Citizen Participation in the EU Democratic System' in Alberto Alemanno and James Organ (eds), *Citizen Participation in Democratic Europe. What Next for the EU?* (ECPR Press 2021) 48).

102 From the perspective of *Alemanno*, '[u]nder the current Treaty framework, the participatory and representative components of EU democracy are like ships that pass in the night' (Alemanno (n 12) 38).

103 Grundmann (n 65) 136.

by the executive. This means that DMPs have to exercise an (admittedly subordinate) form of public power to become a meaningful component of a democratic system. It goes without saying that public accountability has to be proportional to the exercise of public power.[104] On the other hand, it is at the heart of deliberative democratic theory to allow space for the abovementioned *constraint-free force of the better argument*, which would be frustrated if DMPs were in the same way subject to the dynamics of constant public scrutiny elected parliaments are.[105] From the perspective of deliberative quality, it might thus seem alluring to 'insulate deliberators from the harmful effects of the glare of publicity'[106], but this would go along with the complete exclusion of public accountability.

Warren sets out three constellations in which publicity of deliberation is particularly important:[107] if the discussants are endowed with representative functions, when non-public deliberation would be prone to exclude certain legitimate interests, and in the case that the deliberating body can take binding decisions. The question of representation will be discussed below, but it can already be concluded from the foregoing that participants in DMPs should not have representative functions equal to those of elected parliamentarians, in order to allow for constraint-free speech. The last constellation *Warren* cites – deliberative bodies with decision-making powers – has also already been excluded in the present context. However, the possibility remains that legitimate interests are sidelined in the debates. To allow public opinion-formation on the question whether this occurs *systematically* or *deliberately* in the respective case at stake, the process of opinion-formation and will-formation within the DMP should be publicly available. Rather than 'sheltering the process',[108] it would be a reasonable middle-ground to allow the public to comprehend the course of deliberations without, however, any possibility to trace back results to distinct participants.

104 Mark E. Warren, 'Institutionalizing Deliberative Democracy' in Shawn W. Rosenberg (ed), *Deliberation, Participation and Democracy: Can the People Govern?* (Palgrave Macmillan 2007) 281.
105 Lafont (n 37) 104 et seq.
106 Simone Chambers, 'Measuring Publicity's Effect: Reconciling Empirical Research and Normative Theory' (2005) 40 Acta Politica 255.
107 Warren (n 104) 282.
108 ibid.

5. How to Assemble a *European Deliberative Mini-Public*?

The question of how to assemble a DMP on the *European* level, compared to a body on the domestic or regional level, is no less challenging. When it comes to the selection process, research is for the most part focusing on the downstream question of how to select participants from a given set of candidates. In the supranational context, the more intricate question is, however, how to form a pool of candidates in the first place. Where research is engaging with this question, it is often dealt with in a remarkably succinct manner by pointing to the principle of degressive proportionality,[109] known from the elections to the European Parliament, in order to '[ensure] that smaller states have a voice in the proceedings'[110]. Such an approach entails, however, a fundamental misconception on the possible role of a deliberative body on the supranational level. To reduce its function to merely representing the Member States positions on the European level would render it superfluous right from the start for obvious reasons. Moreover, it would seriously undermine its potential to foster the emergence of a *European* public sphere and society, distinct from those on the national level. Regardless of how a selection process would be designed in detail, it would have to safeguard representativeness with regard to the *European citizenry* as a whole, in order to allow for 'discussions to evolve around common (global) goods problems instead of around constituency interest (...)'[111]. Taking into account that some sort of local or regional anchoring might nevertheless be beneficial to public approval of, and interest in a *European* DMP, participants may be selected representing certain (possibly transboundary) regions. As a European public sphere requires to understand the transboundary challenges the Member States are facing as *shared* challenges, overcoming 'national cleavages'[112] which are until today shaping public debates on European issues will be an indispensable prerequisite for unfolding the full potential of any supranational deliberative body.

---

109 For an analysis of recent proposals to reform EU electoral law, arguing in favour of understanding EU citizenship as the basic tenet of active and passive voting rights in the EU, see Sydow, '"In Deutschland gewählte" statt "deutsche" Abgeordnete' (2024) 79 JuristenZeitung 313.

110 Graham Smith, 'The European Citizens' Assembly' in Alberto Alemanno and James Organ (eds), *Citizen Participation in Democratic Europe. What Next for the EU?* (ECPR Press 2021) 146.

111 Fiket (n 6) 205. For a similar account see Eymard (n 93) 140.

112 Mark Dawson and Floris de Witte, 'From Balance to Conflict: A New Constitution for the EU' (2016) 22 European Law Journal 204, 208 et seq.

V. Conclusion

(Very) briefly put, the legitimacy of any exercise of public power can (also) be measured by the extent to which the polity in question 'structurally incorporates and reflects the values that "matter" to its constituents' [113]. As the EU undeniably exercises a considerable amount of public power, this raises the question of *whose* values it should reflect.

In the foregoing considerations, it has been argued that the Lisbon Treaty entails an underlying *deliberative rationale* which should guide the interpretation of Article 2 TEU, and in particular the notion of 'society' therein. On the basis of an interpretation of Article 2 TEU which aims to take this notion seriously, the concept of a permanent *European Citizens' Assembly* has been sketched out (at least in its rough shapes). As '[d]emocracy is not about states', but 'about the exercise of public power (...)'[114], such a plenary may considerably alleviate the notorious democratic deficit of the Union's exercise of public authority. Due to the Union's inherent imbalance towards executive federalism, complementing parliamentary with participatory-deliberative elements may even be more important on the Union level compared to the political processes of its Member States. Even more than its Member States, the Union is in need of 'feedback from the insistent dynamics of a political public sphere and a mobilised civil society'[115].

The fact that the Union's democratic deficit is subject to fierce debates since the *Maastricht* era, but integration has nevertheless only been deepening since then, and the Union turned out as quite an efficient crisis manager over the past one-and-a-half decades or so, could give the impression that all talks about the democratic deficit are of merely academic interest. However, such a conclusion would not only ignore the considerable internal and external pressure on the integration project existing today, but – all the worse – the immense challenges the Union will most likely face in the years and decades to come. Making EU citizens' voices heard by the means of a permanent *Citizens' Assembly* would be an admittedly small, but no less important contribution to enhance the Union's cohesion resilience from within, and thus to its long-term future-proofing.

113 Mark Dawson and Floris de Witte, 'Constitutional Balance in the EU after the Euro-Crisis' (2013) 76 Modern Law Review 817, 819.

114 Weiler (n 3) 100.

115 Jürgen Habermas, *The Lure of Technocracy* (Polity Press 2015) 11.